Matthew

Matthew

Spirituality
for the
80's &
90's

LEONARD DOOHAN

BEAR & COMPANY
SANTA FE, NEW MEXICO

Acknowledgement

I would like to express my thanks to my wife, Helen, for her constant support in my work. My research and writing were done during a sabbatical break granted to me by Gonzaga University, Spokane, Washington. I take this opportunity to thank the administrators and faculty for their support. Scripture texts used in this work are taken from the NEW AMERICAN BIBLE, copyright © 1970 by the Confraternity of Christian Doctrine, Washington, D.C., and are used by permission of copyright owner. All rights reserved.

Bear & Company
P.O. Drawer 2860
Santa Fe, NM 87504

Cover Design: Kathleen Katz
Typography: Copygraphics, Santa Fe
Printed in the United States by BookCrafters, Inc.

9 8 7 6 5 4 3 2

For my daughter, Eve-Anne,
with all my love.

Contents

Chapter Three
MATTHEW'S PURPOSE

Conclusion
**MATTHEW AND CHRISTIAN LIFE
IN THE 1980s and 1990s** 159

Introduction
MATTHEW'S PASTORAL LEADERSHIP

The evangelist, Matthew, was concerned about the crises his Church faced in the 80s and 90s. His community, living about twenty years after the early period of uniform consolidation of Christianity, had become a melting pot of different, and at times divergent, understandings of the Church, of the nature of discipleship, and of the value to be given to former ways of living.

The community's internal differences were intensified by religious pressures from outside. Having committed themselves to a new way of life, many felt tempted to return to old ways and values. This tension between new and old split not only his community, but individual families as well. The result was painful division, dissension, and mutual recrimination.

In addition to this internal confusion, the community faced the possibility of war, with all the fears and concerns brought by such a threat. The community's enthusiastic commitment to outreach in mission was hampered by the nagging thought that all their efforts could be a waste of time, and that catastrophic destruction would overtake them.

Matthew retold the story of Jesus for a Church in crisis; his pastoral success was incalculable. For the best part of a century, the expanding Christian world focused on Matthew's interpretation of Jesus' message and challenge as the most meaningful synthesis for them.

Matthew's spiritual challenge to the 80s and 90s seems to have been especially tailored to the 1980s and the 1990s. The Gospel's awesome ability to challenge different generations anew has proven fresh and vital through the centuries. As history and cultures vary, and national or local circumstances evolve, one or another of the four gospels seems to be remarkably appropriate to the change. For the Church of North America, but for many others too, Matthew's is the gospel that seems to have been written with these times in mind.

A Church's experience of polarization. Less than half a century ago, there was a substantial uniformity in Christian churches, particularly in Catholicism. However, the two decades since the Second Vatican Council have been, for Christians everywhere, a mixture of love and hate, hope and despair. The polarization of the Catholic Church has been experienced by other Christian churches. Some believers have felt called to live Christian lives in new ways, as manifested in new experiences, new forms of doctrine, new structures, and new values. Other believers have felt called to intensify their fidelity to traditional experiences and doctrines, traditional structures and values. There are conservatives committed to the traditions who see discipleship as a call to faithfully live out the rooted values of the past. There are reformers who call for change, seeing discipleship as a challenge to reincarnate past values and as a call to create new values through interaction with a changing world. There are marginally committed Christians who only partially identify with their churches, superficially accepting what they like and rejecting what they do not like. There are other groups, called "underground Christians," who no longer identify with mainline churches at all, living their own way of Christianity and developing their own styles of discipleship, structures, liturgies, values, and teachings. Finally, there are the radical voices of prophetic contestation calling not for reform but for revolution, for total rethinking of values, not modification of them. There is no longer one way of understanding the Church; no longer one primary paradigm to which we can all commit ourselves.

Accelerating the division of the Church into sub-groups is the growing education of people and their varied cultural and social backgrounds. What is sociologically significant to one person may be insignificant to another. The resulting misunderstandings are intensified when the different value systems are held by a Church leader and members of his or her congregation. American Christians today often have different value systems than their European counterparts, and many, very frequently, have radically different sets of values than international Church officials.

The massive uniformity of the past is no longer a Church reality. Even within local Churches, believers are seldom at the same level of faith and commitment. People are no longer at the same stage of faith at the same time.

In the 1980s and 1990s we live, and will continue to live, in a divided Church. Psychological and sociological differences have led to different, and at times divergent understandings of the Church, of the nature of discipleship and of the value to be given to former ways of living.

Matthew retold the story of Jesus for a community divided on the value of the past, on directions for the future, and on the relative importance of different doctrines. His community was complex, and its sub-groups needed to be challenged in different ways. His pastoral leadership and sensitivity were truly exceptional. Faced with the divisiveness in Christianity today, we can refocus on Matthew and his proclamation for the 80s and 90s; learn his skill in discernment and integration; and imitate his empathy and his ability to make the message and its spiritual challenge accessible to all.

New things or old? The Second Vatican Council ended in 1965. Catholics throughout the world were challenged to a renewal which implied much change and adaptation. Forms of personal and communal prayer changed, as did liturgy and ritual. Many priests and religious saw their roles differently than before the Council, and this led to different interactions and relationships with the general faithful. This desacralization of state in life, together with the universal call to holiness and ministry, called laity to a level of responsibility to which they had never before been called. This new understanding of the Church, this new paradigm, had a profound impact: people who had faithfully committed themselves to a prior way of life were called to change—it seemed to them abandon—that to which they had so zealously committed themselves. Renewal was difficult. Changing a Church we loved was no easy task. People of all ages struggled to change, some more reluctantly than others, and within ten to fifteen years much had been done.

A few years ago the brakes were applied, renewal began to slow down, and compromise began. Conciliar developments which had given hope were now interpreted restrictively. Instead of a new approach to law, we ended up with a new set of laws simply replacing the old. This is exactly what had happened to Matthew's gospel, which Tertullian had used as "a new law."

A few years ago there were great hopes for laity; we now seem at a standstill. There were changes in the life and ministry of religious; now there are clear indications of control and oppression. There had been signs of a revaluing of marriage, even in the ranks of the clergy, with the ordaining of married deacons; now, should their wives die, they may not remarry. There had been support for women's equality in the Church; now there is a return to the oppression of previous years, and clergy are informed that it is even wrong to belong to organizations that support women's ordination. Liturgical renewal focused on the desires and needs of the people (as for example in reconciliation); now efforts are underway to return to forms of confession that most people have clearly rejected as unsuitable for our times. Many other examples could be added to this short list.

We, like Matthew's Church before us, are in the midst of a battle for theological control. All positions in the theological spectrum are motivated by faith, commitment, and goodness, but the pressures exerted from without local communities are not unlike those experienced by Matthew's Church.

After Christ's preaching many were converted to his new way of life, and the early Church drew many converts from Judaism. Although they had been committed to their former ways of religion, they courageously left them behind, accepting the renewal to which they were called. As time passed, the religious power-brokers of their day reorganized and closed ranks. The Pharisees of Matthew's time told the people who followed the "way" how their commitment was misdirected; how true religious commitment should be shown by being more faithful to the past. The call went out: "Come back to the way things used to be." The Pharisees told their people that the destruction of Jerusalem was a punishment on the people for their infidelity to the Law, and that they must now leave these new ways of Christianity and return with greater fidelity to the ways of the past.

Matthew retold the story of Jesus to a community suffering from anxiety and tension regarding where their commitment should be directed. Some in his community wished to go back to the way things used to be, and others wished to move ahead with new emphases. His superb insights into Church life, community living, and Christian reconciliation, gave new life to his disintegrating community and can be the catalyst in the healing of our own.

Wars and rumors of war.   In these years of the 1980s and 1990s we hear daily of wars and rumors of wars. The threat of nuclear war is something we live with every day of our lives. It has a paralyzing influence on us all.

Matthew's community did not expect the immediate return of the Lord. His Gospel seems to indicate that his community had already come to an awareness that the second coming would be delayed. However, many of his people had lived through times of expectation of the end of the world. They also knew that the additional threat of war from the great world power of the day could easily have led to their annihilation.

Never since this period of New Testament times have all Christians lived in expectation of the end of the world. History reports many small groups from time to time that had thought God's coming was near. Today is different—the possibility of war and cosmic destruction is more real than at any other time in the history of our planet. And, for once, it is not the result of an interpretation or misinterpretation of a prophecy. It is an ever-present reality of daily life. It can hamper our commitment to righteousness, stunt our service to others, paralyze our Christian mission to the world.

Matthew's community was right in the heart of theological warfare, and unfortunately the attitudes we show in battling for theological ground are part of the larger picture of fear and hate. However, the threat of world destruction imposes levels of daily concern and anguish that must be addressed if life is to be worth living at all.

Matthew brings hope and love to a world filled with fear. At a time of paralysis, he calls for the great Christian mission of outreach to the Gentiles. He challenges all to forgiveness, reconciliation, and peace.

In the 1980s and 1990s Matthew's hope, vision and peace can be the directives we need not only for survival, but also to give new relevance to our Christian way of life.

Matthew: a leader for the 1980s and 1990s.   Matthew is a brilliant pastoral leader who knows how to challenge his people with "new things and old" (Mt 13:52). He is able to call for fidelity, but without legalism. His presentation resists any easy synthesis, complex as it is with various levels and degrees of integration. At times we find seeming inconsistencies, where Matthew is unwilling to impose one new integrated spirituality on a community that is at various stages of identification with Christianity. He respects independence, encouraging interdependence instead of uniformity. He demonstrates discernment, not control.

Matthew's Gospel is not a psychological or sociological analysis of his community's life and development. Rather, Matthew finds enlightenment and guidance for his mission of leading his people in a re-reading and reinterpretation of Scripture and the events of Jesus' life. In Matthew's Gospel, Jesus said he would send "wisemen, prophets and teachers," and the evangelist himself is certainly one of them. "A scribe of the kingdom," he reinterprets the message of the Lord with powerful relevance, embodying a new and irresistible challenge to his own community.

Mark, Luke, and John needed to confront persecutions from outside the community, or mediocrity and disbelief from within. Matthew's task was one of the most difficult and painful that any religious leader needs to face: the healing, rebuilding, and redirecting of a divided and oppressed community.

He sees his Church as a community suffering something like the effects of an earthquake (Mt 8:24). Yet he reminds his followers that they must not become paralyzed with fear or helplessness, for the coming of the Lord Jesus and the challenge he brings is itself the most earth-shattering event of all time (Mt 21:10; 27:52; 28:2).

Matthew's community was not uniform but divided into sub-groups, each with its own theological emphases. Our Church today is very similar to his, and unless we deal with the problem with reconciliation, love and mutual understanding, polarization will increase, the drift away from each other will continue and rigid division will result.

Matthew's community faced the crisis of all renewal and reform: When do you stop? Should changes continue? Have they already gone too far? It is hard to go on when Church officials you have respected say no. Matthew's community must have felt like that too, as their previous leaders, the Pharisees, called them to halt their developments and re-emphasize past values. In circumstances such as these, decisons are not easy; conscience is challenged in the extreme.

Matthew's community, like ours, faced fear and threat of war. Can we, like Matthew, bring peace and increased apostolic commitment precisely when others would expect them to end?

Written for a Church in the 80s and 90s, this proclamation from Matthew is truly good news for all Christians of the 1980s and 1990s. The first evangelist focuses so clearly on a community with needs like those of the North American Church he seems to bring us very close to the Lord Jesus and his call to us today.

Chapter One
THE AUTHOR OF MATTHEW

I shall send you prophets and wisemen and scribes
(Mt 23:34).

Matthew was an exceptional person, a giant among religious
leaders of all time. At a crucial turning point in early Christianity,
he stood out with courage and vision when many around him
had neither He gave new directions to his Church, established
new goals, and synthesized a challenging vision of Christianity
that would inspire Church leaders for centuries.

He guided a Church as polarized as our own, and yet he led it to
healing, reconciliation, and a renewed sense of mission. He was,
very likely, a conservative-minded Church leader, but approached
religious and ecclesiastical issues with an exciting interpretive
skill. Immovable on necessary foundational values, he was equally
committed to flexibility and freedom in non-essentials. He united
his community in a common vision while maintaining an open-
ended understanding of the nature of Church and discipleship.
He had organizational and planning skills in abundance, as his
gospel and theology show; he had the true leader's skill to
dream, imagine, wonder, and create new visions, new methods,
new goals; above all he had the caring skills of a master leader
who can visualize the whole and see how disparate parts can
make up a united community.

The New Testament is not arranged chronologically. However,
the Gospel according to Matthew is well placed first, since he was
the evangelist who best bridged the Old Testament and the New;
his was the first presentation of the Gospel that gained extensive
circulation and acceptance; his was the gospel most quoted by
the Church Fathers. The first gospel is also noted for its completeness and order, as well as for its excellent topical synthesis
of the teachings of the early Church.

Its extensive use was partially due to its value as a complete handbook of early Christianity, and as such, very useful to early missionaries. However, it should be mentioned that Matthew's presentation dealt with common problems of the early Church; so valuable were its assessment and directives to the Church as a whole that Renan referred to it as the most important book ever written.

A key feature of Matthew's telling of the Gospel story is his constant focusing of the message on his own community's needs. Since this is the way we generally read Scripture today, it is enlightening to see Matthew's approach. The message he retells comes out of the living faith of his own community. His concise and insightful synthesis is both a Christology and an ecclesiology at the same time.

The Gospel according to Matthew has had major impact on the Church since the very earliest times. It is a superb synthesis of Jesus' teachings, a handbook for catechesis, a valuble tool for missionary evangelization, a much quoted source for Church leaders of all times, a goldmine of liturgical readings.

In the 1980s and 1990s, this gospel challenges again with equal power and efficacy. Now more than ever, we see Matthew's gospel as a pastoral and spiritual response to a community faced with the problems and crises in which we are now immersed. For the 1980s and 1990s this first gospel could well be again the most important book ever written.

Traditions And Today

Matthew in the early traditions of the Church.   The first book of the New Testament carries the title "Gospel according to Matthew." This title is found not only on our modern gospels but also on ancient manuscripts. In fact, the early traditions of the Church are unanimous in ascribing this book to Matthew. While it was common around New Testament times to show devotion to great figures by dedicating work to them by placing it under their authorship, nevertheless, here in the case of the first gospel, the witnesses were convinced that it was not only dedicated to Matthew and a summary of traditions coming from the preaching of Matthew, but rather they were convinced that Matthew actually wrote the gospel bearing his name.

The evangelists Mark and Luke include Matthew in their lists of the twelve apostles, but without further comment (Mk 3:18; Lk 6:15).

Prior to listing the twelve, both Mark and Luke had described Jesus' calling of a tax collector named Levi, but neither added him to the list (Mk 2:14; Lk 5:27). When the first gospel lists the apostles, it specifies that Matthew was a tax collector (Mt 10:3), and the writer had already modified the calling of Levi to state explicitly that this was Matthew (Mt 9:9). The early tradition of the Church unanimously agreed that the Matthew who authored the first gospel was one of the twelve, and the tax collector personally called by Jesus.

The first direct quote from Matthew's gospel occurs in the writings of Ignatius of Antioch, martyred in 110 AD. In his letter to the Smyrnans (I:1), he quotes from Matthew 3:15. In his letter to Polycarp (II:2), he makes use of Matthew 10:16. In section 19 of his letter to the Ephesians, he recounts a story seemingly based on Matthew's birth narrative. In other places, he gives sayings of Jesus found only in Matthew (E.g. 12:35; 15:13; 19:12).[1] Although Ignatius seems, in places, to be quoting directly from Matthew, he nowhere acknowledges Matthew as his source.

Another great bishop of the early Church was Polycarp of Smyrna, martyred in his own city in 155 AD. In his letter to the Philippians, he quotes on four occasions the teachings of the Lord in forms very close to Matthew's gospel (Mt 7:1; 5:3; 6:13; 26:41).

Scholars have also found allusions to Matthew's gospel in other writings of early Christianity.[2]

The first explicit attribution of the first gospel to Matthew, the disciple of Jesus who had been a tax collector, is in the writings of Papias, bishop of Hieropolis in Asia Minor, who lived around 60-130 AD. The five-volumed work of Papias, *Exposition of the Oracles of the Lord*, has not survived, but sections of it are quoted by Eusebius in his work on the history of the early Church. According to Eusebius, Papias had explicitly stated that "Matthew compiled the oracles in the Hebrew language, and each one translated them as he was able" (Eusebius, *Church History*, III, 39, 16). Eusebius in general was mistrustful of Papias, since the latter was a milleniarist and Eusebius opposed that view. However, he seems unquestionably to accept Papias' statement about the authorship of the first gospel. This statement is repeated by Irenaeus, a disciple of Polycarp, who lived around 140-202. In his work *Against Heresies* (III:1, 1) he stated: "Matthew wrote the Gospel in Hebrew while Peter and Paul

were evangelizing and founding the Church of Rome." Papias'
statement is also found in a series of early writers,[3] and is confirmed by Origen (about 185-254), a Father of the Church who is
generally considered to have been very particular and critical of
his sources.

The long line of early witnesses is impressive. However, the
early allusions to the text of the first gospel in the quotes of Ignatius, Polycarp, and others never include a statement on
authorship. The later apostolic and patristic references are all
based on Papias. Is he the first link in a strong chain, or a weak
first link in a dependent chain? Until recently it had been common to criticize Papias as unreliable. New Testament scholars felt
that Papias did not have facts to go on, but rather was writing
devotional history based on information gleaned from the New
Testament itself, not from additional outside witnesses.
Moreover, he was not considered reliable by some of his successors, and therefore should not be accepted today. In the last
decade, there has been a rethinking of the value of Papias, and a
smaller number of writers now very strongly support the
reliability of his testimony.[4]

Based on these witnesses, Christianity has traditionally considered that Matthew, a tax collector and personal disciple of the
Lord Jesus, was the author of this first gospel. Holders of this
position consider that the only discrepancies in the tradition are
the two names Matthew and Levi. These, it is suggested, can be
reconciled by seeing the latter as a tribal designation rather than
a name. The author of the first gospel was called Matthew and
belonged to the tribe of Levi. Matthew the Levite is sometimes
referred to by name, sometimes by tribal designation.[5]

This convincing chain of external evidence is confirmed, it is
thought, by internal evidence which shows that the writer was
educated, bilingual, rather conservative and legalistic, and firmly
rooted in Jewish tradition: likely characteristics of a tax collector
with connections to the tribe of Levi.

Matthew in the understanding of contemporary scholarship.
Since the seventeenth and eighteenth centuries, and subsequent
developments in biblical criticism,[6] New Testament scholars have
seriously questioned the traditional view based on Papias. The
point of departure for this more recent view is the internal
evidence that Matthew's gospel was not written in Aramaic or
Hebrew, as Papias said, but in Greek. The Greek gospel we have

is not translation Greek, but rather the original language of this first gospel. Moreover, as we shall see, source critics have shown that Matthew is dependent on Mark. It is unthinkable that an eyewitness such as Matthew the tax collector, disciple of Jesus, would be so extensively dependent on a non-eyewitness such as Mark. The Matthew we have was written in Greek, is dependent on Mark, and was written later. This conclusion undermines each of Papias' statements. When Papias spoke of Matthew's Hebrew or Aramaic oracles, he was probably referring to a collection of Jesus' sayings that no longer exists, unless it was a source used by the first evangelist as a smaller part of the work we now have: maybe M or even Q which we will discuss later.

The early Church generally considered that apostolic authorship was necessary for a writing to be considered as Scripture. Christians of early centuries assumed that all our New Testament books were authored by one or another of the twelve apostles. Papias' sincere statements regarding a book we probably no longer have were interpreted by early writers as applicable to our gospel. This would have been done in good faith, with clear convictions that an apostle would have written it anyway. Put simply: Papias' statement was not only what early Christians wanted to hear, but also exactly what they expected to hear. Looking at the first gospel today, it is not possible to view it as having been written by an eyewitness disciple of Jesus. We must look elsewhere for a description of our author.

When we look at the first gospel, we see its sense of order, its completeness and balance. The author was a well educated writer, accustomed to the literary forms and methods of his day. He knew Greek very well, and was an authority on the Jewish religion, its teachings and practices. His ability to bring these two cultures together is one of his outstanding qualities. He writes with skill, care, thoroughness, and ordered planning.

His thorough knowledge of the Old Testament, of Jewish methods of interpretation and rabbinical debate not only permeate Matthew's work, but contribute as well to the organization and structure of his book. In fact, the Jewish coloring of the gospel is so pronounced that until about thirty years ago, scholars were virtually unanimous in considering that Matthew was a Christian of Jewish origin.[7] The first gospel shows constant interest in Jewish society: its law, leadership, sects, customs, traditions, and rituals. It presents Jesus as the Messiah, Son of David and Son of Man, and constantly "proves" how he fulfills the expectations of the Old Testament.

Some recent writers, impressed with Matthew's constant condemnation and rejection of Israel and its leaders, and disturbed at Matthew's inaccurate presentation of Judaism in one or two key places, have begun to propose that Matthew was a learned Gentile Christian, not a Jewish Christian.[8] These objections do not seem insurmountable, and it still seems preferable to accept the virtually unanimous position that Matthew was a Christian of Jewish origin.

In fact, his formula quotations of scripture, his use of rabbinical debating methods, his interest in traditional oral law, his skill in using rabbinical interpretation of Scripture, all point to his having had the skills and background of a scribe or rabbi. A dedicated scribe or rabbi, however, would not have been a tax collector, since the latter were despised by devout Jews. Truly, the author was "a scribe trained for the kingdom of heaven" (Mt 13:52). In fact, *Mathetheutheis*, the Greek word used in this passage to translate "trained for" or "becoming a disciple of," is very similar to *Matthaios* meaning "Matthew."

Matthew, skilled scribe of the kingdom, was above all a disciple dedicated to his Lord. Rooted in a religion he had loved, he faithfully launches out into the unknown, contributing all his skills to the new community of the Lord. He gave it identity, helped it to cope with its new independence, strengthened it against outside attack, fostered its stability, and channelled its ministry. He was a dedicated churchman, possibly occupying an official role in the Christian community. He was so well respected that his written account of the Lord's life and good news became the most extensively used proclamation of the early Church.

We may never know how the author of this first gospel received the name or pseudonym of Matthew; indeed, we may never know how, or even if, this work is traceable to the eyewitness disciples of Jesus. The author known to us as Matthew was not an eyewitness, but a brilliant theologian, highly educated in Judaism and profoundly committed to the Lord. He had been faithful to the religious ways of his earlier life, but had had courage enough to leave, moving in a new direction. Above all, he became an insightful interpreter of Jesus' message, showing how both new and old things can be brought out of a treasure house, together giving life to the community of faith.

Sources And Adaptation

The sources of the first gospel.   Matthew's gospel contains
approximately 1,070 verses, but many of these are also found in
Mark or Luke. In fact, it has become common in this century to
identify three clear sources of Matthew's gospel: First, there is a
large block of Matthew's gospel, more than half, which is also
found in the other synoptic gospels of Mark and Luke. Second,
there are 200 to 235 verses, or just less than a quarter, which
Matthew shares with Luke. Finally, approximately 330 verses,
found only in Matthew but not identified with his own editorial
work, are viewed as drawn from an earlier source. These blocks
of material are understood as three distinct sources from which
Matthew wrote the first gospel.[9]

The source material shared by all three synoptic gospels has,
since the first half of the nineteenth century, been identified as
Mark.[10] Of 661 verses in Mark, Matthew uses ideas from 600,
although he uses only about fifty percent of Mark's vocabulary.
While there have always been proponents of a Matthean priority,
a position strongly re-presented in recent years,[11] the majority of
scholars still insist on the priority of Mark and its use by Matthew.
Matthew's gospel is not Aramaic but Greek, and is not a source
for Mark but rather a polishing of Mark's crude Greek. Matthew's
dependence on Mark is clearest of all in the narrative passages. It
is even insisted that Matthew is dependent on Mark for the story
of the call of Matthew.[12] So clear is this dependence that the
resulting gospel reads like an expansion and interpretation of
Mark for the new needs of a growing community.

There are about 230 verses in Matthew found also in Luke but
nowhere else in the New Testament. The episodes are narrated in
the same order in both gospels, and show similarities in language
and style, indicating the same source for both. Moreover, both
seem to preserve the same style and characteristics of a written
source. Since the source remains unknown, it has become traditional to refer to it simply as "the source," which in German, the
language of the scholars who first proposed it, is *Quelle;* hence
the symbol "Q".[13]

There have always been authors who have firmly rejected Q
altogether.[14] Others have dispensed with the need of Q by sug-
gesting that Luke copies Matthew, and that this accounts suffi-
ciently for their similarities.[15] While such criticisms have helped
refocus on the nature of Q, reminding some scholars that it is

only a hypothesis, nevertheless, most scholars remain unconvinced, and still consider Q the best explanation of the data we have.[16]

In addition to Mark and Q, about 330 verses of Matthew are exclusive to the first gospel. This material, referred to as "M", is often thought to represent special interests in his own community. M includes episodes such as the birth narratives, sections of the Sermon on the Mount, the empowering of Peter at Caesarea Philippi, and parts of the resurrection appearances and final commissioning of the disciples. M contains varied traditions, possibly from the Antiochene Church.[17] In places M seems not only representative of varied strands in the Church, but actually includes contradictory positions. This latter understanding has led to the suggestion of two separate stages in the composition of M.[18]

Matthew, then, uses three major sources: Mark, Q, and M. The first two were written sources and the third could have been. The three sources would probably have been present in the community over a period of time, possibly twenty years, and Matthew's community probably used all three sources in the context of community life: liturgy, education, discipline, and so on.

Mindful of recent challenges to these hypotheses, we should avoid any simplistic approach to these traditions. There was overlap between them, as we can see in the large number of doublets in Matthew. There was interaction and daily application to the needs of a living local community. Eventually, after a couple of decades of living interaction in dialogue or confrontation, Matthew incorporates the three sources into his retelling of the events of Jesus' life. His dependence on other sources is evident; he cannot be viewed as an eyewitness disciple of Jesus.

Matthew's use of his sources.   When Matthew combines his sources, literary and experiential, he stamps them all with his own editorial and theological characteristics. He does not simply merge the traditions, nor does he merely repeat them. Rather, he selects, rearranges, reinterprets, and reapplies the insights of all three.

In his use of Mark, Matthew shows respectful dependence and theological freedom. He builds his new gospel on Mark's general structure of the life and ministry of Jesus. He also preserves most of the content of Mark, in contrast to Luke, who has the "great omission." Matthew also maintains the general flow and order of Mark, following the same order from Mark 6:7 to the end.

However, Matthew demonstrates considerable editorial freedom in his use of Mark. He abbreviates Mark's stories, omits many details, gives a different meaning to some of his sayings, in places substitutes his own dialogues instead of Mark's, and often expands a Marcan text, adding theological applications more appropriate to the Matthean Church.

Matthew's editorial contributions begin with his conscious effort to improve on Mark's Greek. In some places Matthew corrects Mark's verb tenses; in other places whole narratives written in the present tense are rewritten in the past. Matthew's vocabulary is richer than Mark's, over 350 words more, and he substituted classical words for Mark's vaguer diction, conversational vocabulary, or even offensive phrases. Where Mark is clumsy, Matthew refines (Mt 9:3); where Mark's verbs have no subjects, Matthew supplies (Mt 19:26); where technical terms are inaccurate, Matthew corrects (Mt 14:1).

By using the unusual technique of abbreviation, Matthew cuts through Mark's distracting details, emphasizing essential teachings on such crucial issues of spirituality as discipleship, faith, and the person of Jesus.[19] He reduces miracle stories to half their original length, and in other places condenses narratives by 10-20%. He achieves this by omitting many of Mark's distracting details, as in the stories of Jairus' daughter and the woman with a hemorrhage (Mt 9:18-26).

Frequently, Matthew rearranges material found in his sources (Mt 8:1 - 9:34), at times without concern for either the order in which events occurred or their place in the sources. Examples of this would be Chapter 10, which gives instructions for the apostles, or Chapter 13's detailed structuring of seven parables. By weaving together material found in the differing contexts of its several sources, Matthew gives new meanings to stories and sayings.

Sometimes he takes words and phrases from Mark, rearranging them for his own aims (as in Mt 4:23-25). Sometimes he arranges scattered sayings in the form of a discourse (as in Chapter 10). In this case, by the time he has completed his editing, Jesus' discourse is really delivered to Matthew's Church of the 80s rather than the Galilean crowds. Such interpretative editing is a further example of Matthew's pedagogical interests: history and chronology are secondary for him.

It seems reasonable to conclude that Matthew would be at least

as free in editing Q as he was in editing Mark. Q, a collection of
the sayings of the Lord, is that part of the gospel tradition used
by no one but Matthew and Luke. It is thought to have originated
in Antioch and, as we shall see, to have had a close relationship
to Matthew's community. Because of its emphasis on the end
times, it is generally dated as early as 50. Some scholars consider
it an oral tradition, but others are more impressed by the similarity
of vocabulary in the Q sections of Matthew and Luke, and prefer
to accept Q as a written source. Q was obviously an important
tradition in the early Church, and is treated very respectfully by
both Matthew and Luke. Most commentators consider the order
of Q is best preserved by Luke. Matthew, as in the case of Mark,
has here exercised considerable freedom in rearranging the
material to fit his didactic interests, rereading and interpreting
the material in light of the needs of his living community. He
changes the order, as we have already mentioned; arranges
material differently, as he does in the sections of the Sermon on
the Mount which come from Q; unifies dispersed sayings, as
those on discipleship in Mt 10:34-39; and, in general, integrates
the Q material into his own broad theological purposes.

Matthew's own personal source, M, generally deals with
Church discipline, liturgy and apologetic positions. It focuses on
Old Testament texts, supporting Jesus as the fulfillment of Jewish
hopes. In these sections, Matthew quotes the Old Testament,
comments on it, molds his own narrative to biblical phraseology,
chooses themes important to Judaism, and even uses key Old
Testament texts as pins to hold together the fabric of his thought.
Not only does he use Old Testament texts as pivotal points, but
uses as well scribal and rabbinical approaches to explain problem
issues to his community. Midrash is the scribal exposition and
interpretation of scripture; Halakah is the application of the
legal requirements of the Pentateuch to concrete issues; Haggadah
is the pious devotional reflection on scripture, showing its
wonderful fulfillment beyond its obvious meaning. All three are
especially evident in M. Midrashic additions permeate the
material, Halakah can be seen in Mt 17:24-27, and Haggadah in
the infancy narratives.

Gospel sources will no doubt remain a focus of debate.[20]
However, the most convincing and useful hypothesis remains
that Matthew incorporated Mark, Q, and M in his re-presentation
of the life and teachings of Jesus. In weaving these three sources

together, Matthew exercised the extensive freedom traditionally associated with scribal interpretation. His pastoral interest is not the past, but the present. He searches through his storehouse of traditions to bring out new insights and new interpretations, as well as the life and spirit of former times.

Style And Interests

We have looked at what tradition tells us about Matthew, as well as what modern scholarship concludes about him. We have also caught a glimpse of our author in light of the sources he depends on, and how he uses them. Now we turn to the writer's style and interests, as these too reveal much about him.

Polished Greek. The first gospel, as we know it, was written in Greek. Matthew's Greek is much better than Mark's, though not as elegant as Luke's. Matthew has a vocabulary larger than any of the evangelists except Luke, using over ninety-five words and expressions peculiar to the first gospel.[21] Many of Matthew's words and sentence constructions are specifically Greek with no Jewish equivalents, and even some of his plays on words can come only from a skillful knowledge of Greek. He clarifies and specifies Mark's vague vocabulary, and where, on occasions, he retains it, his new contexts create greater attention and focus. For example, the phrase "and then": a vague chronological connecting link in Mark, it is more frequently used in Matthew, but refers to special moments in salvation history, equivalent to "in those crucial days" or "in that critical time."[22] Matthew's work is unquestionably a stylistic improvement on Mark.

Jewish interests. This gospel, written in Greek, also has a distinct Jewish coloring to it. Matthew never explains Jewish customs to his audience, even using many Palestinian expressions and writing styles. Some sections of the gospel have a semitic tone to them, such as the infancy narratives (Mt 1:1 - 2:23) or the empowering of Peter (Mt 16:17-19). Others are presented with the Jewish stylistic procedures of parallelism, use of numbers, chiasm, and inclusion. At times, the whole tone of a passage is determined by frequent Old Testament citations, often introduced with a formula that focuses the reader on Jesus' fulfillment of Messianic prophecy.[23] Elsewhere, the text echoes the Old Testament flavor of promise and warning (Mt 18:5-6), or prophetic challenge and woe (Mt 18:7), or wisdom sayings and proverbial

18 MATTHEW

explanation (Mt 18:8-9).[24] In the narratives of Jesus' debates
with his opponents, the rabbinical style of question (Mt 17:25;
18:12; 22:17, 42; 26:66) and counter question (Mt 12:5; 13:13; 19:9;
21:16; 22:31) is frequently used.

Emphasis on discourse. One of Matthew's notable
characteristics is his emphasis of dialogue and discourse. He
gathers together sayings of Jesus from throughout his ministry,
composing discourses appropriate to his own Church. To do this,
Matthew "uses a large number of 'literary seams,' lines intended
to connect passages previously unconnected."[25] While the component parts of the discourse go back to Jesus, the discourses, as
we know them, are Matthew's. He sometimes rearranges and
reformulates an outline of Mark's, to suit his own theological
aims (E.g. Mt 24:1-36). As a result, we now have a series of
outstanding discourses. These Matthean syntheses of Jesus'
teachings are separated from each other by narratives, the
bridges between them generally provided by one or another of
Matthew's typical formulas (Mt 7:28; 11:1; 13:53; 19:1; 26:1).
Matthew's skill in using the discourses is not only seen in lengthy
summaries. The final speech of Jesus (Mt 28:18-20) is a brief but
excellent Matthean summary of his gospel's major themes. Matthew
is thus able to offer his community the teachings of Jesus in a
way specially synthesized for their needs.

Symmetrical arrangements. In Chapter Three we shall examine
in greater detail Matthew's structuring of his work. Here we can
mention one aspect of his style: symmetry. Not only is the whole
work structured to alternate narrative and discourse (Chapters
1-4 and 5-7; 8-9 and 10; 11-12 and 13; 14-17 and 18; 19-22 and
23-25), but the entire twenty-eight chapters are symmetrically
arranged.[26]

Often the arrangement of passages focuses on the mid-point,
all other parts arranged around it in inverted parallelism. This
method draws the reader's attention to the teaching of the mid-
point, frequently in Matthew the fulfillment of an Old Testament
prophecy.[27]

Another supportive structuring technique is the arranging of
material in numerical groups. There are three divisions of the
genealogy (Mt 1:1-17), three temptations (Mt 4:1-11), three duties
(Mt 6:1-18), three sets of three miracles (Mt chs. 8-9), three signs,
three parables of judgment and three challenges to the scribes

(Mt ch. 22). There are seven parables of the kingdom (Mt ch. 13), seven woes (Mt 23:13-33) and seven parables of warning (Mt 24:32 - 25:46).[28]

Repetitive devices.   Matthew composes his work with considerable attention to stylistic characteristics which will help the reader remember. These mnemonic devices include some common to the other gospels, and some unique to Matthew.

Often he anticipates an event with a programmatic statement, or foreshadows it with a dream; he then describes the event, finally summarizing it in retrospect (E.g. Mt 1:18-25). More frequently he states the teaching twice: first in narrative and then by a clarifying interpretation or explanation (E.g. Mt 8:16-17).

Matthew often employs parallelism, in which the same idea is repeated either in a positive or negative way. While all New Testament writers use this, Matthew cultivates it (E.g. Mt 7:24-27).[29] Sometimes parallelism is used more elaborately whereby an entire section is arranged in parallel (A-A¹, B-B¹, C-C¹) or in inverted parallelism (A B C D C¹ B¹ A¹). A further elaboration of parallelism is the literary technique of inclusion, by which an author stresses the same point of interest at the beginning and the end of a section (Mt 1:23 and 28:20; or 3:2 and 4:17).

Simpler forms of repetitive devices used by Matthew include stereotyped phrases such as "the prophets and the law," "heirs to the kingdom," "the lost sheep of the house of Israel," "blind guides," "let him who has ears to hear listen." Matthew uses these repeatedly.[30] Sometimes he will repeat a phrase two or three times in a short section, thus helping to focus the reader's attention. On other occasions he repeats a teaching with a doublet (Mt 5:29-30 and 18:8-9). Even single words are used by Matthew to focus his readers attention: at times a repeated key word echoes through the passage, reminding the reader of a point of interest (Mt 14:26-33). At times he will use a key word at the end of one section and at the beginning of the next, stitching together two parts of his work and emphasizing his own understanding of the link.

Matthew's editing skills produced a topical, well-organized gospel eminently suitable for teaching. Certainly, several of the stylistic characteristics we have examined make the work an appropriate resource for preaching and teaching. It gathers the teachings of Jesus into discourses already interpreted for the Matthean community. It presents the traditions already compiled for community education rather than private reading. It deals with themes crucial to Matthew's time, even introducing terms never used before but now important to the community, such as "Church," "end of the age," and "gospel of the kingdom." His use of structure, symmetry, and repetitive devices facilitate remembering, useful both in liturgy and in catechesis.

By the time Matthew writes, the eyewitnesses are dead. Others must carry on the tasks of leading and educating in the faith. Matthew offers them the guidance and synthesis they need. He not only recounts history and the teachings of Jesus, but superimposes his community's needs on Jesus' message. He asks of the traditions questions appropriate to his own time, and, with the ability and dedication of a scribe of the kingdom, re-presents the vision and challenge of Jesus with new relevance for the 80s and 90s. His literary and stylistic skills enable Matthew to be a master teacher, a guide of guides, a leader who fosters leadership in others.

Recent Studies In Matthew

We have evaluated Matthew's use of sources and his stylistic characteristics; in this section we turn to the contemporary revival in Matthean studies. Other gospels have held the center stage of research, or been rescued from academic oblivion. Matthew, however, is only just emerging as a focus of contemporary scholarship. This is hardly because his is the only gospel left to scholars! Rather, Matthew has come to the fore for two major reasons. First, his message is very appropriate for the Church today. Second, a series of critical problems in biblical scholarship are well exemplified in Matthew, and the first gospel becomes a natural focal point of debate: the reassessment of source theory, or the development of new approaches to literary structure, or different syntheses of biblical theology, all focus on Matthew.

This century in general, and the last quarter century in particular, have produced a series of fine studies on Matthew.[31] As contemporary scholars research Matthew, they too contribute to our understanding of what Matthew was like. In their attempts to identify the purpose or theology of Matthew, contemporary biblical writers highlight one or another of his many qualities, giving us further glimpses into the kind of leader he was.

Studies of his sources.   The scientific method was first applied to the texts of the New Testament in the eighteenth century. The time prior to this time is referred to as the pre-critical period. In the case of Matthew's gospel, as we have seen, the pre-critical tradition was unanimous in assuming that Matthew wrote in Aramaic, and that his work preceded the other gospels. Most of the early writers were dependent on Papias, and their interpretation of his few comments was consistent in considering Matthew the first evangelist, even though Papias himself had dealt with Mark first.

Most scholars upheld the priority of Matthew until the research of K. Lachmann and C. H. Weisse in the early nineteenth century. The insights of these two source critics were first documented and critically examined towards the end of the nineteenth century in the work of H. J. Holtzmann, and in the early part of this century in the outstanding exposition of B. H. Streeter. These scholars discovered and documented the two-source theory as an explanation of the relationship of the synoptic gospels. The two-source theory is sometimes expanded to a four-source theory including Mark, Q, M, and L. In the case of Matthew, it states that he used Mark, Q, and M. While this hypothesis has been widely accepted, there have always been opponents. In the late eighteenth and early nineteenth centuries, J. S. Griesbach held that Luke made use of Matthew and that Mark was composed from a selection of episodes in Matthew and Luke. More recently, the meticulous work of B. C. Butler and B. Orchard insists on the priority of Matthew.[32] This position did not receive substantial support. In the last fifteen years, however, there have been two interesting developments. One is the reappraisal of the statements of Papias by a small group of scholars who believe him trustworthy.[33] The other is more significant and more broadly based: the growing dissatisfaction with the four-source theory.[34] Some scholars believe M too vague a designation, a catch-all for more than one source.[35] Others think that Matthew uses a Mark, but not our present Mark. Many, as we have seen, reject Q.[36]

In addition to these explicit studies on Matthew's sources, we can also mention some recent redactional studies, as significant for their position on sources as they are for their theology.[37]

Studies of his literary structure.   The literary structure of Matthew's gospel was first emphasized by B. W. Bacon, who suggested that it was divided into five books in imitation of the Pentateuch.[38] This understanding, still accepted in at least a modified form, by a surprisingly large number of writers, now

receives mixed reactions. More recently, other writers have moved
away from this literary structuring for apologetic purposes, tend-
ing to stress such structuring in support of a geographical plan
(W. Trilling), a salvation-historical perspective (G. Strecker), or a
developing Christology (J. D. Kingsbury).[39]

Scholars, such as O. L. Cope and R. Gundry, have emphasized
the importance of the Old Testament in the literary structuring
of Matthew. The former stresses the mid-point technique, in
which narratives hinge on an Old Testament mid-point, and
claims that the passages are to be viewed and interpreted in light
of the Old Testament quotation placed at the center of the narrative. Gundry considers Matthew so steeped in the Old Testament that he claims he is imitating the targums, and should be
interpreted accordingly.[40]

There have been several changes of emphasis in biblical studies
in the last twelve years, and one such change has been from
history to story. The writers are seen as having fictionalized
history, and Matthew too is seen as a storyteller or epic writer.[41]

Studies of his editing.   After 1950, biblical scholars turned
their attention to the editorial contributions of the evangelists.
Redaction criticism, as this analysis is called, considers each
author a creative writer who, through final editing of the oral
traditions, imprints his own theology on the gospels. Each
evangelist editor integrates all his sources into his own
theological vision. While contemporary authors differ in the
theological emphases they ascribe to Matthew, all agree that
Matthew is a great theologian who has filtered the traditions
through his own theology as an answer to what he discerned
were Church needs. Four emphases are common in redactional
critical studies of Matthew:

1. J. Rohde, W. Trilling, G. Strecker, F. V. Filson, and others,
stress an ecclesiological motivation for the writing of the first
gospel. They consider Matthew's gospel to be a response to the
needs of a community which had just come to recognize its own
independence from Judaism. In this context, Matthew gathers
material from his sources and chooses, orders, and arranges it to
stress the origins, authority, life, discipline, and nature of the
Church.[42]

2. G. D. Kilpatrick, K. Stendahl, and O. L. Cope see the distinct
involvement of a scribe in the composition of the first gospel.[43]
Kilpatrick and Cope see Matthew as a Christian scribe

thoroughly acquainted with the life, teachings, law, and inter-
pretational skills of the Old Testament. They believe he reworks
the source material of his gospel and is himself a Church official,
or at least has ecclesiastical support for his venture. Kilpatrick
considers the origin of the final document to be in the liturgical
context of a reflection on Mark, Q, and M. Stendahl broadens
Kilpatrick's view in two ways: from liturgy to catechetics, and
from Matthew being one scribe to being a school of scripture
interpreters.

3. G. Bornkamm, J. D. Kingsbury, and E. Schweizer are three of
the many writers who emphasize a strictly theological motivation
in Matthew's final redacting.[44] Bornkamm deserves special mention as the first redactional critic of Matthew's composition. He
sees Matthew's theological emphases to be an integration of
Christology, ecclesiology, and eschatology. Kingsbury, one of the
outstanding Matthean scholars of recent years, has stressed
throughout his writings the Christological syntheses of Matthew.
Schweizer too stresses Jesus' centrality in Matthew. He sees
Matthew as a Jewish Christian highlighting the role of Jesus as
the new interpreter of God's law.

4. The final group of commentators to be mentioned here includes W. Thompson and J. P. Meier, who see Matthew's redactional work specifically directed to the upbuilding of his community. Thompson stresses Matthew's concern to deal with the
problems his community had to face because of the challenge of
Jamnian Pharisaism.[45] Meier sees Matthew's editing as focusing
on the need for mutual understanding among the four subgroups
of Matthew's community, and on the need to establish lawful
authority, especially in moral matters.[46]

A revival of interest in Matthew. The variety of scholarly
work on Matthew in the last twenty-five years mirrors the
richness of the first gospel. The 1980s continue to witness the
publication of outstanding major commentaries.[47]

Matthew's gospel presents both scholars and believers with
significant problems: Did he break away from Judaism, or not?
Did he abandon the Law as Paul did, or did he just reinterpret it?
Did he confirm the primacy of Peter, or the primacy of the community? Did he document ecclesiastical authority, or a Church
without structure? These are a few of the many serious questions
which pour down on the attentive reader of Matthew. The future
research of scholars and the reflective integration of believers

will continue to focus on Matthew, giving promise of exciting years ahead.

The recent scholarly emphasis on Matthew has brought to light his creative use of his sources. It has helped us appreciate Matthew's desires, hopes, and convictions as seen in the literary structuring of his work. It has highlighted his pastoral sensitivity, leadership skill, and theological synthesis.

Although unquestionably more at home with conservative positions, Matthew emerges as a courageous pastoral leader. He can now be seen as one of the wisemen, prophets, and teachers that Jesus had promised to his Church (Mt 23:34).

The Spirituality Of Matthew

We have developed a portrait of Matthew from the contributions of Church traditions and contemporary analysis. We have seen something of the kind of Church leader he was from an examination of his sources and his use of them. We have identified some of his exceptional artistic, literary, and leadership qualities in the ways he composed his work. Finally, we have reviewed how contemporary writers see and appreciate Matthew.

The spirituality of Matthew.   During a period of multiple crises for his community, Matthew was able to proclaim the centrality of Jesus and the originality of his message. In times of theological crises, such as those described in chapter 23, Matthew saw the Church as needing three forms of the ministry of leadership. For such times, Jesus promised prophets, the wise and scribes (Mt 23:34). This promise is still future in Luke (Lk 11:49-51), but a present reality in Matthew's Church. Matthew himself embodied this threefold charism. He gave Jesus' message renewed life and vitality through his scribal interpretation and skill. He made himself a channel for personified Wisdom, bringing to his community the youthful freshness of the new, the perennial vitality of the old. He became for his own community a prophetic voice of challenge and vision. Before anyone can exercise these ministries of scribe, sage, and prophet, he or she needs to embody in their own life and commitment the stuff of which such ministries are made. The focus of Matthew's teaching is also the focus of his own life and commitment. Jesus' call to repentance and a redirection of life became Matthew's own inspiration, means of growth, vision of commitment, and measuring rod of authentic Christianity. Matthew was dedicated to his Lord and to

his own ecclesial community, responding to the latter's needs by
presenting the past of Jesus in such a way that it challenged the
present situation of his own Church. Matthew's spirituality, the
secret of his own life and authenticity, became, through his interpretation of Jesus' message, the spirituality offered to his
Church. Given the similarity of our crises to his, Matthew's
spirituality can become the basis for our discipleship and ecclesial
response today.

A prophetic ministry.   Prophecy is the ministry of speaking
God's words of denunciation and challenge, of consolation and
encouragement, of renewal and community building. Matthew
denounced hypocritical Pharisees and half-hearted Christians
with the force and vigor of Amos (Mt 23:1-39; 22:11-14). He encouraged and consoled his oppressed "little ones" with the sensitive feeling of Second Isaiah (Mt 25:31-46; 19:13-15). Like the
post-exilic prophets Haggai and Zechariah, Matthew called his
community to renewal and upbuilding (Mt 18:1-37).

His own conversion from the Judaism he loved was an experience
filled with sorrow and hurt, yet he had the courage to leave the
security of a known and cherished past to proclaim a new direction, a new vision, and a new corporate sense of mission.

He offered no easy solutions to the crises of his Church.
"Matthew's material refuses with the obstinacy of granite to integrate itself into an easy and accessible presentation. The
author's personality is complex, just as his religious and ecclesial
experience is rich."[48] Yet no suspicion was ever attached to
Matthew's gospel. Radical though it is in places, it was
wholeheartedly accepted by the wider Church as Jesus' call to
their times.

A ministry of wisdom.   Matthew's gospel is the only one to
identify the Wisdom of God with Jesus (Mt 23:34, 39; 11:28-30).
Wisdom, best described in the book of Wisdom (7:22 - 8:1), is
shared by men and women as a practical charism of experience,
understanding and skillful guidance.[49]

Matthew was a highly educated, pastoral leader whose experience, understanding and counsel made him a truly wise
leader in a turbulent Church. His community lived at different
levels of identification, was polarized and certainly not open to a
uniform presentation of teaching. Matthew could appreciate all,
accept the practical contradictions of daily living, and affirm the
different groups who made up his Church. Contradictions in

Matthew are indicative of contradictions in his Church (Mt
12:1-14 and 5:19; 28:19 and 10:5; 23:13, 16 and 23:3). He could be
pro-Gentile (Mt 2:1-12; 4:14-16; 12:21; 28:19) and anti-Gentile (Mt
10:5; 18:17). He could be pro-Jewish (Mt 5:17; 22:34-40) and anti-
Jewish (Mt 12:6; 21:28-32; 27:25). He could call for a new direction
for the Church, and still be the only evangelist who also wants to
keep the old (Mt 9:17). He had the strength and stature to give his
community a sense of identity, stability and independence. He
also had the caring skill to unite diverse groups into a peaceful,
reconciled community. It would have been easier for him to take
sides or drift to one of the extremes, particularly a more conservative position, but instead he rose above petty, party positions,
steering a middle course. His dedicated ability and skillful
counsel reconciled a divided Church.

A ministry of teaching.   A scribe was both scholar and intel-
lectual, both custodian and interpreter of the law. He was not a
historian, but rather a spiritual director showing others the
perennial vitality and obligatory force of God's will. Matthew
was a custodian of his sources who realized that their form must
change for their essence to remain the same. In order to make
the spiritual challenge relevant to his community, Matthew often
alters the stories to apply them better; he drops names from
historical episodes to make them more universal; he constructs
artificial settings for Jesus' teachings to make them concrete for
his own Church. His structure of narrative and discourse com-
municate consistent attitudes to essential problems of his own
Church. Matthew sees Jesus as the definitive interpreter of God's
will. As new problems arose from the pressure of Jamnian
Pharisaism, or from Christians who were against the law, or from
enthusiastic charismatics, Matthew returns to Jesus' teachings,
bringing that teaching alive for his own day.

Biblical spirituality.   In any generation, the way we live our
Christian calling must always be rooted in the biblical call of
Jesus. Each book of the New Testament presents us with a
specific community's understanding of that call and their concrete interpretation of its message. Each gospel is already a
school of spirituality defining the nature of discipleship, Church,
worship, and Christian service.

Matthew's biblical spirituality is a rich synthesis of Jesus' foundational teachings and the evangelist's inspired interpretation of
them. A living witness of prophecy, wisdom, and interpretation,

he called his own community to renewal through reconciliation. His approach was so powerful, his attitudes so sincere and authentic, and his teaching so carefully and sensitively presented, that he became the most successful evangelist of the early Church.

Matthew's challenge echoes again for our Church of the 1980s and 1990s, calling us to reconciliation and a Christ-centered life. To achieve this in our times requires similar discipleship and leadership as in Matthew's. Now, as then, we need Matthew's charisms and ministries of prophecy, wisdom, and interpretation.

Chapter Two
MATTHEW'S COMMUNITY

He got into the boat and his disciples followed him.
Without warning a violent storm came up on the
lake, and the boat began to be swamped by the
waves Jesus. . .stood up and took the winds and the
sea to task. Complete calm ensued (Mt 8:23-24, 26).

Matthew is the first evangelist to describe the Church as a boat.
For him, discipleship means following Jesus into the boat of his
Church. However, at the time Matthew is writing, it seems that a
storm has developed without warning, tossing the boat of his
Church, the disciples within feeling abandoned and helpless.
Jesus rises and reminds them all to have courage in facing their
common hardships, and faith in him as the Lord who guides his
boat to safety.

On a closer reading of this passage, we see that Matthew has
slightly but significantly changed Mark's account. The latter
naturally speaks of a "bad squall" on the lake (Mk 4:37), whereas
Matthew, unexpectedly, uses the word "earthquake" to describe
the catastrophe.[1] This is the first of four uses of the term "earthquake." The second describes the impact on Jerusalem of Jesus'
arrival and solemn entry (Mt 21:10). The third earthquake occurs
at the death of Jesus (Mt 27:52), the fourth "mighty earthquake"
at his resurrection (Mt 28:2). At the time of the first earthquake,
the disciples ask: "What sort of man is this?" (Mt 8:27). At the second earthquake, the whole city of Jerusalem asks: "Who is this?
And the crowd kept answering, 'This is the prophet Jesus from
Nazareth in Galilee' " (Mt 21:10-11). The third earthquake draws a
powerful response from the Gentile centurion at the foot of the
cross: "Clearly this was the Son of God!" (Mt 27:54). After the
fourth and last earthquake, an angel proclaims to the world: "Go
quickly and tell his disciples: He has been raised from the dead"
(Mt 28:7).

The community of disciples whose Church seems shaken as if by an earthquake are reminded three times by Matthew of the cosmic earthquake experienced by the universe at the arrival of Jesus. The disciples, according to Matthew, should feel no fear in their turmoil, but their very crisis ought to be an occasion to refocus their faith "that even the winds and the sea obey him" (Mt 8:27). Such an earthquake can be lifegiving to their community.

During their exile in Babylon, at a time of lost hope, discouragement, and oppression, the chosen people had been called by the prophet Ezekiel to rise up to a new awareness of the life and power which God had given them. Ezekiel foresaw a great earthquake, when God would raise people from their graves and give them new life as his chosen people. These events seem to be in Matthew's mind as he uses the symbolism of the earthquake.[2]

Matthew's community is faced with serious problems. It seems that the boat of his local Church is tossed by a violent storm and swamped by destructive waves (Mt 8:24). Matthew likens the community's hardships to an earthquake which is not destructive but lifegiving; filled with the spirit of God; an opportunity for new life and commitment to the Lord's mission; an occasion for a new sense of identity as God's chosen people.

This chapter considers the influences on Matthew's Church of the political, social, and civic developments of the Palestinian and Syrian regions. It was a community in transition to a new set of religious values, with all the usual hurtful effects of such a shift. It was a community in the 80s and 90s, possibly located in a major city, with all the power, culture, wealth, and immorality attendant thereto.

Matthew's community was certainly one of the most difficult, yet interesting and challenging, groups of early Christianity. In reflecting on its influences, needs, problems, date, and location we will keep an eye on our own Church communities. Matthew's call to his community echoes in our own, tossed as we are by the earthshattering events of our times.

A Community In The Midst Of World Events

A region under seige.   In the summer of 323 BC., Alexander the Great died in Babylon at the age of thrity-three. By brilliant military strategy, he had consolidated control over an empire that extended throughout the Mediterranean, Persia, and India. His conquests were not only military, but cultural as well. His vision included uniting the world in common appreciation of classical Greek culture. After his death, Alexander's empire was divided by his two great generals, Seleucus and Ptolemy.

The Roman Republic began to expand eastward around 200 BC., defeating the Seleucid king Antiochus III in 190 BC., annexing Macedonia in 148, North Africa in 146, and Asia Minor in 133. By 63 BC., Rome had established the imperial province of Syria, with its capital in Antioch. This last expansion included the regions of Galilee, Judea, and their neighboring areas, which were under Roman rule though governed locally by Maccabean monarchs. One of the latter, Hyrcanus II, had an advisor, Antipater, whose second son was Herod, later to emerge as a powerful puppet king who ruled the land of the Jews from 37 BC. to 4 BC. Both Herod the Great and the sons who acceded to his divided kingdom were tyrannical, violent, immoral, and corrupt. Herod Agrippa I died in 44 AD., and, since his son was only seventeen, the Roman Emperor Claudius used the occasion to transform the land of the Jews into a Roman province. Nine years later, however, under Nero, the young king was again the governing figurehead in the northern parts of the country.

Since 63 BC., the land of the Jews had been governed from Antioch in Syria, where the Roman military governor, or legate, was stationed. It was, however, common practice that some smaller difficult areas be governed directly by the emperor through his prefect or procurator, and this had been the case with Judea, Galilee and the surrounding regions. From 6 to 66 AD., unfortunately, most of the fourteen procurators were second-rate administrators, incompetent and cruel. The last of them, Gessius Florus, governed from 64-66 AD. In May of 66, he demanded seventeen talents from the temple treasury. While probably within his rights, this request was viewed as robbery and sacrilege by the Jews. Tension escalated, fighting broke out, and the Jews gained early victories. Eventually, the legate of Syria intervened, and he too was routed. Rome could not tolerate this local revolt, and Nero sent the commander Vespasian and his son Titus to subdue the rebels. Galilee was reconquered by 67, and most of Judea by 68. The fighting then stopped due to Nero's death, and was not resumed until the spring of 70 when Titus began the five-month siege of Jerusalem. In September of 70, the city and temple were sacked, the country became an imperial province, and even its name was changed, to "Palestine," land of the Philistines, to symbolize the Roman extinction of the Jewish nation.[3]

A nation under oppression.   A nation that tried to resist the Roman military believed it was God's chosen nation. The land had been given to their ancestor Abraham, and they had re-entered it after their slavery in Egypt in the thirteenth century BC. They had been attacked many times, but believed God had protected them through the leadership of their judges, early prophets, and kings. Assyria had exiled them twice, in 733 and 722 BC., but they had rebuilt their nation. Three times their kings were personally exiled, and on three other occasions in 598, 587, and 582 BC., thousands of skilled people were led to exile in Babylon, leaving only the poor and uneducated behind. Some of these, against the law, intermarried with the Canaanites, and were later segregated as Samaritans. In 538, Cyrus of Persia conquered Babylon, releasing the Jews to return to their land. From August 520 to February 519, the two prophets Haggai and Zechariah challenged the people to rebuild their city and temple, the latter being completed in 515 BC.

The history of the chosen people was a history of faith and suffering. Even after their return from exile, they would become again a small buffer state between great powers. Before the exile, the warring powers were frequently Assyria, Egypt, and Babylon. Later the Jews would find themselves between Alexander the Great and the Persians, or the Seleucid kings to the north and the Ptolemies to the south. In 167 BC., the Jews, led by the Maccabees, revolted against Antiochus Epiphanes IV, who had begun to persecute those Jews who would not accept his hellenizing policy.

The Jews believed Yahweh had chosen them to bear witness to him by their faith and obedience to his Law. They believed Yahweh was the Lord of history and their own destiny, and that his will was carried out in them. They lived in hope that Yahweh's Messiah, or anointed one, would come to save them and re-establish his rule.

The Jews believed in God's choice and guidance of them. When oppressed, they saw their suffering as punishment for their infidelity to the way of life God had given them as revealed in the scriptures of the Law and the prophets. Following the Law was not easy for the ordinary person, since even religious leaders argued among themselves regarding the content and interpretation of God's Law. The Sadducees, a priestly group, accepted only the first five books of the Bible, centered their faith on the temple and its worship, and rejected all oral tradition. They were conservative and generally very politically involved. The Pharisees were a lay group who accepted many books as scripture. They were more liberal, opposed political involvement, and centered all Jewish religious life on fidelity to the Law. Both Sadducees and Pharisees had supporters skilled in interpreting the Law. These teachers or scribes would later emerge as the key rabbis.

At the time of Jesus and the early Church, varied interpretations of God's Law had led some to reject society altogether to live as strict ascetics, called Essenes, some of whom lived in Qumran on the edge of the Dead Sea. Others grouped together to restore their religious freedom by military conflict with the Romans, these were the Zealots.[4]

A region under constant siege, a nation under oppression; this was the the historical setting of early Christianity.

A people of dispersion.   During times of political and military conflict, as also during periods of persecution, the Jewish people had fled their homeland for havens of security, or, having been exiled, remained behind in the cities of their imprisonment, setting up new homes. There were over a million Jews in Mesopotamia by the first century, especially in Babylon, and over a million in Egypt, especially in Alexandria. Asia Minor held over a million, a hundred thousand each lived in both Italy and Northern Africa, and many others were scattered throughout the Mediterranean.

In the early Church, Christians too were forced to disperse, first from Jerusalem after the death of Stephen (Acts 8:1), and later, in 66 AD., in anticipation of the attack on Jerusalem, many Christians fled to Pella, in the Decapolis.

When early Christian preachers went on mission throughout the known world, they met many Jews of the dispersion to whom they preached Jesus as Messiah. This initial contact with people who held similar beliefs was generally fruitful, although negative reactions were frequent.

Among the Gentiles, the missionaries met people who believed in the usual Greco-Roman pantheon, especially the prominent gods Jupiter, Juno, and Minerva. The traditional and official piety of Greece and Rome was now mixed with newer religions from the east. Other people balanced the emphasis on distant deities with the popular personal experiences of the mystery religions, such as those of Osiris, Dionysius, or the Eleusinian cult. Yet other people, disbelieving the myths, had turned to a philosophical interpretation of the universe, and with the decline of Platonism came the appeal of Stoicism, Epicureanism, and eventually Gnosticism.

When Matthew wrote his gospel, the Mediterranean world, especially the provinces of Syria and Palestine, was facing up to the Jewish-Roman crisis. For those with Jewish background, it was another period of suffering and of questioning the ways of God. All major cities of the region, such as Jerusalem, Antioch, Caesarea, Tyre, and Sidon, had experienced recent war, and were struggling to adapt to a changing world. The might of the legions, the politics of Rome, the culture of Greece, and the religious presence of the Jews were daily experiences for all.

People throughout the region struggled with issues of political obedience, redistribution of wealth, mutual tolerance, and religious belief. It was a time of searching for some new unity in personal and social life, for answers to the power of a hostile universe, for an explanation of human suffering, for an appreciation of the secrets of life, a revelation of an accessible God: truly a yearning for a savior.

A Community In Internal Crisis

Matthew's community was situated in a region which had experienced recent war, including among its members many converts from Judaism. It was a time of searching for a new identity, not only for this community, but for the whole region. Like many others, this community felt the need to consolidate: to identify structures and authority, to be assured of authentic interpretation of God's will, and to find a new sense of purpose.

Several of the author's emphases give us insight into the kind of community for which he wrote. In establishing its structures, the community experienced tension as individuals vied for power. The community was made up of several parties that at times were mutually intolerant, and lived in ways that led to divisiveness, conflict, scandal, betrayal, and hate. Faith and commitment had grown cold, and the community needed to be called to renewal and a reaffirming of their faith in Jesus. Finally, the community was struggling to discover a new sense of mission in a changing world.

Searching for structures.   Matthew's gospel is written at a turning point in early Christian history. As Christianity spread, its members had to face up to its separation from Judaism. It had also to cope with its own growth, since it was no longer a small group but a universal Church. These kinds of developments needed organization and structure. When we look at Matthew's Church, there is clear opposition to the previous organizational structures of Judaism, which are no longer considered as having any authority in the new community (Mt 5:20; 15:1-11; 16:5-12; 23:1-36). However, Matthew's Church still seems to be without a clearly defined structure. There is no mention of bishops, elders, or deacons.[5] Even the Twelve apostles whose ministry is referred to in chapter 10 are never described as exercising any specific form of authority such as we find in the Acts of Apostles (Acts 1:15-26; 6:1-6; 15:6-22). Moreover, the power given to Peter in 16:19 is also given to the whole community in 18:18.[6]

Times of crisis and transition are generally occasions for the surfacing of self-appointed leaders. Matthew, in a major discourse against the leadership of the scribes and Pharisees, digresses to add a warning to his own community not to seek titles or positions such as those of rabbi, father or teacher (Mt 23:8-12). This "yearning for titles presupposes a community in the course of development and already more or less established."[7] The rivalry among the Twelve, described in the request of the mother of the sons of Zebedee (Mt 20:20-28), is edited by Matthew to show "the brotherly service one member of the community owes another," and to emphasize that "the disciples are to learn what it means to live in the community of Jesus."[8]

One of the emerging authorities in Matthew's Church is the charismatic prophet (Mt 5:12; 10:41; 23:34). While this ministry is positively appreciated by Matthew, he also stresses the destructive influence of false prophets (Mt 7:15-23; 24:11). The latter may work miracles, but they do not produce good fruit, leading the good lawlessly astray.

Matthew's Church is already facing community problems, as the selective list in chapter 18 clearly shows. These problems of Church order can be complemented with the needed directives for preaching and missionary work detailed in chapter 10.

Moreover, the community also sees itself as the only serious con-
tender challenging the Pharisees' claim to represent God's will to
the people. Yet with all these forms of order and discipline, the
authority structures remain undefined. We shall see in chapter
five that Matthew's is not a leaderless community, but for now it
is sufficient to see the early struggles and search for authentical-
ly recognized leadership and authority.

Appealing for reconciliation.   Many of the members of Matthew's Church had been very committed to the Judaism of their
ancestors. However, as we have already seen, there were serious
divisions in Israel in Matthew's time. More confusion and tension
resulted when Gentiles came into the Church. However, "simplistic
solutions which set all Jews against all Gentiles in deciding on
the nature of the Matthean church are out."[9] Certainly, he had to
deal with "the opposing forces of conservatism and radicalism,"[10]
but between the two extremes there were several levels of identification with Judaism, and several levels of identification with
the Gentile world.[11] Trying to unite this mixed Church is a major
undertaking for Matthew, who would like to preserve both the
new wine and the old wineskins (Mt 9:16-17). Unfortunately conflict remains, polarization increases, hate and mutual betrayal
continue (Mt 10:21; 24:9), and persecution is anticipated (Mt
10:23; 28-33). Some want to welcome the Gentiles (Mt 28:19-20),
others want to get rid of them (Mt 15:23-24). Some want to
preserve old ways (Mt 5:17; 15:1-2), others wish to abolish them
(Mt 16:5-12). Among the various groups, there is ambition, scandal, opposition, mutual rejection, lack of forgiveness, and spite
(Mt 18:1-35). At times the tension is so strong that the community
can see Jesus' words verified in them: "My mission is to spread
not peace, but division" (Mt 10:34b).

As a response to the harmful divisiveness of his community,
Matthew compiles two great discourses from Jesus' words: the
sermon on the mount (Mt 5:1-7:28) and the community discourse
(Mt 18:1-35). The former begins with an awareness of the community's suffering and persecution (Mt 5:10-12), and a realization
that they are called to be salt and light (Mt 5:13-16). The disciples
are then challenged to avoid scandal and false teachings (Mt
5:17-20), and urged never to use abusive language, but to live in
reconciliation and forgiveness (Mt 5:21-26). They are reminded
that they must choose not revenge, but mutual forbearance and

love (Mt 5:38-48). All are called to quietly build up the commmunity through good works of alms, prayer, and fasting. In the culminating teaching on the Lord's prayer, they are reminded yet again that the disciples' only contribution to the growth of the community is mutual forgiveness (Mt 6:12).

In the community discourse, Matthew calls his Church to avoid ambition (Mt 18:1-4) and scandal (Mt 18:5-9). Rather they should take care of each other (Mt 18:10-14), correct each other when necessary (Mt 18:15-20), and show limitless forgiveness (Mt 18:21-31).[12]

Focusing on renewal.   All three Synoptic gospels describe the end of the world and the troubles which will befall the Church in those times. Matthew is the only writer to sorrowfully acknowledge that many will apostasize and, "because of the increase of evil, the love of most will grow cold" (Mt 24:12). This verse is the only time in the gospel that Matthew uses the word "love." He sees that the community's loyalty to true righteousness, which should be maintained by their love, is actually weakening. During his ministry, Matthew's Jesus says to the disciples: "0 weak in faith!. . . How little faith you have!. . .What an unbelieving and perverse lot you are!" (Mt 6:30; 8:26; 17:17). Faith which will be challenged in the final cosmic upheaval seems already to be strained in Matthew's Church.

Their religious commitment must not be some outward empty show (Mt 6:1-5; 7:15), but must lead to the fruits of good living (Mt 12:33; 21:20-22). In Matthew and Luke, we have the parable of the return of the evil spirit to the exorcized man (Mt 12:43-45; Lk 11:24-26). Because the man remains empty and does not act to fill his empty life with good, the demon returns. Matthew alone adds: "And that is how it will be with this evil generation" (Mt 12:45). Later, in narrating the parable of the marriage feast (Mt 22:1-14; Lk 14:16-24), Matthew adds the short parable about the person who was invited and came, but was not suitably dressed (Mt 22:11-14). For Matthew it is not enough to respond to the call—the Church must manifest that response in the quality of living (Mt 7:15, 24-25; 21:28).

In Matthew's Church, there are members who seem unwilling to live out the implications of their discipleship (Mt 22:11-14; 25:1-13). They have heard Jesus' call, but are not building on a good foundation because they are not putting those words into action (Mt 7:24-25). This leads some to try to serve two masters

(Mt 6:24), others to disown Jesus (Mt 10:32-33), and still to others betray their community to save themselves (Mt 24:10).

To this internal crisis of faith, Matthew's gospel "is a clarion call back to basics — and the basics are the words of Jesus, the only solid foundation on which the Church can build (7:24-27)."[13] Matthew, therefore, calls his community to a renewal of the quality of their faith.

Identifying a mission.   During his ministry, Jesus stated explicitly: "My mission is only to the lost sheep of the house of Israel" (Mt 15:24). He sent the apostles on mission with the same directive (Mt 10:5b). The vision seemed clear: Jesus came to work for the salvation of Israel. This does not mean that Jesus had no contact with the Gentiles. The Gentile magi recognized him at his birth (Mt 2:1-12), and the faith of Gentiles had, at times, amazed even Jesus (Mt 8:10; 15:28). During his preaching, moreover, Jesus had hinted that changes would come. The parables of the two sons, the tenants, and the marriage feast (Mt 21:28 - 22:14) had all focused on the infidelity of the Jews and the passing of salvation to others (Mt 21:43).

By the time Matthew writes, the mission to the Gentiles is a major issue of Church policy. When describing the end of the world, only Matthew's Jesus states explicitly that "this good news of the kingdom will be proclaimed throughout the world as a witness to all the nations. Only after that will the end come" (Mt 24:14). Matthew calls his Church to an extended mission, reminding them that the end will not come until the mission to the Gentiles is accomplished. Although limited to Israel during the life of Jesus, Christian mission in the post-Easter period is a broad, all-embracing commitment to all nations of the world. The risen Jesus, endowed with full authority, commands and missions his followers to make disciples of the world (Mt 28:19). "Exegetes have long recognized that the final commission 'to make disciples of all Gentiles' (28:16-20) dominates Matthew's historical and theological perspective."[14]

As Matthew's community struggles with its own sense of identity and purpose, Matthew unites them in a common sense of ministry to the world. His call and vision imply a new sense of Church, and energize his followers to corporate action.

As Matthew's community began to consolidate and expand, it became profoundly aware of its own authority, and struggled to identify structures through which that authority could be channeled.

Composed of several groups, each with its own value system, Matthew's community needed him to call them all to a spirit of reconciliation and a sense of communion.

As a reaction to outside pressures and persecution, the faith of many weakened. The Church needed to be called back to an appreciation of the centrality of Jesus and the need for a living, fruitful faith in him.

Finally, in the changing world of the post-Easter Church, the loss of a sense of purpose and direction needed to be challenged. Matthew refocused his community's commitment, launching out to a visionary mission of world conversion.

A Community In Religious Transition

Changing religious scene.   Christianity began within Judaism, and its early leaders no doubt hoped that Israel would be won over to Christ (Lk 24:21). In the early years of the Church, Christians continued to frequent the temple (Acts 2:46), seeing themselves as the Jewish nation chosen by God (Mt 15:13-21). The early entrance of Gentiles was received with amazement (Acts 10:45; 11:17-18) and doubt (Acts 15:1-2). Christianity, however, was soon seen as a sect within Judaism. It had the typical characteristics of any sect: protest against the establishment, rejection of the dominant culture, an attitude of equality for all, a spirit of love and acceptance for its members, emotional religious experiences, converts by free choice, a challenge to total commitment, and the expectation of an imminent end.[15]

When Christianity started, Judaism was based on the temple, and governed principally by the High Priest and the Sadducees. There were other groups too: the Pharisees, the Essenes, and the Zealots.

By the time Matthew writes, the religious scene has changed. The temple and its worship is no longer a component of religious life. In fact, temple worship seems to have come to an end (Mt 27:51), and Matthew explicitly claims that we now have someone greater on whom to center our religious life (Mt 12:6).

Moreover, by the time of the first gospel, the power and authority of Judaism has changed. The Sadducees are never mentioned by Matthew as an independent authority group.[16] Likewise, the Zealots and Essenes are never referred to as having an effective voice in the religious development of Palestine. The only religious authority in Palestine at the time of the first gospel is the Pharisees.

The first gospel presumes the growing independence of Christianity and the need for organization, because of the new understanding that the Lord's second coming will be delayed (Mt 24:14). It also presupposes the end of temple worship, the destruction of the temple (Mt 23:38), and even the fall of Jerusalem (Mt 22:7). The events of those years led to the end of the power of the Sadducees, the destruction of the Essene communities, and the slaughter of the Zealots.

By the time this gospel is written, the stage is set for a major confrontation between Christians and the Pharisees.

External religious oppression.   Matthew's is the most Jewish of all the gospels, and he seems reluctant at times to introduce change. There are still several places where a Jewish commitment is presumed (Mt 10:6; 23:2; 24:20). However, what seems to have been a natural desire on Matthew's part to remain linked to his roots has been strained to the breaking point. The failure of the mission to the Jews is a fact for his Church. Instead of union in one people, there are clear indications of bitter conflict. The previous leaders, the Pharisees, are now referred to as "frauds," "hypocrites," "vipers' nest," "brood of serpents," "blind guides," "fools," "sons of the prophets' murderers" (Mt 23:1-36). This abusive language seems to indicate that Christians have reached a point of no return in their mission to Israel. Objectivity, let alone a sense of dialogue, would now seem to be impossible on either side. We can expect that controversies will be magnified in this context, shortcomings generalized into major grievances.[17]

One of the earliest measures taken against Christians, probably around 80, was to include a condemnation against them in the daily prayers of devout Jews. Reciting the "Eighteen Benedictions" morning, afternoon, and evening, as was expected of every Jew, now became impossible for Christians.[18] This was followed, around 83-85, by the formal excommunication of Christians from the Jewish synagogues. By the time Matthew writes, it is clear that the synagogue is no longer an institution frequented by Christians. It is always referred to as "their" synagogue.[19]

This gospel not only presumes antagonism, curse and excommunication, but consistently speaks of the Jewish persecution of Christians (Mt 5:10-12; 10:16-33; 22:6; 23:29-39). "They insult you and persecute you and utter every kind of slander against you because of me" (Mt 5:11). "They will hale you into court, they will flog you in their synagogues. . . Do not let them intimidate you. . . Do not fear those who deprive the body of life. . ." (Mt 10:17, 26, 28). "Woe to you scribes and Pharisees. . . Some you will kill and crucify, others you will flog in your synagogues and hunt down from city to city" (Mt 23: 29, 34). While some of these statements are probably colored by the mutual hate of the two groups, it remains unquestionable that Matthew's community faced external religious oppression in the form of controversy, ridicule, excommunication, and general persecution.[20]

Early religious debates.   Much of the early Christian struggle with Pharisaic Judaism centered on theological debate. Some of the questions asked of Jesus in the first gospel are more likely to have been points of debate between the Matthean Church and the Pharisees: the Beelzebul controversy (Mt 10:25), the issue of the Sabbath observance (Mt 12:1-13), and the demand for authenticating signs (Mt 12:38-42).[21]

There are three major areas of debate between Mathew's Church and Pharisaism. "In the first place, Christians questioned the central symbols of Jewish solidarity."[22] These included the Holy City, the temple, the Torah, purity, food laws, circumcision, and the Sabbath. Matthew's debate with the Pharisees of his own time is woven into many passages (Mt 5:33-37; 12:1-8; 15:1-20; 17:24-27; 21:12-17; 23:16-23).

A second focus of debate was the Christians' outreach to the Gentiles, which implied a rejection of the Jews' exclusive claim to be God's chosen people. This was certainly a sore point (Mt 21:45), but it punctuates the narrative, especially the parables (Mt 21:1 - 22:14), and is stated explicitly in the final mandate of Jesus (Mt 28:18-20). Matthew's Church, like all early Christianity, was becoming an increasingly Gentile movement, and would be condemned for this by the Pharisees.

A third area of debate was the authentic interpretation of the Law. Jesus had condemned the legalism of the Pharisees (Mt 23:23), specifically attacked some of their interpretations (Mt 12:1-8; 23:16-23) and promised that life under his yoke would be easy (Mt 11:28-30). The Pharisees were anxious about observance to the point of scrupulosity, but the Matthean Jesus tells his followers not to be so anxious (Mt 6:25-34).

The fall of Jerusalem, the destruction of the temple and the collapse of the power of the Sadducees created a vacuum in authoritative interpretation. The Pharisees reorganized, and, with the permission of Vespasian, founded a school in Jamnia for the study of law. Under the leadership of its founder, Rabbi Johanan ben Zakkai, the Jamnian school regained control over Judaism, organized synagogue worship, codified the scriptures, and consciously confronted Christianity.[23]

Much of Matthew's gospel becomes a two-pronged attack against Jamnian Pharisaism. First, he condemns the sages and undermines their authority (Mt 5:20; 15:1-11; 16:5-12; 23:1-36), and second, offers his own gospel as a new interpretation of the Law.

Matthew's Church is immersed in theological debate, redirecting its followers to new outward forms of religion, new ways of understanding God's salvific will and new sources for the interpretation of his will.

Open confrontation.   Matthew's gospel presents not only debate, but also open confrontation with Christianity's opponents. Sometimes these opponents are referred to as the "Pharisees and Sadducees" (Mt 3:7; 16:1-12), a designation which for Matthew denotes the Jewish leadership in the time of Jesus. On most occasions, he speaks of the Pharisees and scribes, a designation for "the rabbis and synagogue authorities with whom Matthew was in conflict in his own day."[24] The gospel's anti-Pharisaism is, in places, so violent that it must reflect recent hostility in the early Church. Matthew modifies his sources to put the Jewish leaders in bad light (Mt 3:7 and Lk 3:7; 6:39; Mt 12:33-35 and Lk 6:43-45). They are consistently presented as uncaring and unmerciful leaders (Mt 12:7; 23:15), portraying the exact opposite of the beatitudes.[25]

In Matthew's understanding, Christianity's confrontation with the Pharisees mirrors and repeats Jesus' own confrontation with the Jewish leaders.[26] They criticized him when he cured the needy (Mt 9:32-34; 12:22-24), but he challenged their reaction (Mt 12:25-37). They criticized his disciples (Mt 12:1-2), but Jesus defended them (Mt 12:3-8). As we have seen, he openly confronted the Jewish leaders with the powerful parables of the two sons, the wicked tenants, and the guests for the marriage feast (Mt 21:28 - 22:14). When they tried to trip him up with questions on taxation, resurrection, and the great commandment, Jesus' answers were so disarming that "no one dared, from that day on, to ask him any questions" (Mt 22:46).[27]

Not only is the Pharisees' opposition openly confronted by the Matthean Jesus, but they are blamed as being unreformed (Mt 3:8) and empty of goodness (Mt 12:43-45). Matthew explicitly blames the Jewish leaders for deliberately plotting the death of Jesus (Mt 12:14; 16:21; 21:45-46; 26:14-16), encouraging the treachery of Judas (Mt 26:14-16), instigating the clamoring of the crowds (Mt 27:20-23), and urging Pilate to condemn the Lord (Mt 27:11-14).[28]

On his last great day of public teaching (Mt 21:23 - 23:39), Jesus makes his final appeal and challenge to the Jewish leaders. Five controversial issues are debated in the typical question and answer form of rabbinical debate (Mt 21:23 - 22:46). The scribes and Pharisees refuse to listen, all further attempts at reconciliation are ended, and the break is now final (Mt 23:1-39).

Outright rejection. The tenants of the vineyard (Mt 21:33-44) did not produce the fruits everyone had a right to expect. Mark and Luke end the parable by focusing on Christ, whereas Matthew ends by focusing on the need for new leadership of God's people. In Matthew's judgment, the scribes and Pharisees are worthless teachers whose leadership is now ended (Mt 16:6). With a little material from his sources, Matthew constructs a formal condemnation of the Pharisees which is "the most severe attack and condemnation of the entire New Testament,"[29] "a masterpiece of vituperation."[30] The Pharisees are accused of hindering people's journey to God; of making their converts wicked by their misguided interpretations of the Law; of hypocrisy in their observance; of being unmerciful legalists; of living in ways that make them unclean to the godly; of murdering the just. Matthew's "woes" express grief, rejection, and a warning of punishment for the Pharisees.

Matthew goes on to insist that not only are the Jewish leaders worthless, they are blind and ineffective as leaders. In Matthew's understanding, "their deeds are few," "they bind heavy loads. . .on other men's shoulders," "their works are performed to be seen" (Mt 23:1-7). Although they claim to be teachers of the Law, they miss its important challenges (Mt 23:23-24), emphasize outward petty legalism (Mt 23:25-38) and thereby actually fail to teach the heart of the Law (Mt 15:12-14). For Matthew, the Pharisees simply no longer represent the authentic interpretation of the Law. They are blind guides (Mt 23:17, 19, 24, 26). "The accusation that they are blind leaders of the blind strikes them at the heart of their effort, for it means that they are blind to the actual will of God."[31]

The Pharisees are not only worthless leaders and blind guides; Matthew rejects them as absolute failures. With their failure, the Judaism they represented is now ended as the channel of God's will to the people. They failed to see God's will, persecuted his messengers (Mt 13:57; 23:29-36), and embodied the spirit of apostasy. All future guidance of the people is now over (Mt 15:13-14). "Thus the condemnation of the Pharisees. . . shades almost imperceptibly into a condemnation of the people as a whole."[32] The whole tree is condemned: "Never again shall you produce fruit" (Mt 21:19b). The first son is rejected, and Jesus adds: "Let me make it clear that tax collectors and prostitutes are entering the kingdom of God before you" (Mt 21:31b). The tenants are thrown out, told that "the kingdom of God will be taken away from you and given to a nation that will yield a rich harvest" (Mt 21:43).

By the time Matthew writes, the centrality of the Sabbath is over, for "The Son of Man is indeed Lord of the Sabbath" (Mt 12:1-8); the destruction of the synagogue system, symbolically portrayed in the fall of Bethel (1 Kings 13:1-10), is affirmed (Mt 12:9-14); Matthew adds that "Jesus was aware of this, and so he withdrew from that place" (Mt 12:15). Even the temple's power is finished (Mt 23:38; 24:1-2) and the Holy City destroyed (Mt 22:7).

Matthew's unrelenting condemnation of the leaders of his people and the generation they represented, anticipated from the first pages (Mt 2:18 and Jeremiah 31:15; Mt 8:11-12), climaxes in the poignant cry of national rejection of Jesus in the passion account (Mt 27:25). The rejection is complete, there is no promise of future conversion, no hope of a remnant. In Matthew's vision, God's choice has passed to his own community, which is now challenged to be faithful to the call (Mt 5:20).

The changes in post-war Palestine led Matthew's community to a new sense of identity and independence.This led to external oppression, excommunication, and persecution on the one hand, and a firm struggle in theological debate on the other. Unfortunately, the inevitable break between Christianity and Judaism soon came, followed by open confrontation and outright rejection.

Matthew's condemnation of his opponents seems to come out of real personal hurt and anger. Being rejected after one has loved deeply produces greater hurt. These seem to be the sentiments of Matthew and his Church, who, having loved the Old Testament origins of the faith, have been cut off and rejected. Unfortunately, they in turn attack their oppressors.

A Community In A Large City Of The 80s And 90s

The milieu of the 80s and 90s. Matthew's gospel was in use by Bishop Ignatius of Antioch around the year 110. As we have already seen, this is the earliest witness to the first gospel as a respected source. However, since a work takes time to gain respect and reverence, we could possibly date Matthew, at the very latest, at around 100. In order to be more precise in establishing the period of community development to which this gospel is a response, we need to find not only its latest date but also its earliest.

Matthew's gospel no longer expects the immediate return of the Lord (Mt 24:48; 25:5, 19). This second coming, expected by the early Church, has already been reinterpreted, and Matthew proposes an understanding of salvation history which presumes extended future ministry (Mt 24:1-35; 28:18-20). This gospel is therefore later than the 60s.[33]

We have seen that Matthew uses Mark. As the most widely accepted date for Mark is 65-70, Matthew must therefore be later; since it would take some time for Mark to be accepted and revered by the early Church, it would therefore not be out of place to suggest for Matthew a date in the 80s.[34]

While nowhere explicitly stated, Matthew, by deliberate modification of the text, hints at both the fall of Jerusalem and the destruction of the temple (Mt 22:7; 23:37). Moreover, even if not reported explicitly, there are indications that Matthew is giving a theological explanation and interpretation of those events (Mt 21:33-45; 27:25). This gospel also presumes the exclusive power of the Pharisees and the end of the influence of other Jewish groups. A certain distance from the events is implied, the peace and opportunity to reflect would, again, place this writing no earlier than the 80s.[35]

In the last section, we saw the painful effects of Christianity's break from Judaism. The curse against heretics and Christians was introduced into the "Eighteen Benedictions" probably in the 80s, the excommunication from the synagogue following, at the earliest, in 83-85. The major confrontation with Jamnian Pharisaism came around 90. The bitterness of Matthew's reaction indicates that these events are not in the distant past, but alive and hurtful at the time of writing. These realities would place the gospel in the late 80s or early 90s.[36]

Matthew's gospel reflects tension in the debate between Pharisaic Judaism and Christianity; the problems of Israel's rejection of Christ and the future status of Gentiles are of on-going importance. Thus the gospel is not as late as John's when these points are already dead issues.[37]

Matthew's community is gaining independence and a sense of identity. It is ordered, and consolidating to face opposition. It shows signs of laxity and of need for renewal. It is at a considerable distance in time from the events of Jesus, not in a period of early fervor.

Matthew's discourses synthesize and interpret past teachings. The final discourse for example (Mt 23:1-25:46), combines the passion events, the resurrection, and the history of the early Church up to 70 or 80. This section, like many other parts of Matthew, is written by a leader looking back over an extended period.

This gospel is earlier than 100 but later than the 70s or early 80s. The most likely date is late-80s to mid-90s.

City life.   Although Matthew's gospel has a strong Jewish interest throughout, it is written in Greek. His audience, while including many Christians of Jewish origin, speaks Greek and lives outside the immediate region of Palestine, where Aramaic would have been spoken. Admittedly, Matthew could have written in Greek for the benefit of the universal Church. However, as we have seen, the problems he confronts are local issues.

Matthew's gospel is well ordered: a handbook or public lectionary, possibly prepared for ecclesiastical use. Considering the cost of writing materials in the early centuries, we must presume a reasonably large Church. The immediate and extensive respect for the gospel also points to an influential Church.

The community was probably urban. Matthew uses the word "city" twenty-six times and the word "village" only three times. His preference is supported by a comparison with Mark, who uses "city" eight times and "village" seven times.[38] These statistics are "all the more striking when it is observed that several occurrences of the word 'city' seem to relate to circumstances in Matthew's own time (Mt 10:11, 14, 15, 23; 23:34; also 5:14)."[39] Commentators have made various suggestions, emphasizing particularly the coastal cities of Caesarea, Tyre, and Sidon.[40] The preference for these cities has no doubt been influenced by their proximity to Jamnia and its impact on Matthew.

There are indications that Matthew's mixed community was relatively wealthy. The amounts of money referred to in Matthew are much larger than those of the other evangelists (Mt 25:14-30 and Lk 19:11-27; also Mt 10:9 and Mk 6:8). Matthew speaks of "the poor in spirit," not "the poor" (Mt 5:3 and Lk 6:20) and omits "poor" from those invited to the wedding feast (Mt 22:9 and Lk 14:21). In Mark and Luke, Jesus tells the rich young man to sell all he has to give to the poor (Mk 10:21; Lk 18:22), but Matthew alone adds that this is necessary "if you seek perfection" (Mt 19:21). In this context, it is natural that Matthew should make a personal appeal to his community: "Do not lay up for yourselves an earthly treasure" (Mt 6:19-20),[41] and to offer his wealthy disciples the model of Joseph of Arimathea, to whom only Matthew refers as "a wealthy man...another of Jesus' disciples" (Mt 27:57).

Syrian Antioch.   Matthew's gospel is written for a wealthy, urban community in the midst of world events; a community with internal crises to resolve and external pressures to face; a community dated in the 80s and 90s. "Matthew's church seems to be situated somewhere between Jewish and Gentile spheres of cultural influence, with a foot in each camp."[42] Though it has strong Jewish influences, the absence of emphasis on Jewish ceremonial law indicates that the community is outside the immediate regions of Jerusalem.

The most likely place for the writing of the first gospel is Antioch. Founded shortly after the death of Alexander the Great in 323 BC., Antioch was a major center of power, wealth, and culture. Since the death of Stephen, Christians had established a Church there. The only major city in the eastern part of the empire, Antioch was a melting pot of pagan, Jewish, Gnostic, and Christian religious thought. In this complex and unstable setting, "Antiochene Christianity developed its own strongly-marked features."[43] By the late 90s, during Trajan's policy of expansion, Antioch was again the eastern center of military and political power.

Matthew's concerns are those we know to have been present in Antioch. He changed "Tyre and Sidon" to "Syria" (Mt 4:24), yet rural Syria was Aramaic speaking; Antioch was a cultural center and Greek speaking. It experienced serious disturbances between Jews and Gentiles which eventually led to revolt.

Moreover, it is probable that "Syria was of special concern to Jamnia," and that "Christians in Antioch and other Syrian cities felt Pharisaic opposition with special force."[44]

We have dealt with the internal crises of conflict between the various group reactions to the Jewish/Gentile issue. Antioch certainly reflects this kind of conflict, with some Christians who lived there insisting on "full observance of the Mosaic law", others requiring "some Jewish observances" but no circumcision, a third group feeling no need of any Jewish prescriptions, and a fourth group rejecting any "abiding significance in Jewish cult and feasts."[45]

Not only is the history and religious background of Antioch similar to that out of which the first gospel emerges, but Matthean interests are well situated in Antioch. In addition, we should note the first gospel's interest in Peter, whom the early Church considered the first bishop of Antioch (Ga 2:11), and the use of this gospel by Ignatius, also a bishop of Antioch. Moreover, the great influence of the Antiochene Church could well account for the great respect given to Matthew, and since Antioch was the departure point for early missionary work, could also account for the widespread use of the first gospel.

In short, the interests that permeate Matthew are those of the late 80s and early 90s; there are some slight indications that it is written for a wealthy community; and the problems it deals with and the issues it confronts are well placed in Syrian Antioch.

A Community Of The 1980s And 1990s

Matthew's insights are very much directed to our communities of the 1980s and 1990s. The disciples in the boat with Jesus cried out: "Lord, save us! We are lost!" (Mt 8:25b). This appeal is never far from the hearts of committed Christians today, as we deal with the hurtful divisions of the post-Vatican II period. Storms and destructive waves seem appropriate descriptions of some of the crises we have faced. Matthew, however, presents Jesus as the Lord who calms the storms our boat encounters.

His community was not a group of withdrawn ascetics, but rather a community that had participated in significant historical events, and had in turn been conditioned by those events. His people could look back over a century or more to unbelievable tragedy, regional oppression, and a few hard-won victories.

Reactions to some of the major events, both religious and social, had divided Matthew's people into all shades of conservative and liberal. His community showed not only pluralism, but at times even contradictory positions on important issues; Matthew, while probably not agreeing with them, left the differences intact. He strove for reconciliation, renewal, and a corporate sense of mission.

Matthew's community lived at a turning point in Christianity, and had to make decisions that brought them hardship and social persecution. They debated with their opponents, confronted them, and eventually rejected them. Unfortunately, it seems that they did not succeed in maintaining an objective view of the opposition, and, as is often the case in theological warfare, what they attacked did not correspond to reality.

Matthew's Church was part of a capital city, "Antioch the golden," whose power, architectural splendor, wealth, and cosmopolitan culture never ceased to amaze them. Antioch was the emerging Church in miniature, embodying in itself the tensions and conflicts which would plague and challenge the whole Church.

Our communities of the 1980s and 1990s have many of these same characteristics. Matthew presents Jesus to us to calm the storms of our communities, reminding us that divisiveness is a sign of little faith. Christianity's place is still in the midst of world events: the tragedies, oppression, joys, and hopes of humankind. There will always be differences among us, but if we are constantly committed to reconciliation, renewal, and a sense of mission, they can at least be controlled and managed.

We are now again at a turning point in Christianity. There are clear indications of theological warfare, some signs of hardship, and social or religious persecution imposed on one group by another within the Church. Like Matthew's community, we need maturity and objectivity to face our differences, qualities his people seemed to lack. Matthew speaks to us, as to them, with power, relevance, and challenge.

Chapter Three
MATTHEW'S PURPOSE

*"Have you understood all this?" "Yes," they
answered; to which he replied, "Every scribe who is
learned in the reign of God is like the head of a
household who can bring from his storeroom both
the new and the old" (Mt 13:51-52).*

It is difficult to identify a unifying purpose throughout the
whole of Matthew's gospel Although we have already seen some
of his interests, and the series of community concerns which influenced his work, we have seen that Matthew contains contradictory positions. Moreover, the author of this long gospel emphasizes so many ideas that it is not easy to pinpoint his overriding theological perspective. Rather, his wholistic approach integrates many vitally necessary component parts.

Although it has been suggested that Matthew does not seem to
have written the gospel to present one main theological idea or
purpose,[1] most commentators do nevertheless try to identify an
overriding aim. Some of them stress the Christological aims of
Matthew: "His purpose was to make clearer to his readers the
claim of Jesus to be believed and to be obeyed."[2] The first gospel
thus announces "the news which saves or condemns, that is
revealed in and through Jesus," in whom "God has come to dwell
to the end of time with his people the Church."[3]

Other commentators stress the ecclesiological purpose of Matthew, considering that he sees his task as one of defending the
Church as the true Israel;[4] or rooting the authority of the missionary Church in the authority of Jesus;[5] or challenging the
persecuted Church to maintain its evangelism;[6] or basing the way
of life of an ascetic and charismatic Church in Jesus, "the prototype of such charismatics"[7]; or awakening in the Church a new
self understanding, in light of the challenge of Jamnia.[8]

A third group of commentators emphasizes the pedagogical aims of Matthew. They suggest that the first gospel is written as a lectionary for liturgy,[9] or a handbook for catechetical instruction.[10] Matthew's "immediate aim is to provide the Church's teachers with a basic tool for their work . . . He seeks chiefly to support the work of faithful teaching,"[11] by providing his Jewish-Christian Church with "a manual of instruction in the Christian way of life."[12]

Some commentators stress a fourth purpose, "the believer's understanding of and attitude to law, ethics, mission and service."[13] This understanding sees Matthew moving from Christology and Jesus the teacher, to ecclesiology and the authority of the Church, to morality. "The specificity of Matthew's gospel was the nexus between Christ and his church...this nexus between Christ and church is the foundation on which Matthew builds his presentation of Christian morality."[14]

In this chapter we will focus on the new theological directions which Matthew has introduced into the tradition. We will also examine his major themes and compositional contributions. We will then study the outline and structure of his work, concluding the chapter with a consideration of what motivated Matthew to serve his Church through this gospel.

Matthew's New Theological Directions

Matthew retells the story of Jesus for his mixed Antiochene community. As he does so, he challenges his people to a new level of consciousness regarding their Church and its mission. These new levels of awareness, these new theological directions, include a reinterpretation of history, an emphasis on Christianity as a new creation, together with a stressing of the continuity of blessings and a focusing on the responsibilities of the Church for community growth.

A reinterpretation of history   Many members of Matthew's community had understood all previous history as a preparation for the coming of the Messiah, who was to have set Israel free and fulfilled all the prophecies to the glory of the chosen people. Unfortunately, this had not happened. For a short period, possibly two decades, believers thought that Jesus was to return again in glory. Unfortunately, this had not happened either. It was in this context that Matthew wrote, trying to explain to his community both the meaning of the past that they valued, and the roots of their hopes for future expansion to the Gentiles.[15] Although Matthew's Church was the hinge between the predominantly Jewish past and the new future, it is significant that Matthew's understanding of history is centered not on the Church, but on Christ.[16] The whole of the history of Israel culminates in Jesus, referred to as the "son of Abraham" (Mt 1:1-17). The whole ministry of the Church is also centered on Jesus: "Know that I am with you always until the end of the world!" (Mt 28:20b). Jesus is the center of history, the fulfillment of the hopes of Israel, and the judgment on the future fidelity of the Church.

The birth of Jesus is interpreted as the climax of Old Testament expectations and the ushering in of the period of fulfillment. Jesus' life becomes the measure both of past hopes and future fidelity. His death, like his birth, is a major moment of transition to a new period of history. Matthew, by a series of apocalyptic events, indicates the cosmic significance of Jesus' death and resurrection (Mt 27:51-28:3).[17] This major historical break leads into the time of the Church. Instead of ascending to heaven to return in glory at the end of the world, the risen Jesus of Matthew appears in glory to his Church and assures them of his permanent presence in their period of mission, to the end of time (Mt 28:16-20).[18]

Salvation history is divided by Matthew into three periods: Old Testament expectation, the fulfillment in Jesus' life and the universal ministry of the Church. This threefold division gives Matthew the opportunity of dealing with some of the practical pastoral concerns of his community, allowing him to include material of Jewish interest, stressing its importance for history and its fulfillment in Christ. It lets him accept, in two distinct historical periods, both the restricted ministry of Jesus to "the lost sheep of the house of Israel" (Mt 10:6; 15:24) and the expanded Gentile ministry of the Church (Mt 28:19).[19] It also facilitates an explanation of the roles of Israel and the Church, and when the transition from one to the other took place.[20]

Matthew's concept of salvation history is a theological explanation of the centrality of Christ, of the natures of Old Testament expectation and ecclesial ministry. When the stages are kept in mind, some of Matthew's pastoral concerns, and even some seemingly contradictory statements, can be better understood.

Continuity in a new creation.   The first words of Matthew's

gospel introducing the time of Jesus are similar to those which
begin the Book of Genesis, and recall the creation of the world.
In fact, the first evangelist deals with world history from Genesis
to the end of time,[21] seeing the coming of Jesus as a new order of
creation heralded in his birth (Mt 1:1), ritually celebrated at his
baptism (Mt 3:1-17), and publicly confirmed in the new life of the
Sermon on the Mount (Mt 5:17-48). When the Lord's work is complete and the kingdom established, the resulting situation is
again described as a new creation (Mt 19:28).

Moreover, the transition to the time of the Church is also
presented as the beginning of a new age. Apocalyptic imagery
describes the dissolution of the old order and the beginning of a
new creation of world salvation. The veil of the temple is ripped,
and an earthquake leads to the resurrection of the new Israel.[22]

Each period of history begins and ends with the creative work
of God. However, the three periods also clearly portray the continuity of God's blessings. The prophecies of the time of expectation are fulfilled in the time of Jesus (Mt 1:22-23; 2:5-6, 15, 17-18,
23; 4:14-16; 8:17; 12:17-21; 13:14-15, 35; 21:4-5; 27:9-10), and
Jesus prophesies developments in the Church (Mt 21:18 - 22:14). In
the Old Testament, wisdom guided the chosen people; now
Wisdom is Jesus himself, who guides his Church (Mt 11:25-30;
23:39). The authority of God is established in Jesus (Mt ch. 1-9;
28:18), who shares that authority with his Church in the work of
the twelve (Mt ch. 10). The very reign and kingdom of God come
in Jesus (Mt 3:1-2; 4:17, 23; 9:35) and are proclaimed in the mission of the Church (Mt 10:7; 24:14; 28:20). God's will, pro-
mulgated in the Law, is manifested in the fidelity of Jesus (Mt
5:17-19), and the very heart of that Law is retrieved by Jesus (Mt
15:3-6; 23:2-3), taught to his Church (Mt 5:17-48) and proclaimed
to the world (Mt 28:20). Some of the disciples of the Lord
recreate in their own sufferings the persecutions of the prophets
of old (Mt 5:12), while others are reminded that they continue
the infidelities of the past (Mt 7:21-23; 13:41-42; 23:13-36;
24:9-12).

The developments associated with the coming of Jesus and the
establishing of his community are so radical they can be referred
to as a new creation. Yet this does not imply an uncreation of
God's previous work—rather a preservation of the best and a
continuity of the blessings, for the new order is not a destruction
of the past, but a fulfillment of it (Mt 9:17).

Responsibility for community growth. The first gospel is an outstanding educational tool. It is the most serviceable collection of Church teachings in the New Testament. Material dealing with the same topic is synthesized in appropriate blocks, accessible to all. A manual for personal instruction and a handbook for the ministry of Church leaders, its structure, order, and topical arrangement indicate the author's interest in the educational needs of his Church. Coming at a time of major transition in early Christianity, the first gospel demonstrates its author's awareness of his community's need for consolidation, for the bridging of the educational gaps in new converts, and for those who were coming from other religious traditions.

Matthew is so well organized, detailed, and explicit that some authors believe it written for public use in the liturgical assembly. From one angle, it is "a revised lectionary, improving and expanding Mark and Q for liturgical reading and preaching."[23] Not only does it give the Word to be proclaimed in the liturgy, it teaches the formulas and rituals for the sacraments (Mt 26:26-28; 28:19). Its aid in the development of the liturgical life of the community possibly accounts for some of its conservatism, since congregations are easily distracted and disturbed by changes in the liturgy.[24]

Matthew's awareness of the need for community growth not only leads him to develop his gospel for the catechetical and liturgical needs of his community, but also to present his insights regarding the life and discipline of this new Church. The community discourse (Mt ch. 18) is a fine synthesis of practical issues of community discipline, while the Sermon on the Mount is a superb integration of the new life and responsibilities of the growing community (Mt 5:1-7:28).

Besides its educational, catechetical, and community responsibilities, Matthew's Church needed a sense of its urgent evangelistic and missionary obligations in this new age,[25] and Matthew skillfully sensitizes his people to these responsibilities. He presents both Jesus' commitment to his own people (Mt 10:6; 15:24), and his openness to missionary expansion (Mt 8:10; 15:28; 21:43). He locates the community's responsibility in God's plan for the world (Mt 24:14), and climaxes his gospel with Jesus' call for the expansion of their ministry (Mt 28:16-20).

Matthew's gospel, among other things, challenges the people to new levels of awareness regarding religious issues. He calls his people to an awareness of a new interpretation of salvation history, with Jesus its center. The new creation in Jesus builds on the old, affirming the fidelity of God and the continuity of his blessings. The new levels of awareness introduced by Matthew give us a first glimpse of his theological thrust, aims, and concerns.

Matthew's Major Compositional Contributions

Matthew is a highly skilled author who imprints his own style on his collection of the teachings of Jesus. He selects from the oral tradition those teachings which he believes faithfully present Jesus to his community and their needs. He arranges and structures the work with his skills as an author, reshaping the tradition to achieve his theological aims. Some of his compositional contributions are particularly telling: his use of the Old Testament is both extensive and unique to him; the great discourses are of his own personal composition; the parables, a recognized characteristic of Jesus' ministry, are used in a particular way; miracles are modified and interpreted to achieve his own aims. An examination of these editorial features will be a further step toward clarifying our author's main purpose in writing his gospel.

Using the Old Testament. We have already seen some of the Jewish features of Matthew's gospel. Although written in Greek, the many recognizable Jewish expressions, styles of speech, forms of debate, and themes of interest show Matthew's great reverence for Moses and the prophets, and his concern to show the boy Jesus reliving the history of his people, and his interest in exodus, covenant, Law, and Pentateuch. His dialogues with Pharisees, scribes, and rabbis reveal one who has had similar training.

Matthew often paraphrases the Old Testament, thus creating an Old Testament atmosphere in his work. He explicitly quotes the Old Testament sixty-one times: twenty of these are not found in the other synoptics, and ten of them nowhere else in the New Testament. On eleven occasions, Matthew uses the Old Testament to show that its hopes are fulfilled in Jesus.[26] On occasions, the Old Testament is used as a focal point for a larger teaching on Jesus. Matthew thus skillfully employs Old Testament quotes at mid-points of long passages as "structural keys" to open up the full meaning of entire sections. Several portions of the gospel are organized around Old Testament texts to be understood as fulfilling it and giving it Christian meaning.[27]

Christians soon became convinced that the Old Testament was written with Christ in mind, and they interpreted it in light of the life and teachings of Jesus. Matthew, accustomed to Jewish traditions and methods of interpretation, gave Christian meaning to the Old Testament, showing how Christian events fulfilled Old Testament prophecies. This was not unethical or irreverent, since the scribes of Qumran and the rabbis themselves showed similar freedom in their use and interpretation of the Old Testament.

Matthew uses the Old Testament more than the other synoptics. This deliberate dependence stamps his work with a conviction of religious roots, the realization of hopes, and the fulfillment of God's promises.

Composing the discourses. The central section of Matthew's gospel is made up of five great discourses: the Sermon on the Mount (ch. 5-7), the Missionary discourse (ch. 10), the Parables of the Kingdom (ch. 13), the Community discourse (ch. 18), and the Eschatological discourse (ch. 24-25). Each of these discourses is preceded by a narrative section which prepares us for the discourse which follows. Moreover, the five speeches are arranged in inverted parallelism, or chiasm: the first and the last deal with the blessings or woes in store for those who accept or reject the kingdom; the second and fourth deal with aspects of the life of the new community; the central discourse deals with the nature of the Kingdom of Heaven.

Not only does the structure of this section stress Matthew's understanding of the nature of life under God, but each discourse is the result of his compositional work. Undoubtedly based on the mind of Jesus, they are the result of Matthew's selection and arrangement of the traditions. He ends each discourse with the same conspicuous concluding formula (Mt 7:28; 11:1; 13:53; 19:1; 26:1).

It is possible to see these five great discourses as Matthew's attempt to present a new Pentateuch: the five biblical books of the teachings of Israel. The same recurring themes are stressed throughout the discourses. In fact, "a particular and consistent attitude toward the Pharisees, the disciples, the law, eschatology, and ecclesiology characterize Matthew's discourses."[28] He contrasts the hypocritical Pharisees with the discerning disciples; interprets the Law from a Christian perspective; sees that the final judgment will be made on the observance of Christian love; and understands the Church as the true Israel.

This Matthean editorial feature of the discourses is again a technique he uses to focus on his aims. Moreover, the focus he gives in the discourses is very similar to that he gave by his use of the Old Testament.

Selecting the parables.   Jesus often teaches the disciples about the nature of the Kingdom in parables (Mt 13:44-50). On occasions, when he speaks to the crowds, he gives explanations only to the disciples (Mt 13:4-23, 36-43). In fact, in Matthew's understanding, the very purpose of parables is to clarify the mysteries of the reign of God for the disciples, and to further confound disbelievers (Mt 13:10-15). Thus, for Matthew, the use of parables verifies the prophecy of Isaiah (Mt 13:14-15) and further shows the rewards of belief in Jesus. Disciples of Jesus understand the nature of the kingdom, but by rejecting Jesus, the crowds reject their only chance of understanding.

Matthew contains twenty-four parables, four of which are also found in Mark and Luke, ten of which are found in Luke, and ten of which are special to Matthew.[29] Parables, however, are used by our author as another editorial feature which contributes to the clarification of his general theological aim. These parables, "a fragment of the original rock of tradition,"[30] manifest a very personal style. We have no parables from Judaism before Jesus, and even those contemporary with or after Jesus compare poorly with his own masterly presentations. As with Jesus' other teachings, the parables are transformed in the process of transmission; frequently the audience changes, extravagant embellishments are introduced, and allegorical interpretations are added.

There are several constant themes in Matthew's parables; themes which emphasize yet again his main theological concerns. A series of parables are used to stress the disinheritance of those who reject Jesus (Mt 20:1-16; 21:28-44; 22:1-10; 24:32-35; 25:1-13). Others teach the importance of the acceptance of Jesus (Mt 7:24-27; 11:16-19). The major collection in chapter thirteen deals with the nature of the Church (Mt 13:3-46), and these are complemented by several parables describing the life of the

Church (Mt 13:24-30, 47-50; 20:1-16) and the disciples' need of reconciliation (Mt 5:25-26; 18:12-14, 23-35), commitment (Mt 12:43-45; 22:11-14), and vigilance (Mt 24: 43-51).[31]

In places, Matthew interprets or allegorizes the parables, using them to present an overview of salvation history culminating in the Christian Church (Mt 21:28 - 22:14); or to reflect on the centrality of Jesus' words for fruitful growth (Mt 13:36-43); or to identify the problems of apostasy from Jesus (Mt 22:11-14).

By his selection, explanation of purpose, and interpretation of teachings, Matthew uses parables to lead his audience in the direction of his major aims.

Interpreting the miracles. Matthew's gospel contains twenty-four miracle stories, none of them exclusive to him. Although he abbreviates the miracle stories by 50%, he nevertheless highlights their miraculous elements. In places, he gives general summaries of Jesus miraculous activity (Mt 8:16-17; 12:15-21; 14:34-36; 21:14) insisting that the really outstanding miracles are not even recorded (Mt 11:20-24). As in the discourses, the parables, and the Old Testament, Matthew's compositional contribution here is significant.

In the Sermon on the Mount, we are presented with the transforming power of Jesus' word; the succeeding narrative section presents us with the transforming power of the miracles. As teacher and healer, Messiah of word and deed, Jesus heals sin, sickness, social divisions, and natural catastrophes. These miracles are not propaganda to persuade the disbelieving, but rather, "the broad significance of the miracle-story is that it portrays Jesus as bringing. . .the gracious, saving power of God's eschatological rule."[32] Through the miracles, Jesus shows that he is Israel's Messiah. He heals two men who acclaim him Son of God (Mt 8:28-34), and two who acclaim him Son of David (Mt 9:27-31), two being required for authentic witness.

In the narrative section presenting Jesus as Messiah of deed and power, Matthew offers ten healing miracles to parallel the ten harmful plagues that had historically led to the liberation of the people. Later, on the mountain, the usual place of divine revelation, Jesus cures all who come to him (Mt 15:29-31). The image of the healing Messiah is highlighted by Matthew's technique of abbreviating the supportive narrative and focusing on the essential teaching of the miracle, which for Matthew is the person of Jesus and the nature of our response in faith and discipleship.[33]

Jesus the healer takes initiative to cure (Mt 8:15), shows a sense of urgency to heal (Mt 9:19, 32), and is willing to expose himself to criticism in order to heal the needy (Mt 8:7; 9:20-22). He did not work miracles for the disbelieving (Mt 13:58). However, those who received cures were Gentiles (Mt 8:5-13; 15:21-28), religious outcasts (Mt 8:1-17), the ritually unclean (Mt 9:18-34), those excluded from participation in temple worship (Mt 21:14), and social outcasts (Mt 8:1-4). Jesus' only destructive miracle shows the condemnation awaiting unfruitfulness and rejection of his word (Mt 21:18-21).

Jesus bypasses laws to show his healing presence (Mt 12:10), and Matthew seems to establish new criteria of life before God. Jesus shows the power of the new age: responding to people's needs because "his heart was moved with pity. . .They were. . .like sheep without a shepherd" (Mt 9:36), and so "he cured every sickness and disease" (Mt 9:35). He would later command his Church: "Cure the sick, raise the dead, heal the leprous, expel demons" (Mt 10:8). The crowds formulate Matthew's own conclusion regarding Jesus' miraculous activity: "Nothing like this has ever been seen in Israel" (Mt 9:33). "The result was great astonishment in the crowds . . They glorified the God of Israel" (Mt 15:31).

By means of these editorial features, Matthew succeeds in focusing his readers' attention on the roots out of which Christianity grew; on the hopes it realizes; on the discerning disciples and their new law of love; on the nature and privilege of life in the kingdom; and on the mercy of the Messiah of power, who welcomes all to his healing and salvation.

Matthew's Recurring Themes

In the following chapters, we will consider the major teachings of Matthew on God, Church, discipleship, and mission. However, at this point it would be useful to identify some of the author's recurring themes in so far as they are an indication of his interest and purpose. At times, Matthew relies on his sources, making them his own. On other occasions, the prominence of the themes is due to his own editorial contributions. Four broad topics are emphasized throughout his work: community, authority, faith, and response.

Community. We have already seen Matthew's concerns for his community. His motivation, however, is not sociological but theological. He addresses himself to the nature of community life under God's rule, using the concept of "Kingdom" or, more specifically, "Kingdom of Heaven." He uses the latter 32 times; no other New Testament writer ever mentions it. In all, the notion of kingdom is used 51 times. It is "the single most comprehensive concept in the first Gospel . . . It touches on every major facet of the Gospel, whether it be theological, christological, or ecclesiological in nature."[34]

Matthew understands that Israel had been called to life under God, but that through poor leadership, the community had rejected Jesus, in whom alone God draws near to the people (Mt 1:23; 11:25-30; 12:28). As a result, the vineyard or kingdom is given to others (Mt 21:43; 8:10-12).

While Matthew loves his people and speaks of them nobly,[35] he also insists that the Church, the community of the disciples of Jesus, is the true Israel and inheritor of the kingdom (Mt 21:33-43; 28:16-20). The new community is organized by faith in Jesus (Mt 16:13-20), led to understand the true nature of the kingdom (Mt 13:10-13), and taught its ethical (ch. 5-7), missionary (ch. 10), community (ch. 18), and eschatological (ch. 24-25) demands. Moreover, even though Matthew's community may be oppressed, they live in the reign of God (Mt 5:3, 10).

The new community is made up of those who accept Jesus (Mt 12:38-42) and live fruitfully in him (Mt 12:43-45). God's will is revealed in Jesus, and those who totally obey that will are the new community of God (Mt 12:46-50). This kingdom is the essence of Jesus' preaching (Mt 4:23; 9:35), and must be so for the disciples (Mt 10:7). While this kingdom is a reign of mercy, it is also one of judgment for the disciples (Mt 22:11-14; 25:31-46).

Authority. Closely connected with the theme of community is that of authority, which, like the former, is woven into the whole tapestry of the first gospel. There is constant comparison between Jesus and the Pharisees. The latter are criticized as hypocritical (Mt 23:1-36), their teachings to be avoided (Mt 16:5-12), and they themselves not to be followed (Mt 15:1-11). They criticize Jesus' works of mercy (Mt 9:32-40; 12:22-24), and try to trap the Lord in debate (Mt 22:16-39).

One of the basic questions that Matthew wants his community

to answer regards Jesus' authority: "Who do you say that I am?"
(Mt 16:15). Jesus is presented as an authoritative teacher who
claims exclusive obedience (Mt 28:20). He does not abolish the
previous demands of the law (Mt 5:17; 19:17-19), but explains
their fulness and essential meaning (ch. 5-7; 23:13-23). Matthew
wants his community to realize that Jesus "left the crowds spellbound at his teaching. The reason was that he taught with
authority and not like their scribes" (Mt 7:28-29).

The new community now builds on the authoritative words of
Jesus (Mt 7:24-27), for he is the sole source of the Father's will
(Mt 11:25-30). His authority, however, is not maintained by the
control of law (Mt 9:13; 12:7), but by a personal commitment to
him (Mt 11:28-30).

Jesus, endowed with full authority, remains permanently with
his Church (Mt 28:18-20), is active in its ministers (Mt 10:40-42),
and is the assurance of their authority (Mt 16:17-20; 18:18). During his earthly life, Jesus is the only teacher (Mt 23:8), but he
shares with the twelve his authority to heal and to preach (Mt
10:1-10). At his post-resurrectional appearance, that solemn coming to his Church in glory, he shares also the authority to teach
(Mt 28:18-20). For Matthew, authority over the new community
is rooted exclusively in Jesus and shared by his Church.

Faith.   Throughout the gospel of Matthew, a series of Gentiles
are praised for the quality of their faith (Mt 2:1-12; 8:10; 9:22;
15:28; 27:54). Unfortunately, the chosen people to whom Jesus
was sent (Mt 15:24) are generally portrayed as rejecting the Lord
(Mt 11:20-24; 27:25), even though there are also some fine examples of faith among them (Mt 9:2, 18, 22, 28; 17:15).

In Matthew, faith is personalized: it is faith in Jesus himself (Mt
18:6). Those who do not have this personal faith in Jesus are condemned (Mt 12:38-42; 23:37-39; 26:23-24). Even the disciples,
those who believe in him, are frequently criticized for the
weakness of their faith (Mt 8:26; 14:31; 16:8; 17:20; 21:21; 28:17).
If it were stronger, they could calm the storms their Church
faces, cure the sick, appreciate Jesus' power, and do wonders in
his name. Faith is not simply an oral acknowledgement of Jesus
(Mt 7:21), nor is it even working miracles in his name (Mt 7:22),
but a living faith that leads to deeds (Mt 7:24; 22:11-14). In fact, it
is possible that this living faith be present in people who do not
know Jesus personally, even though they live the life to which he
calls all (Mt 25:37-40).

Faith is tested under persecution in the storms of life (Mt 8:26; 14:31), personal anxieties (Mt 6:30; 16:8), and attacks of the evil one (Mt 17:20). Matthew's community in particular expects intense suffering because of their faith in Jesus (Mt 24:4-12), and so Matthew has meticulously documented for his community that Jesus fulfills scripture, is the authoritative guide and Messiah of Israel. Twice he tells his community that Jesus is the Son of God, whose every word should be obeyed (Mt 3:17; 17:5). Moreover, the disciples must persevere in this living, obedient faith, for only the one "who holds out to the end...will see salvation" (Mt 24:13).

Response. The new community which accepts Jesus' authority, committing itself in faith to him, is expected to live a quality of holiness that "surpasses that of the scribes and Pharisees" (Mt 5:20). This holiness must be each one's exclusive concern (Mt 6:33). It implies a willingness to be spiritually poor, to accept life's hard experiences, to live without complaint or bitterness, to hunger for growth, to be merciful, peacemakers, singleminded in commitment and willing to accept persecution (Mt 5:3-12). This faithful response needs to be total, including not only the externals of social and religious life, but thoughts and attitudes as well. The disciple avoids not only murder but anger, not only adultery but lustful looks, not only false oaths but all swearing. Each believer should not only reject revenge but cultivate availability, not only love neighbors but also enemies (Mt 5:21-48).

The disciple's faithful response must include action in Jesus' name (Mt 12:33), including good works of almsgiving, prayer and fasting (Mt 6:1-18).

Above all, Christian response shall be in love. This is the essence of all law (Mt 7:12; 22:39), and the quality on which the community will be judged (Mt 25:31-46).

This response in holiness to faithful acceptance of Jesus' authority over the community is absolutely essential and exclusive (Mt 7:24-27; 28:20). All are judged by this, and those who do not respond to Jesus' call are condemned (Mt 25:45-46; 22:13), refused forgiveness (Mt 6:15; 18:35), and judged harshly (Mt 3:10; 11:24). The somber judgment scenes of Matthew seem designed to stress the exclusiveness of commitment to Jesus as the way to fulfill God's will.

These recurring themes of community, authority, faith, and

response focus the reader's attention on issues crucial to Matthew. They contrast the old Israel and the new, the authority of the scribes and that of Jesus, the faith of the disciples and the unbelief of others, the responsive commitment of the Church and the inadequacy of disbelievers. These themes, like Matthew's new theological directions and editorial features, contribute to the general picture of his theological plan and overriding aims.

Structure Of Matthew's Gospel

The general outline of Matthew's work expresses his purpose as well: he alternates narrative and discourse; arranges the discourses in chiastic structure, balancing them not only in content but also in length; and uses consistent introductory formulae and concluding refrains for the discourses. It seems clear that his intentions were to mark off the discourses and their accompanying narratives into five major blocks, the birth narratives preceded by a solemn introduction, the passion-resurrection narrative followed by a solemn conclusion. Lest "introduction" and "conclusion" be interpreted as secondary, it might be more desirable to see the gospel unfolding in three movements: the birth narratives as creedal anticipations of the life and death of Jesus, the ministry as the gradual unfolding of Jesus' life and teachings, and the passion and resurrection as the salvation events revealed and taught by the preceding section.

The whole gospel is centered on the person Jesus; a general overview follows, which will be expanded and utilized in this book.

General overview of Matthew's gospel

Introductions. Life based on Jesus
      "The Shepherd of my People Israel."

I. A. Jesus the source of holiness—early preparations
      "Prepare the way of the Lord."

    B. Disciples are called to a life of holiness
      "Blest are they who hunger and thirst for holiness."

II. A. Jesus the foundation of ministry—early work in Galilee
      "I have come to call."

B. Disciples are called to a life of ministry
   "He who welcomes you welcomes me."

III. A. Jesus reveals the Father's kingdom
   "In his name the Gentiles will find hope."

   B. Disciples are called to a life in the kingdom
   "To you has been given a knowledge of the reign of God."

IV. A. Jesus establishes his Church
   "Follow in my footsteps . . . lose life for my sake."

   B. Disciples are called to a life in community
   "Where two or three are gathered in my name, there I am in their midst."

V. A. Jesus passes judgment
   "If you seek perfection . . . come follow me."

   B. Disciples are called to a life under constant judgment
   "Stay awake . . . you must be prepared."

Conclusions. Life based on Jesus
   "Clearly this was the Son of God."

Some commentators prefer to see the gospel in seven sections rather than the five indicated above.[36] Recently, it has been suggested that the five-fold division focuses too much on the Church, and a three-fold division could highlight Matthew's christocentric concerns.[37]

While a five-fold division recalls the Pentateuch and could suggest a deliberate modeling by Matthew, some writers consider it unnecessary to embrace such an interpretation. However, many writers still find the five-fold division the most persuasive interpretation of Matthew's intentions,[38] and this formal association with the Pentateuch is presumed in the detailed outline which follows.

As Matthew's new theological directions, major editorial features, and recurring themes underline his theological purpose in writing the gospel, the outline can likewise be seen as the scaffolding which supports his theological, pastoral, and spiritual enterprise.

Outline Of The Gospel Of Matthew

The powerful Jesus
>   Three exorcisms over evil powers 8:23-9:7
>   His authority was awesome—a summary 9:8
>   A call to ministry 9:9-13

The healing Jesus
>   A controversy and interpretation 9:14-17
>   Four cures 9:18-34
>   A call to corporate ministry 9:35-38

B. SECOND DISCOURSE—SERMON ON MISSION
>   A call to ministry
>   "He who welcomes you welcomes me."

Major characteristics of ministry 10:1
A personal call to ministry 10:2-4
Instructions for ministry 10:5-15
Warnings on the dangers in ministry 10:16-33
Tensions and hardships in ministry 10:34-39
A ministry of the presence of Jesus 10:40-42

Conclusion 11:1

BOOK THREE 11:2-13:53

A. GROWING REJECTION BY OPPONENTS
>   "In his name the Gentiles will find hope."

An expected Jesus 11:2-15
An unexpected Jesus 11:16-19
A rejected Jesus 11:20-24

Jesus reveals the Father's will 11:25-30

Jesus debates Sabbath observance 12:1-8
>   Heals on the Sabbath 12:9-15a
>   Jesus the merciful 12:15b-21

Jesus brings the kingdom of God 12:22-37
>   Signs of fruitfulness 12:38-45
>   Jesus and his true disciples 12:46-50

B. THIRD DISCOURSE—PARABLES OF THE KINGDOM
>   Life in the Kingdom
>   "To you has been given a knowledge of the reign of God."

The community of the Kingdom is built on the word
>   Parable of the sower 13:1-23
The community of the Kingdom is mixed

Parable of the weeds 13:24-30
The community of the Kingdom is small but will grow
  Parables of leaven and mustard seed 13:31-43
The community of the Kingdom is worth everything
  Parables of the treasure and the pearl 13:44-46
The community of the Kingdom awaits judgment
  Parable of the net 13:47-50

Conclusion 13:51-53

BOOK FOUR 13:54-19:1

A. GROWING ACKNOWLEDGEMENT BY HIS DISCIPLES
"Follow in my footsteps . . . lose life for my sake."

Jesus at Nazareth 13:54-58
Death of John the Baptist 14:1-12
Jesus the miracleworker
  Jesus feeds the 5000 14:13-21
  Jesus walks on the water 14:22-33
  Jesus heals all 14:34-36
Jesus the compassionate
  Jesus rejects interpretations of the Parisees 15:1-20
  Jesus cures a Gentile of faith 15:21-28
  Jesus heals the rejected 15:29-31
  Jesus feeds the 4000 15:32-39
Jesus the suffering servant
  Jesus rejects the teachings of the Pharisees 16:1-12
  Jesus gives authority to the believing Peter 16:13-20
  Jesus foretells his death 16:21-23
  Jesus calls to follow the cross 16:24-28
Jesus the Messiah
  Jesus is transfigured 17:1-8
  Jesus and his Elijah 17:9-13
  Jesus and the need for faith in him 17:14-21
Jesus the obedient Son
  Jesus foretells his death 17:22-23
  Jesus obeys the requirements of law 17:24-27

B. FOURTH DISCOURSE—SERMON ON THE CHURCH
Life in community
"Where two or three are gathered in my name, there I
am in their midst."

Avoid ambition 18:1-4

Resurrection
  Women at the tomb 28:1-10
  Coverup by the guards 28:11-15
  Return in glory to his Church 28:16-18
  Final commission to evangelize 28:19-20

Matthew's Purpose

Matthew's concerns.   Matthew's reinterpretation of history
focuses the whole of salvation history on Jesus, whose teachings
and prophetic call are now continued in the Church. While
rooted in Judaism, this new creation of the Lord's community
must take upon itself the responsibility for its continued life and
ministry. Matthew sees his community as the true Israel, rooted
in the hopes and call of the Old Testament. However, as he re-
presents the teachings of Jesus, he does so in light of his own
community's needs; refocusing the teachings of Jesus in the
discourses, emphasizing the newness and exclusiveness of the
Christian community in the parables, and, in the miracles, stressing the messianic power of Jesus the Lord. The recurring themes
of community, authority, faith, and response stress the newness
of the Church and the substitution of the authority of Jesus for
all other authority.
  The structure of the gospel indicates Matthew's conviction that
Jesus is the new Moses guiding his new Israel. He challenges his
community to a new understanding of what it means to live in
the reign of God, raising them to new levels of awareness of their
calls to holiness, ministry, community, and vigilance.
  Commentators have emphasized the christological, ecclesiological, pedagogical, and moral aims of Matthew. Certainly each
of these is of major concern to him. However, his focus in each
case is to interpret the teachings for the new circumstances of
his Church. He is a learned scribe who can give the "old" new
meaning and vitality by interpreting the essence of its call in new
situations, and who can root the "new" in the traditions of the
past (Mt 13:51-52). He is the prophet, wiseman, and scribe who
wants to make sure that his people have truly understood the
teachings of the Lord so that they can live them out with renewed
vitality in changed times.
  Matthew is not an ultra-conservative who will not change, nor
is he an ultra-liberal who disregards the values of the past.
Rather, he shows a conservative commitment to the essence of

traditional faith, and a liberal freedom in finding new ways of living that faith from the past. He is a liberal conservative who bridges the generations, guiding them through transitions at a critical point in Church history

The importance of tradition.   Matthew has, at times, been called "legalistic," calling disciples to more rigorous obedience than the Pharisees practiced. If a legalistic approach to the first gospel is taken, then Jesus' words, exclusively found here, are hardly verifiable: "Your souls will find rest, for my yoke is easy and my burden light" (Mt 11:29-30). However, a rigorous Christian imposition of commandments is not a correct understanding of Matthew's pastoral directions. It is true that at times he is very sensitive to the expectations of Jewish Christians (Mt 5:17-20), but such statements must be understood in the general context of the gospel, and of the specific needs of groups within his community.

"Law" for the Jews referred to God's providential guidance and the saving events of their history. This instructive guidance is found in the Pentateuch, principally an historical account of the way God dealt with his people. "Law" helped Israelites appreciate their covenantal relationship to God, his faithful care of them, and their righteous response. Laws are concrete regulations governing correct response, and as such are only a part of "Law."

Matthew criticizes the burdening accumulation of laws (Mt 23:4), the emphasis on laws before people (Mt 12:1-15), and any hypocritical observance of laws (Mt 15:1-20; 23:23). Generally, Matthew uses "Law" to mean the revelation of God's dealings with his people (Mt 11:13; 12:5; 22:36). This "Law" is also passed on through the insightful interpretations of the prophets (Mt 5:17; 11:13; 22:40), and now the providential guidance of God is fulfilled in Jesus (Mt 5:17; 12:8). For Matthew, therefore, there is an ongoing historical interpretation of "Law."

Where Matthew deals specifically with laws, he highlights Jesus' concern for the inner spiritual attitude which the laws were intended to protect. Compassion, reconciliation, respect, simple sincerity, availability, and universal love are the essential challenges of the "Law," rather than the minimalistic attitudes governed by laws (Mt 5:21-48).

The basic blessings and guidance of "Law" are protected by laws, but, over time, these very laws can become hindrances to the essential spirit of the "Law" they were meant to protect. When this happens laws must be abandoned to safeguard the "Law" (Mt 12:9-15; 15:1-20; 23:23).

The Matthean Jesus also points out that changed circumstances necessitate a different understanding of laws (Mt 5:32, 37, 39), although this does not necessarily imply relaxing or watering down their demands (Mt 5:18-19).

Moreover, when needing to confront changed circumstances in his own community, Matthew has no qualms in presenting teachings as coming from Jesus even when they dealt with situations that the historical Jesus never had to confront (Mt 18:15-18; 23:8-12). The spirit of Jesus must continue to live on afresh as new circumstances develop in the community (Mt 28:20b).

For Matthew, fidelity to tradition is neither legalism nor conservative fundamentalism. The great Tradition of the Law must be preserved first of all by fidelity to the priority of all that is human, raised and dignified as it is through the covenant. Laws which support human response should be maintained as long as they work, done away with when they become hindrances, changed as history progresses, and reincarnated as circumstances change. The criteria of the community is fidelity to the inner spirit of the "Law," and the measure of all guidance and instruction is now exclusively Jesus.

Interpretation as the essential function of Matthew. In chapter two we saw the internal and external crises of Matthew's Church, and something of his pastoral skill in reconciling and guiding his people with his contemporary interpretation of the message of Jesus. "Matthew emerged as the 'liberal conservative' who creatively redacted his sources in order to meet the identity-crisis of the Antiochene church."[39] His gospel is not just a retelling of the story of Jesus, but a theological, pastoral, and spiritual response to his community's need for new understandings of the present and new directions for the future.

He was appreciative of the past, and sensitive to those who loved it (Mt 5:17-19; 23:2). He frequently collected traditional material valued by those suffering from the paradigm shift to Christianity. However, the whole social and religious context was different after the events of the 70s, and God's call had to be understood in a new light. "It was Matthew's task to embrace, reinterpret, and synthesize the competing traditions of Christian Antioch, to make them speak to a new day."[40] While affirming his commitment to the Law, he brought about a profound change in the community's approach to it.

For the Jewish leaders at the time of Matthew, Law was not static but was developed by interpretations called Mishnah. After 150-200 AD., even the Mishnah became the object of further interpretations called Gemara. Matthew's approach was very like that of the Jewish leaders, but he presents Jesus' life and teachings as the authoritative interpretation of the Law (Mt 5:17-20; 12:18), and his own gospel as the Church's further interpretation of Jesus' teachings (Mt 28:16-20). We have already seen Matthew's scribal training and methods, and identified his constant use of midrash, haggadah and halakah. He has the scribe's convictions on the authority of scripture, sees the essential need to support that authority, but shows equal commitment to ongoing interpretation. Laws fossilize, but the call of Law is perennially fluid and vital.

The Matthean Jesus stresses that rules and regulations do not give life in the kingdom (Mt 23:2-4). What the Church must pass on in Jesus' name (Mt 28:20) is first a requirement of wholeness in our self-gift to God (Mt 11:25-30), a wholeness that reincarnates the attitudes of covenantal relationship (Mt 5:3-12). This wholeness is complemented by inwardness: the dedication of our thoughts, feelings and attitudes (Mt 5:21-48). This leads us to live the golden rule in our dealings with others (Mt 7:12) and to exemplify the basic attitudes of the covenant, those "weightier matters of the law, justice and mercy and good faith" (Mt 23:23; also 9:13; 12:7; 25:31-46).

Jesus' interpretation then becomes the spirituality of Matthew's community. The essence and criteria of all Law is love (Mt 22:34-40), and the Matthean Jesus' constant emphasis on this reality makes Matthew's interpretation not too unlike Paul's life under grace.

If interpretations do not change, they lose their ability to sustain faith. Matthew claimed that a wise interpreter, "learned in the reign of God," would know how to bring to his people "both the new and the old" (Mt 13:52). His gospel is an exercise in interpreting the old in light of the new, and that "new" is not only Jesus' teaching, but Matthew's application of it as well. "This disciple who understands, it is implied, is a well-trained scribe, who can pass on what he himself has learned and develop new thoughts out of it."[41]

By means of his new theological directions, major editorial features, recurring themes, and general structure, Matthew emphasizes his aims of presenting both Jesus, and later Jesus in his Church, as ongoing interpreters of the nature of life under God.

Chapter Four
IMAGES OF GOD IN MATTHEW

*"Go and make disciples of all the nations. Baptize
them in the name of the Father, and of the Son, and
of the Holy Spirit" (Mt 28:19).*

No one can really be called good except God (Mt 19:17). In Matthew's
vision, this all-good God came to dwell among us (Mt 1:23), and
remains with us permanently (Mt 28:20). For each of us, God is
lifegiving (Mt 22:32), knows what we need (Mt 6:32), and is
generous in taking care of us (Mt 7:11). Jesus reveals God to us in
a way that Matthew claims is original and exclusive At his final
solemn coming to his Church, Jesus calls all disciples to immerse
themselves in the reality of God, calling all nations to this commitment (Mt 28:19-20).

Our Christian life and spirituality focus essentially on God,
drawing us to himself and calling us to personal and community
growth. The image we have of God determines the style and
quality of our religious commitment, our attitudes towards other
religions, and our world of increasing unbelief.

The Father And His Plan And Will

God the Father.   In Matthew's gospel, God is the One, the Good
(Mt 19:17), the living God (Mt 16:16), the Creator (Mt 19:4), the
God of Abraham, Isaac and Jacob (Mt 22:32), and the King (Mt
18:21-35; 22:1-14). He speaks through the scriptures and prophets
(Mt 1:23; 4:4), is master of marriage and family life (Mt 19:6), con-
trols evil and the Evil One (Mt 4:1). God is all-powerful, requires
the homage and adoration of humankind (Mt 4:10), and must not
be put to the test (Mt 4:7).

In Matthew, God is referred to as Father forty-five times. This
compares to four times in Mark, and seventeen in Luke. This

special concern is highlighted even more by comparison with the
Old Testament, where the Psalms speak of God as father only
twice, and devout Jews in their formal daily prayers addressed
God as father on only two occasions.[1] In the first gospel, Jesus
speaks of God as "father," "my father," and even "your father."[2]
The "father in heaven" or "heavenly father" are favorite expressions, combining the familiarity due "father" with the respect
and awe attendant upon his "heavenly" abode.

The heavenly Father has a plan for humankind, a plan of
universal salvation (Mt 18:14) revealed through Jesus (Mt
11:25-27) and, on occasion, to specially chosen disciples (Mt
16:17). His providential care is for all, the just and the unjust (Mt
5:45), but is especially directed to the little ones, whose angels
are always in his presence (Mt 18:10). He looks after everything in
nature (Mt 6:26; 10:29), but his special love is for humankind (Mt
7:11; 18:10). He is interested in our growth (Mt 15:13), knows what
we need (Mt 6:8, 32), grants our requests (Mt 7:11), especially
when we make them together as his children (Mt 18:19). His
kingdom, however, is reserved for those who acknowledge his
Son (Mt 13:43; 10:32-33).

While the Father could conquer the world with his legions of
angels (Mt 26:53), his will called for a quality of life that implied
suffering for his Son (Mt 26:29, 39, 42) and his Son's disciples (Mt
20:23). The Father gave everything to his obedient Son (Mt
11:27), even sharing his own glory (Mt 16:27). Now we await the
Son's return in the Father's glory (Mt 16:27), when the Father will
judge all on their commitment to his Son (Mt 10:32-33), rewarding
proportionately (Mt 25:34). The time of the end, however, is
reserved to the Father (Mt 24:36).

The Father has entrusted his plan to his Son, who knows all
about the Father, revealing him to the disciples (Mt 11:25). Jesus
tells the disciples to call God their Father (Mt 6:9; 23:9),[3] and to
imitate the perfection of God (Mt 5:48). Their righteousness is
not to be mere vocal acclaim of God (Mt 7:21), nor empty outward demonstration (Mt 6:1, 4, 18); rather, their prayer, deeds,
and commitment are to be shown in simple sincerity seen only by
the Father (Mt 6:6). Baptized in the name of the Father (Mt 28:19)
and obedient to his will (Mt 7:21; 12:50), disciples are also committed to treat others as children of God, forgiving each other,
reconciled to each of the Father's children (Mt 6:14-15). The
disciples' good lives will lead others to praise the Father (Mt

5:16), and they can be courageous in their witness to the Lord, for the Father has given them his own Spirit (Mt 10:20).

In Matthew, the Father is the awesome, heavenly God who gives life and takes care of all. He expects trust, commitment to his Son, and a spirit of reconciliation among his children.

The will of the Father. Matthew presents us with a theology of the will of God. In a context of universal love, Jesus calls disciples to be perfect as the Father is perfect (Mt 5:48). They are to be singlemindedly committed to the Father's way of holiness (Mt 6:33), treating all else as secondary. In fact, as disciples, they are especially distinguished for their obedience to the will of the Father (Mt 6:10; 7:21; 12:50; 18:14; 21:31).

The Father's will was revealed to the chosen people in the Law and brought to complete fulfillment in Jesus (Mt 5:17-20). The Father's will is carried out in detail in the infancy account; it is explained, reinterpreted, and reapplied in the teaching ministry; it is faithfully accepted in the passion, even when it includes the cup of sorrows. Jesus, the obedient Servant of the Lord (Mt 12:17-21), calls his disciples to imitate his obedience to the will of the Father, insisting that this very obedience makes one a disciple of his (Mt 12:50).

The emphasis on the will of the Father is complemented with an awareness that it is Jesus alone who now places us in contact with the divine will. To this needs to be added the realization that all will be judged on the quality of their fidelity to God's will (Mt 10:42; 25:34). The parables of the tenants, wedding guests, and two sons, each an allegory of salvation history and the will of God, end with judgments on both past and present infidelities. The theme of judgment pervades Matthew's presentation. Any hypocritical obedience to the will of the Father is condemned (Mt 6:1, 16b); lack of forgiveness toward others is met by a similar judgment from the Father (Mt 6:14-15). In fact, obedient life in the Father's kingdom is constantly contrasted with the kingdom of outer darkness reserved for those who are unfaithful to the will of the Father (Mt 7:23; 22:13). Matthew generally refers to this place as a "fiery furnace," where the disobedient "wail and grind their teeth" (Mt 5:22b; 7:19; 13:42, 50; 25:41, 46).

While the portrait of God is essentially that of Father, there is also an awesomeness to it, since the Father requires obedience to his sovereign will. The Father is loving and just. He rewards obedience but condemns the refusal to live a fruitful obedience. At times "the punishment of the damned is described in far more vivid terms than the bliss of the blessed   The terrors of the Day of Judgment hang perpetually over the heads of Matthew's readers."[4]

Along with his call to follow the will of the Father, Matthew's emphasis on judgment is consistent with his usual pastoral practice of challenging his community to a realization of the exclusiveness of Christianity and warning them of the consequences of rejection. The will of the Father now comes through Jesus, "the supreme arbiter of the will of God."[5] The Father, who wills that none be lost (Mt 18:14), has constantly guided and shepherded his people, and in Jesus has come decisively to be with his little ones (Mt 1:23). His call is fatherly, his hopes are compassionate, and his love is perfect. When disciples respond to the Father by obedience to his will, they enter into joy. When they refuse, they impose upon themselves an alienation described as judgment.

The Son—The Chosen Servant

Jesus' life and teaching.   The earthly life of Jesus is divided into three main periods: the period of preparation for ministry; the ministry proper (beginning at 3:1, or explicitly at 4:17); and the events of the passion (anticipated from 16:21, but beginning at 26:2). These three sections are integral parts of Matthew's gospel, forming a three-fold presentation of who Matthew believed Jesus to be. We will first look at each of these three periods, identifying Matthew's gradual revelation of his beliefs. Then, we will synthesize Matthew's portrait of Jesus.

The Shepherd of my people—The period of preparation

Matthew's infancy narratives are an integral part of his gospel. While the gospel could easily begin at chapter three with little loss noted, it is most unlikely that it ever did. As time passed after the work of Mark, further needs and questions arose in the early Church to which the infancy accounts were an excellent response.[6] As growing numbers of converts came to the Church, it was necesary to educate them concerning the origins of Jesus, and in some way to anticipate the conclusions of the gospel narrative. Luke had done something similar, and while both evangelists are "largely in agreement in what they are really trying to say," they are "historically irreconcilable."[7] It seems most unlikely that Matthew has any intention of writing history. He tells the reader about the origins and theological understandings concerning Christ, and "this can be done by means of non-historical narratives as well as by means of those which are historical."[8]

Matthew, writing as he is for an audience under strong Jewish influences, anticipates this understanding of the person and mission of Jesus in hints and suggestions from the Old Testament. His belief in Jesus is supported by Old Testament quotations, some of which are modified to suit his aims, and one of which cannot be found anywhere.[9] In fact, none of the quotes seems intended to prove anything—rather, they are pious, devotional applications to Jesus. The reflective use, application, and commentary on biblical quotations is called "midrash," and many commentators today see Matthew's infancy narratives as exemplifying midrashic techniques.[10]

The genealogy stresses the continuity of the life and mission of Jesus with the history of Israel. Generally, a genealogy begins with the key figure, but this one is transformed into a "Christological statement" that "portrays Jesus as the goal and fulfillment of the Old Testament."[11] It is presented in three groups of fourteen names, fourteen being the numerical value of the name "David." The end of the first fourteen is King David, the end of the second group of fourteen is the exile and loss of kingship, and the third group climaxes in Jesus the Christ and King.[12]

The genealogy, with its strong davidic emphasis (Mt 1:1, 6, 17), also shows how God directed world history toward Jesus. In fact, the genealogy can be seen as six groups of seven names: six is the Jewish number for anticipation, and seven symbolizes fulfillment. Matthew's new six days of creation await the culminating new creation in the greatest Jubilee year of all.[13]

The genealogy also mentions four women, none of whom are among the great women of the Old Testament. Instead of Sarah, Rebecca or Leah, we have four women from Gentile families, each involved in some scandalous and immoral relationship. Their presence in the genealogy underlines Gentile contributions to the lineage of the Messiah, the initiative of women in God's plan, and the necessary background for Mary's role in the birth of Jesus.[14]

The regular form of the genealogy is changed in the case of Jesus, and now reads: "It was of her (Mary) that Jesus who is called the Messiah was born" (Mt 1:16). The account of the birth of Jesus goes on to explain this unusual form. The passive "was born" (Mt 1:16) and "is conceived" (Mt 1:20) suggest divine intervention. In the narrative, "the miracle of the virgin conception is not told, but presupposed."[15] Matthew seems to be familiar with the tradition and, as is his usual practice, goes on to show how this fulfills scripture (Mt 1:22-23). Since the virgin conception would place Jesus outside the davidic line, Matthew's narrative emphasizes how this was secured through Joseph's betrothal to Mary.[16]

Matthew and Luke agree that Jesus was born in Bethlehem during the reign of Herod. The latest possible date would therefore be 4 BC, a more likely date being 6 BC. Instead of being announced by the Lucan angels, Jesus' birth as king was heralded by a star in the heavens, signalling the birth of Wisdom.[17] The Gentile magi come to worship the Messiah, disturbing the whole city, and king, scribes, and Pharisees take counsel against the newborn (Mt 2:3-4), as they later will against the Lord when he returns to the city (Mt 21:10; 27:1).

The child is portrayed as reliving the key stages of Jewish history: The patriarch Joseph, a man of dreams, went to Egypt, but his children were badly treated by a wicked pharaoh who slaughtered children, while Moses was protected. Now a New Testament Joseph, another man of dreams, goes to Egypt, and the wicked Herod slaughters children, but the new Moses is protected. The flight into Egypt is given the additional symbolism of the exile to Babylon by mention of Rachel in Ramah, a town the Babylonian exiles passed on their journey to slavery.[18] The infancy narratives end with the return from exile and the locating of Jesus in Nazareth of Galilee.

The infancy narratives are a telescoped presentation or sketch of who Jesus is, the details of which will be filled in during the rest of the gospel. Matthew retells the whole of history leading up to Jesus, whom he calls Son of David (Mt 1:1), Son of Abraham (Mt 1:1), Christ (Mt 1:18), Jesus (Mt 1:21), Emmanuel (Mt 1:23), King of the Jews (Mt 2:2), Shepherd (Mt 2:6), the Son (Mt 2:9, 15), and a Nazarene (Mt 2:23). Matthew's skillful editing presents Jesus as the heir of David, the Son of God, the new Moses, the King of the Jews, and the true Israel. Matthew narrates the birth and anointing of the Lord, his rejection by his own people, his passion, death, and resurrection, and his acceptance by the Gentiles.

Matthew challenges his community to faith in Jesus, awareness of his messianic origins, the realization of the risks of rejection, and a willingness to accept the Gentiles. For a divided and polarized community tempted to reject a new focus in religion, he presents the image of a Joseph who responds to the call to protect the threatened new life, for it is truly begotten of the Holy Spirit.[19]

The presence of the Father—the Ministry of Jesus

The general outline of Jesus' ministry as found in Mark is preserved and imbedded in Matthew. However, the latter is more extensive, since Matthew has additional material from Q and from his own source M to add to Mark's brief outline. Furthermore, Matthew's gospel lays greater emphasis on the discourses, building up the narratives from episodes selected because of their significance in relation to the discourses. Matthew has no particular interest in the chronological accuracy of the ministry, but rather constructs it for theological and pedagogical purposes.

Having prepared his readers with the proclamation of the infancy accounts, Matthew turns to Mark's opening episode on the preaching of John the Baptist. Matthew is not, as was Luke, interested in any relationship between John and Jesus; this meeting is presented as John's first encounter with the unknown Jesus, with John as the Elijah who heralds the coming of the Messiah (Mt 11:14; 17:13; 2 Kings 1:8). In Matthew alone, John claims to be preparing for the arrival of the kingdom (Mt 3:2), acknowledges Jesus as the expected one (Mt 3:14), and immediately condemns, not the multitudes as in Luke, but the unfruitfulness of the Pharisees and Sadducees (Mt 3:7-10). Matthew shows continuity between the Old and New Testaments by presenting Jesus' preaching as identical to John's (Mt 4:17; and 3:2). Moreover, Matthew alone stresses Jesus' obedience by stating that Jesus desires baptism to fulfill all of God's demands (Mt 3:15). This public proclamation by Jesus of fidelity to the will of God is a summary of his life and ministry, and is confirmed by the descent of the Spirit and the acknowledgment of God: "This is my beloved Son. My favor rests on him." (Mt 3:17).

In this first episode of his public ministry, Matthew's Jesus takes the initiative to show himself to the people as one faithful to the will of God, preaching a message rooted in their prophets, welcomed by Elijah, and acknowledged by God as his Son.

Like the chosen people in their journey from Egypt, this "son of Abraham," having passed through the waters, now enters the desert of temptation. Matthew here expands Mark, portraying

Jesus as expressly going to the desert to challenge Satan and confront him on his own ground. In imitation of Moses, the leader of the nation, Jesus fasts forty days and forty nights (Mt 4:2 = Exodus 34:28; Mt 4:8 = Exodus 34:1-4). He faces the temptations of his people during their wanderings. However, as the true Son of God and the true Israel, Jesus triumphs over the Evil One and proclaims his commitment to the fundamental creed of Israel (Mt 4:4 = Deuteronomy 8:3; Mt 4:6 = Dt 6:16; Mt 4:10 = Dt 6:13).

The infancy narratives present Jesus as Emmanuel, the expected one, who relives the history of his people. This is complemented by the baptism and temptations showing Jesus as the obedient Son of God, the obedient Israel strong enough to conquer evil (Mt 12:29).

Having crossed the waters and faced the desert temptations, Jesus, like Moses before him, ascends the mountain to present to the people the will of God.

Matthew followed Mark in chapters 1-4 and will do so again in chapter 12. But in chapters 5-11, Matthew leaves Mark to present his own interpretation of the three dimensions of Jesus' ministry: teaching, preaching, and healing (Mt 4:23; 9:35). This summary is expanded throughout chapters 5-11. After his initial preaching ministry (Mt 4:17), Jesus' reputation spread, and crowds followed him. The Sermon on the Mount presents Jesus as the new teacher of the people. Matthew's summary of Jesus' teachings is a masterly call to holiness of life and greater righteousness (Mt 5:1 - 7:27). Jesus the preacher and teacher is next presented as the healer with power over sickness, evil spirits, and nature itself (Mt 8:1 - 9:34). This section on the personal ministry of Jesus ends with such resounding success that Jesus shares his preaching and healing ministries with his disciples, and, in a major sermon on mission, prepares them for their work (Mt 10:1-42).

Chapters 11 to 13 portray a growing rejection of Jesus by his opponents. Cities reject his message (Mt 11:20-24), the Pharisees challenge him (Mt 12:1-15) and even accuse him of blasphemy (Mt 12:22-37). Doubts and questions lead to hostility: the Pharisees demand a sign from Jesus—Jesus demands fruitfulness from the Pharisees (Mt 12:38-50).

Chapters 5:1-13:52 describe only four days in the ministry of Jesus, a clear indication of Matthew's lack of concern for chronology. However, by the time we come to chapter 13, the early enthusiasm has gone, and the opponents in the conflict are lined

up. The more universal call of the Sermon on the Mount gives
place to the restricted presentation of the Sermon on the Kingdom.
The following section portrays the growing acknowledgement of
Jesus by his disciples, and the growing rejection of him by his
opponents. A series of miracles strengthen the former's faith,
while controversies highlight the latter's rejection.

The ministry began with the designation from God (Mt 3:17),
and as it draws to an end in Galilee, God proclaims the same
words on the occasion of the transfiguration (Mt 17:5). The
Galilean ministry ends with the Sermon on the Church, a Church
already understood as distinct from Israel as a whole. The short
ministry of Jesus has given rise to hopes and fears, to community
and division.

Jesus now begins his last journey to Jerusalem. Matthew
basically follows Mark, with some insertions of his own. This is
Jesus' only journey to Jerusalem in Matthew, and even though
individuals recognize him as the Son of David (Mt 20:30), crowds
giving him an enthusiastic welcome (Mt 21:1-17), he is acknowledged as nothing more than a prophet from Nazareth (Mt 21:11).
When he performs a gesture of messianic symbolism, the
religious leaders challenge his authority (Mt 21:23), which leads
to three confrontational parables (Mt 21:28 - 22:14). Even this
late in the ministry, the Pharisees question Jesus, trying to trap
and ridicule him (Mt 22:15-40), and Jesus is still trying to persuade
his opponents (Mt 22: 41-45). Unfortunately, opposition is firm,
rejection mutual, and the ministry ends with the final sermon on
judgment (Mt 26:1).

Jesus' whole ministry is presented as a perfect example of
obedience to the Father's will. This Son who "would fulfill all of
God's demands" (Mt 3:15) is twice confirmed by his Father as his
favored Son, and all are called to obey him. He is Emmanuel,
who founds his Church, and will always be Emmanuel for his
disciples (Mt 1:23; 28:20). The Matthean Jesus is truly the
presence of the Father.

Clearly the Son of God

On three occasions, Jesus had predicted his passion and resurrection (Mt 16:21; 17:22-23; 20:17-19). When he entered Jerusalem
for the last time he did so from the east, as the Messiah was expected to do (Ezechiel 43:1-9; Zechariah 9:9), then performing
three final prophetic signs: his entry (Mt 21:1-11), the cleansing of

the temple (Mt 21:12-17), and the cursing of the fig tree (Mt 21:18-22). Although "the whole city was stirred to its depths" (Mt 21:10), it did not accept the protective presence that Jesus brought (Mt 23:37),[20] and within three days Jesus was dead.[21]

Matthew's passion account follows Mark's very closely, but he nevertheless adds some theological emphases of his own. The general flow of the account again follows themes from the Old Testament, including reflections on the selling of the patriarch Joseph into slavery.[22] Matthew integrates fifteen of Mark's seventeen Old Testament quotes and adds five of his own. He also makes slight changes in his sources to make them reflect Old Testament themes, which he sees as fulfilled in Jesus' death (Mt 26:54).

After we are informed of the plot to kill Jesus, there follows the anointing in the house of Simon (Mt 26:6-16). The woman's act is the first indication of what is really happening. Her devotion contrasts with Judas' treachery: he sells Jesus, the Son of David, for thirty pieces of silver, the price of a slave.[23]

Throughout the passion account, Matthew emphasizes the Lordship of Jesus: Jesus' foreknowledge is stressed both at the anointing and during the supper (Mt 26:10-13, 18, 21, 25). He is Lord for the disciples, but unfortunately still only a rabbi for Judas.

In the account of the institution of the Eucharist, Matthew makes two minor changes in Mark which probably reflect ritual practice in his own Church. During the trial and passion, he adds: the death of Judas, the intercession of Pilate's wife, the handwashing of Pilate, the guard at the tomb, and the miracles at Jesus' death.

With slight editing, Matthew's theological emphases emerge. He sees that the events of the passion are controlled by God (Mt 26:2, 18, 29, 42), and that Jesus goes to his death freely (Mt 26:42, 52-53). Jesus is presented in royal dignity (Mt 27:27-31), as the innocent one (Mt 27:4, 19, 24), and as the Son of God (Mt 26:63; 27:40, 43, 54). His death brings the forgiveness of sins (Mt 26:28; also 20:28), and entrance into a new era of world history (Mt 27:51-53).

It is interesting that Matthew, who had consistently placed the Pharisees in bad light, finds no reference in Mark to any involvement of the Pharisees in the death of Jesus. Matthew, however, modifies his account to heighten the responsibility of the Jews

(Mt 27:25), portraying the Pharisees as involved in the deceitful cover-up of the resurrection (Mt 27:62-66).[24]

Matthew had not only stressed the predictions of the passion, but also predictions of the resurrection (Mt 16:21; 17:23; 20:19; 26:32). His account of the resurrection differs more noticeably from Mark than did the passion: Matthew presents the resurrection as an established fact. He does not prove it, even though he does include a retort to an objection that must have circulated at the time (Mt 28:11-15). Matthew's resurrection account is a fine integration of christology and ecclesiology (Mt 27:52-53). Although precautions had been taken by the Pharisees (Mt 27:62-66), a mighty earthquake and the descent of an angel herald the wonderful appearance of the risen Lord. The disbelieving guards are struck with fear, while the disciples, gifted with peace and joy, worship their Lord (Mt 28:4-8).

The risen Jesus, having appeared to the women, then comes in glory to his Church (Mt 28:16-20). This epiphany of the Lord is like the enthronement of a king. Supreme authority has been given to Jesus, and sharing it with his Church, he assures them of the permanence of his presence. Although in the narrative these words are addressed to the eleven, they are all dead when this addition is made. Clearly Matthew sees it as Jesus' pledge of continuing guidance to his future Church. The risen Lord then commands his Church to expand, to begin a universal mission.

Jesus is presented throughout the final events of his life as the obedient Son who trusts in God and fulfills his will. By slight editorial modifications, Matthew gives new perspectives to the account. Jesus emerges as a figure of power, foreknowledge, obedience, and trustful commitment. He is seen as Son of God, Son of Man, Messiah, and King. Both his disciples and his enemies approach him with reverence. In the end, however, all abandon him, even his disciples, and Matthew admits that "all the disciples deserted him and fled" (Mt 26:56). Without the Lord, they again experience the fear and anxiety of his absence (Mt 14:22-27).

Though some abandon him and others doubt (Mt 28:17), Jesus remains faithful: ever obedient to his Father, ever supportive of his Church. He has experienced in his ministry the hardships and brokenness of humanity, its temptations, poverty, rejection, sufferings, anguish, and death. Now he returns as Lord, received with liturgical reverence for "Clearly this was the Son of God" (Mt 27:54).

Matthew's portrait of Jesus.   Each of the New Testament
writers, desiring to show how special Jesus was, used titles and
religious concepts familiar in their cultures. Matthew is no exception. He applies to Jesus an extremely rich variety of titles
throughout the three stages of Jesus' ministry, each of them
affirming something special about the Lord's relationship to his
people. Jesus fulfills our hopes, heals our ills, teaches us life,
binds us to each other, calls us to God, and is our Lord and judge.

Jesus fulfills our hopes

Matthew's audience is predominantly, but not exclusively,
Christians of Jewish origin. He presents Jesus as the fulfillment
of the hopes of the chosen people: he is of the house of David,
relives their history, is heralded by Elijah, teaches like Moses,
and suffers like the Servant. Matthew's constant use of the Old
Testament clearly shows his conviction that Jesus fulfills these
hopes. Jesus himself claims that his teachings and deeds confirm
that he is the One "who is to come" (Mt 11:3). To all of struggling
and searching humanity, Jesus affirms that his yoke is easy (Mt
11:29), his call is for compassion (Mt 12:7), and his understanding
is for sinners (Mt 9:13). He speaks sympathetically of the poor,
the sorrowing, the lowly, the hungry, the merciful, the singlehearted, the peacemakers, the persecuted, and the alienated; his
kingdom is for them all. Jesus heals us, protects and guides us,
teaches us to love God as a father and each other as family. The
aspirations of humanity are met in the universal appeal of Jesus.
He promises peace (Mt 11:28-30), happiness (Mt 5:3-12), and providential care (Mt 6:26-34), insisting that these be for all
(Mt 28:18-20).

The Old Testament referred to the expected one as Messiah,
and, as we have seen, Matthew shows Jesus as the Messiah of
word (ch. 5-7) and deed (ch. 8-9). He is also energetic in stressing
that Jesus is the Messiah by his use of the title on at least fourteen occasions, eleven of which are due to his editing.[25] Not only
does Matthew tone down Mark's "messianic secret," but publicly
proclaims Jesus' messiahship (Mt 16:20), introducing additional
motifs and titles to clarify the originality of his interpretation of
Messiah. Matthew's insistence that Jesus is the Son of Man, Son
of God, King, Emmanuel, Servant, Shepherd, and Lord also
clarifies the special way in which he sees Jesus fulfilling human
hopes beyond those contained in the concept of Messiah.

In the infancy account, Matthew links together the titles of Messiah and Son of David (Mt 2:1-6). He goes on to affirm that Jesus is the Son of David eight times, seven of which result from Matthew's redactional work.[26] Unfortunately, those whose hopes Jesus came to fulfill are blind to who he is. Ironically, Jesus is recognized as the Son of David by two blind men (Mt 9:27-31), a blind mute (Mt 12:22), a Gentile woman (Mt 15:21-28), two more blind men (Mt 20:29-34), and the blind, lame, and children in the temple (Mt 21:14).[27]

Jesus is the one who fulfills all our hopes and brings salvation (Mt 1:21). Many awaited his coming, but Matthew, with his usual pastoral concern and skill, warns us that those who awaited him rejected him. The Baptist's question of "Are you 'He who is to come' or do we look for another?" (Mt 11:3), and Jesus' appeal: "who do you say that I am?" (Mt 16:15) are answered forcefully and energetically by Matthew, who shows Jesus as the fulfillment of all human hopes.

Jesus heals our ills

Joseph's betrothal to Mary guarantees davidic descent to his child; he is told by the angel to call him Jesus, "because he will save his people from their sins" (Mt 1:21). Matthew, quoting psalm 130:8, changes "Israel" to "his people," a potentially broader concept. Already, the saving power of Jesus is for all those who are "his people."

Jesus' mission is to save us from our sin (Mt 1:21; 26:28). In a culture that saw sickness and the catastrophes of nature as the results of evil spirits, it was natural that this saving ministry take on a broader, integral dimension. Jesus' ministry of saving from sin merges into cures from sickness, exorcisms of evil spirits, and control over nature.

Jesus cures many individuals from all walks of life (Mt 4:24), but Matthew also stresses that he "cured all who were afflicted," in fulfillment of the scriptures (Mt 8:16-17). He adds a summary that "he cured every sickness and disease" (Mt 9:35); inserts the idea that "Many people followed him and he cured them all" (Mt 12:16); and presents Jesus on the mountain of revelation curing the needy of the world (Mt 15:29-31). We have seen that Matthew abbreviates the miracle stories, omitting secondary features and focusing on the power and immediacy of Jesus' cures. He omits from his sources any indications of human techniques that may have facilitated the cure (Mk 7:31-37; 8:22-26). Rather, Matthew's

Jesus cures with his word (Mt 8:16), and the results are immediate (Mt 15:28; 21:19).

Jesus, whose compassion is for all (Mt 14:14), indicates that faith is necessary for his saving grace to come to fullness (Mt 17:19-20). He praises those who have such faith (Mt 8:10; 9:2, 22, 28; 15:28) and heals them (Mt 8:3, 13; 9:22, 30; 15:28). Jesus' healing and saving grace are not given where faith is absent (Mt 13:58).

Jesus is also the strong one who can plunder the realm of Satan (Mt 12:29-30), and does so in a series of exorcisms (Mt 8:28-34; 9:32-34). Even events of nature are under his control, responding to his saving word (Mt 8:23-27).

Besides bringing healing and purification, Jesus assures us of healing knowledge, peace, rest, harmony (Mt 11:28-30), and mutual love (ch. 18). He challenges us to avoid anger (Mt 5:21-26), lust (Mt 5:27-30), retaliation (Mt 5:38-42), selective treatment of others (Mt 5:43-48), and rash judgment (Mt 7:1-5). Life lost for Jesus is truly regained in all its authenticity and wholeness (Mt 16:25).

All Jesus' healing grace is part of the integral salvation he brings, the total removal of sin and its replacement with good (Mt 12:43-45). The healings are an outward sign of his power to forgive (Mt 9:6). His healing activity culminates in the forgiveness of sin, for which he comes, commits his entire life, and dies (Mt 1:21; 26:28).

When he enters the world he is greeted with the name "Jesus," meaning "Yahweh is salvation." When he enters Jerusalem, he is greeted with "Hosanna," a cry for deliverance: "Save now!" Disciples of all times cry out in their troubles "Lord save us! We are lost!" (Mt 8:25), and Jesus with his healing grace assures us "Peace...I am with you always" (Mt 28:20).

Jesus teaches us life.

Jesus preached in public and taught his disciples in private, like any rabbi of his day. Also like them, he debated, interpreted the Law, and blessed the children. Many people acknowledged him as a teacher and sought his guidance. For Matthew, Jesus is more than a rabbi, since he teaches with an authority they simply did not have (Mt 7:29). In fact, he "left the crowds spellbound at his teaching" (Mt 7:28). We have seen how Matthew presents Jesus as the only teacher (Mt 11:28-30; 23:8-10; 28:20), a new Moses who interprets the Law, modifies it, and even rescinds it.

The future must be built on the solid rock of his teaching (Mt 7:24-27), for only he has access to the will of the Father (Mt 11:25-30).

Although Jesus is the great teacher endowed with full authority from his Father (Mt 28:18), he is never called "teacher" by his true disciples. Pharisees, Sadducees, scribes, lawyers, and strangers address Jesus as "teacher."[28] Even the disbelieving Judas twice speaks of Jesus as his teacher (Mt 26:25, 49). True disiciples know that Jesus is more than a great teacher, and without exception they address him as "Lord" (Mt 26:22). They listen to his word because he is the Messiah and Son of God (Mt 3:17; 17:5).

Many of the crowd also see Jesus as more than a teacher, speaking of him as a prophet (Mt 16:13-14; 21:11, 46). Certainly his birth and early life give indications of a prophetic ministry. Those who heard him and were impressed by his preaching thought he was something of an Elijah or a Jeremiah (Mt 16:14), and there are indications that Jesus spoke of himself as a prophet (Mt 13:57). Even the solemn designation of Jesus as the Son who has God's favor has overtones of the great prophet foretold by Moses (Deuteronomy 18:15).

Some commentators see traces of Jesus' teaching authority rooted in the fact that Matthew sees Jesus as Wisdom incarnate (Mt 11:28-30 and Lk 11:49). Even his rejection is paralleled to the rejection of Wisdom itself (Mt 23:37-39).[29]

Jesus—the teacher, prophet, and manifestation of wisdom—speaks with authority because he knows the Father and reveals him to us (Mt 11:25-27). He is our teacher by his very life: "I will refresh you... learn from me" (Mt 11:28-29). For the believer, Jesus is teacher because he is the prophet, wisdom, the davidic Messiah, Emmanuel. Above all, he teaches us life because he is the favored Son of God.

Jesus binds us to each other

The fact that Jesus knows the Father and reveals him to us indicates his mediational role. Part of this function is to gather us together as God's people. Matthew speaks of Jesus as "a ruler who is to shepherd my people Israel" (Mt 2:6). During his ministry, Jesus spoke of himself as a shepherd (Mt 9:36), and saw his death with its resulting misfortune for the sheep, as that of a shepherd (Mt 26:31). This portrait of Jesus as the shepherd implies the leadership role of gathering his sheep together (2 Samuel 5:2),[30] and is closely connected with the title of King.[31] This latter designation, with its political overtones, is modified by Matthew's portrayal of Jesus' kingship as a humble service of suffering for his people (Mt 21:5; 27:27-31). His death on the cross as king (Mt 27:37) shows how he saved others by being unwilling to save himself (Mt 27:42).

Jesus' ministry shows the concrete steps taken by the shepherd-king to establish and build up his people. He clarifies the nature of his kingdom (Mt ch. 13) and attitudes necessary to belong to it (Mt 5:1-7:28). He calls and trains his disciples, shares his authority with them (Mt 10:1-42), and assures them of his perennial guidance (Mt 28:20).

Those he gathers into his community he calls to reconciliation, benevolence, love, and forgiveness (Mt ch. 5-7). He also calls for the cultivation of humility, care for others, avoidance of scandal and nurturing of the group through care for those who stray, reconciliation of the wanderer, and limitless forgiveness (Mt ch. 18). Finally, he describes the last judgment as a shepherd separating out those sheep he knows (Mt 25:31-46).

Jesus, the Shepherd-King, through his humble life of service and suffering, gathers his people together (Mt 2:6). This he did in history and continues to do in his Church: "Where two or three are gathered in my name, there am I in their midst" (Mt 18:20).

Jesus calls us to God

Jesus is the Shepherd-King, miracle worker, teacher, Messiah, and Son of David. Matthew also understands Jesus as the Servant of God. In fact, when Mark makes mention of the messianic secret (Mk 3:12), Matthew uses the occasion to express his understanding of why Jesus "ordered them not to make public what he had done" (Mt 12:16). It was to fulfill the words of Isaiah that the Messiah would carry out his saving ministry with the silence of the Servant (Mt 12:17-21; Isaiah 42:1-4).

The Servant's acceptance of suffering, his silent witness and his service to the weak, are aspects of Jesus' ministry. As the Servant-Son, he is twice welcomed by his Father (Mt 3:17; 17:5).[32] This servanthood of Jesus gives a specific interpretation to his other titles.[33]

The notion of Servant, which can also be translated Son, merges naturally into the designation of Jesus as "Son of God." In the temptations which preceded the ministry, the tempter twice refers to Jesus as "Son of God" (Mt 4:3, 6). Demons at Gadara (Mt 8:29), the high priest at Jesus' trial (Mt 26:63) and

those who ridicule Jesus on the cross (Mt 27:40, 43) all speak
ironically of Jesus as Son of God. These contrast with three occasions of solemn profound faith, when the centurion once (Mt
27:54), and the apostles twice, acknowledge Jesus as the Son of
God (Mt 14:33; 16:16). The title itself does not mean much more
than adoption or divine designation for service or holiness. The
contexts, however, indicate that for Matthew, if not for the par-
ticipants, this title refers to actual sonship. This is underlined
even more by some of the uses of the absolute "Son" (Mt 11:27;
21:38; 24:36; 28:19), and Jesus' references to his Father. The
resulting picture, which certainly highlights Matthew's redactional work,[34] shows that "Son of God" is a major Matthean
understanding of Jesus.

Matthew also emphasizes this divine sonship in the way he
establishes Jesus' absolute fidelity to the will of God, roots his
authority in the Father (Mt 11:27), identifies his power over evil
(Mt 12:28), and claim his teachings over the laws. Jesus also
presents himself to his disciples as "I am," which is generally
understood as a self-proclamation of God (Mt 14:27). In the
transfiguration story, the cloud that overshadows Jesus recalls
the divine presence, the *shekinah,* that indicated the glory of
God (Exodus 40:35; 2 Maccabees 2:8).

While debating about the Messiah with the Pharisees during
his last days in Jerusalem, the Matthean Jesus pointedly asks:
"Whose son is he?" (Mt 22:42). This is a crucial question for
Matthew, and the answer to it determines one's understanding of
all other descriptions of Jesus. At his birth, at his baptism, during
the temptations, at the transfiguration, and at the crucifixion
Jesus is acclaimed as Son. Believers faithfully proclaim him as
such, and as such do disbelievers blaspheme him. This title
"is easily the most comprehensive title Matthew employs."[35]

Jesus the Son, endowed with glory, lives his life as the Servant.
Only true disciples who see the Servant can acknowledge that
"Beyond doubt you are the Son of God" (Mt 14:33).

Jesus is our Lord and Judge

One of the most frequently used titles for Jesus in Matthew's
gospel is "Lord." This is not simply an expression of courteous
address, since Matthew is diligent about adding it to his gospel
where it was absent in his sources (Mt 8:25 and Mk 4:38; Mt 17:4
and Mk 9:5; Mt 20:33 and Mk 10:51). "Lord" in Matthew is the

cultic title of the early Church, expressing reverence and majesty.
We have seen that this is the title most frequently used by
believers who approach Jesus. When others call him teacher, rabbi
or sir, believers express their faith in Jesus as Messiah, Son of
God, and Son of David by calling him "Lord."[36] In fact, non-
believers only address Jesus as Lord on two occasions, both of
which describe scenes of judgment (Mt 7:22; 25:44).

Lord is a title that conveys awe resulting from the awareness
that the many ways of designating Jesus are all facets of the same
transcendent person. It manifests faith, homage, and a true
sense of worship. Matthew omits Marcan references to the
human feelings of Jesus and to any indication of lack of
knowledge on his part. On the fifty-two occasions Matthew
speaks of people "approaching" Jesus, he uses a verb which
means "showing respect," or "doing homage," or making a
ceremonial approach.[37] His disciples, questioners, scribes,
Pharisees, those who seek cures, the betrayer Judas, and even
the devil, all do cultic homage as they approach the Lord.

This image of Jesus as awesome Lord is complemented by the
title "Son of Man," which Matthew uses thirty times to Mark's
fourteen and Luke's eight. Based on Daniel's reference to the
eschatological judge,[38] it describes Jesus' power and universal
authority (Mt 24:30; 26:64). At times in Matthew, Jesus identifies
the Son of Man with himself (Mt 16:13-15). Although as Son of
Man Jesus has authority on earth to forgive sin (Mt 9:6), this title
is basically an emphasis on his authority and an indication that
his authority extends to the final judgment (Mt 13:41; 25:31).

As Lord and Son of Man, "all the nations will be assembled
before him" (Mt 25:32), Jesus can judge evildoers (Mt 7:22-23;
25:44-46) and reward his faithful disciples with power (Mt
19:28-30). Those who recognize him as Lord and build on his
word (Mt 7:21-27) will welcome his coming in glory (Mt 23:39).

Matthew's presentation and understanding of Jesus, both in
the ministry and in his christological synthesis, is more insightful
and mature than that of Mark or Luke. He has reflected on the
significance of the person Jesus and his life, teachings, death,
and resurrection. He presents Jesus to his Church as the Messiah
and Son of David who fulfills all our hopes; as the healer of all
our ills; as the prophetic teacher of true wisdom; as the shepherd
who builds up his congregation; as the Servant-Son of God who
draws us to his Father; and as the Son of Man and Lord, the
universal judge.

The Holy Spirit—The Sign Of The Kingdom

The presence of the Spirit.   Matthew refers to the Holy Spirit twelve times, only two of which are his own personal additions (Mt 12:18; 28:19). The rest are taken from his sources, with only one indicating a deliberate Matthean specification of the work of the Spirit (Mt 12:28), and one reflecting a more apocalyptic context for the presence of the Holy Spirit (Mt 3:11).

Although Matthew is writing mainly for Christians of Jewish origin, his work does show signs of Hellenistic Judaism rather than Palestinian Judaism, and this is reflected in his understanding of the role of the Spirit of God.

The Holy Spirit is traditionally seen as the source of inspiration for scripture and the prophets (Mt 22:43), but there are also indications that this inspiration is seen in the preaching ministry of Jesus (Mt 12:18-20), and in the bold proclamation of a persecuted Church (Mt 10:20).

Hellenistic Judaism not only saw the Spirit as the instrument of inspiration, but also as the generative principle of life.[39] Twice we are told that the conception of Jesus is the result of the creative Spirit (Mt 1:18, 20). This teaching, recalling the Spirit's presence in the creation stories of the Old Testament (Genesis 1:1-2), is highlighted again at Jesus' baptism (Mt 3:16).

The prophetic and creative Spirit is also seen as the sign of God's anointing. The Spirit descends on Jesus at his baptism (Mt 3:16), leads him into the desert (Mt 4:1), and is God's gift for his Servant ministry (Mt 12:18).

Finally, the presence of the Spirit is seen as a sign of the kingdom and an authentication of the power of God in the healing ministry of Jesus (Mt 12:28). This is the only occasion where Matthew adds the idea of the Spirit to a source which lacked it.

The Spirit's presence in Matthew is one of prophetic inspiration, creative blessings, powerful anointing, and a sign of the kingdom.

The Spirit and Jesus.   Our reflections on Matthew's gospel have shown how forcefully the author centers on the person Jesus. This centrality of Christ absorbs most of the teaching on the Father or the Spirit which can be found elsewhere in the New Testament. Matthew includes those references to the Holy Spirit which highlight the exceptional nature of Jesus, and so we read that he was conceived by the Holy Spirit (Mt 1:18, 20), endowed with God's prophetic and anointing Spirit at his baptism (Mt 3:16), led into the wilderness by the Holy Spirit to face his nations temptations (Mt 4:1), and consecrated by the Spirit in his ministry (Mt 12:18, 28).

Although these texts emphasize the exceptional nature of the person Jesus, Matthew takes care that nowhere do these texts subordinate Jesus to the Spirit of God. When Mark says: "the Spirit sent him out toward the desert" (Mk 1:12), Matthew changes it to "Jesus was led into the desert by the Spirit" (Mt 4:1). He thus preserves Jesus as the agent in control of his own actions.

The only text on the Spirit found exclusively in Matthew deals with the fulfillment of the Servant prophecy of Isaiah (Mt 12:18). If the post- resurrection Matthean Church was encountering people who disbelieved Jesus because of his silent, suffering Servant ministry, Matthew stresses that even here Jesus emerges as the fulfillment of the prophecies. In fact, the one unforgiveable sin is to deny the Spirit's presence and divine power in the ministry of Jesus (Mt 12:31, 32).

The Spirit and the Church. In both John and Luke the Holy Spirit mediates Jesus' presence to the Church, and in Luke the gift of the Spirit constitutes the disciples as Church. Matthew's view is different: Jesus is present to his Church now (Mt 18:19-20) and always (Mt 28:20). The Church is made up of those who recognize his authority (Mt 28:20), build on his word (Mt 7:24-27), and accept his yoke (Mt 11:28-30). The risen Lord is present and active in his Church. In fact, he never left it to return in glory, but came in glory at his resurrection to stay. Therefore Matthew sees no need to present the Spirit as mediating Jesus' presence, rather he "is so convinced of the presence of the risen Lord in his church that he avoids cluttering the purity of that insight by presenting the Spirit as the medium of that presence."[40]

Besides this theological preference of Matthew, there seems to be a further pastoral concern of his that leads to a restricted presentation of the role of the Holy Spirit: namely, his concern for the divisive charismatic activity of false prophets. By rooting the ongoing presence of Jesus in the community of the Church and its leaders, he effectively reduces the claims of self-styled leaders to be guided by the Spirit.

In Matthew, not even the final commission includes the outpouring of the Spirit on the disciples. The major Matthean conviction remains: Jesus has all authority, and the Church teaches in his name because he is always present in the Church.

Although Matthew's pneumatology is veiled, it bursts into a climactic statement on the personhood of the Holy Spirit in the liturgical formula of the final commission: "In the name of the Father, and of the Son, and of the Holy Spirit" (Mt 28:19). This gives expression to the advanced liturgical and creedal tradition of Matthew's community, complementing his discreet statements with a glimpse into the richness of the Church's later expressions of faith. To have reached this powerful vision of God by the 80s and 90s merits respect and wonder.

Matthew calls us all to a deeper appreciation of Jesus as our shepherd, the very presence of the Father, and the Son of God, who as our Lord satisfies our hopes, cures our ills, teaches us life, draws us together, and calls us to God. Jesus teaches us about the Father and his will, and about the Spirit and his powerful presence to us all.

Chapter Five
CHURCH IN MATTHEW

"The farmer sowing good seed is the Son of Man; the field is the world, the good seed the citizens of the kingdom" (Mt 13:37-38).

Matthew's ecclesiastical gospel is the only one to use the word "Church" (Mt 16:18; 18:17), and his whole presentation is shaped by his teachings on the Church. He deals with Church authority both in Peter (Mt 16:13-20) and in the community (Mt 18:16-18), and reacts against challenges to that authority from false prophets (Mt 7:15; 24:11, 24). He alone gives a special discourse on the Church and its discipline (Mt ch. 18), and gives an ecclesiological interpretation to the parables.   We have seen how he is interested in showing both a transfer of leadership from the Pharisees to his own community, and a similar local centering of the fulfillment of messianic hopes. Matthew has so overlayed his gospel with Church interests that it has become very like a gospel and Acts in one.

Matthew's gospel is not only interested in the Church, but, as we saw in chapter one, no gospel has had so much influence on the Church. Since early times, it has exercised educational, disciplinary, and normative influence on Church life.

Focusing on the nature and need of the Church was no easy task in a community that had previously expected the end of the world. The early Christians understood that the divine plan was soon to reach an apocalyptic end, and many Jewish members of Mathew's community expected the Messiah to establish his community within the chosen people. Matthew claims that neither expectation will be realized, and, by the time he writes, his community too had serious doubts that their hopes would be realized in the way they had expected. Some died with unfulfilled hopes, while others tired of waiting for Christ's dramatic return and apostasized (Mt 24:12). Some saw messiahs everywhere (Mt 24:23), others followed false prophets (Mt 24:11), and still others weakened in their commitment, giving up obedience to any law (Mt 5:17-20).

Molding a community out of such disparate groups and giving it a sense of purpose challenged Matthew's leadership ability. His approach to Church is a combination of theological vision and pastoral directives: He calls the lawless and undisciplined to an awareness of the demands of the Sermon on the Mount. He condemns false teachers and shows how his ecclesiology depends on his christology, for the Church is the community who believes Jesus is the only teacher. He reminds people from different cultural and religious backgrounds that God is the father of all, calling them to life together.

Matthew, like spiritual leaders of every generation, directs his people to an awareness that God is not present to them in the way they think he should be. In fact, God is not the god people create him to be, nor does he act in the way people prescribe for him. Matthew refocuses his people's hopes, showing how God realizes those hopes in the Church.

In this chapter, we will study the nature of the Church in Matthew, the characteristics of life in both kingdom and Church, the roles of Church leadership and authority, and finally the ecclesial spirituality of the first gospel.

Kingdom And Church

The Kingdom.   The Kingdom was the central theme of Jesus' preaching. Matthew uses "Kingdom" approximately sixty times, only five of which do not have a specifically religious meaning. On two occasions, he speaks of the Kingdom of the Son of Man (Mt 16:28; 20:21), and on five occasions refers to the Kingdom of God (Mt 6:33; 12:28; 19:24; 21:31, 43). The phrase he uses most frequently, thirty-two times, is "the Kingdom of Heaven," a phrase found nowhere else in the gospels.[1]

Although the concepts at times overlap, the Kingdom can be seen more globally as the sovereign reign of God, realized fully at the end of time, but anticipated in Jesus. Matthew sees the Church as the door to the Kingdom, not the Kingdom itself. Rather, the Church draws others to the Kingdom. The notion of Kingdom is a complex one: it is otherworldly, since it calls us to eternal life with God; it is also very this-worldly and political, since it implies human liberation and growth.

Kingdom is never described as a past reality. John the Baptist considers that it is close at hand (Mt 3:2). Jesus too stressed its imminence (Mt 4:17, 23), proclaimed the good news of its arrival

CHURCH IN MATTHEW

101

(Mt 9:35), described the conditions for entry (Mt chs. 5-7), and insisted that his miracles confirmed its arrival (Mt 12:28).

Jesus states that although everyone is called to the Kingdom, some will be found unworthy of it (Mt 8:11-12). He sees his ministry as directing others to the Kingdom (Mt 4:17; 9:35). Unfortunately, some oppose his work, shutting out those who wish to enter (Mt 13:41; 23:13; 25:10), while many even undertake violence in their attempts to enter (Mt 11:12).

The nature of the Kingdom is described in Book III of Matthew's gospel (Mt 11:2 - 13:53). Here is a clear presentation of Matthew's conviction that the Kingdom is focused on Christ, for not only does Jesus announce its arrival, but actually brings the Kingdom (Mt 11:2-6; 12:28). Those who enter are especially blessed (Mt 11:11), those who reject it condemned (Mt 11:20-24). Jesus reveals that the reign of the Father is one of mercy, forgiveness (Mt 11:25-12:21), and judgment (Mt 11:20-24).

Matthew's parable discourse (Mt 13:1-53) is based on Mark's (Mk 4:1-35), but our author has changed his source and included five additional parables. Unlike Mark, Matthew deals with the nature of the Kingdom, expressing his understanding in the two stages of a simple structure that, again, portrays Matthew's christological and ecclesiological interests. The first part of the discourse (Mt 13:1-35) is addressed to the Jewish crowds, who "listen but do not hear or understand" (Mt 13:13). The second part (Mt 13:36-53) is addressed to the disciples, to whom "has been given a knowledge of the mysteries of the reign of God" (Mt 13:11).

The parable of the sower shows the different responses of people to the word of the Kingdom. The parable of the weeds presents a mixed community where children of the Kingdom live in the midst of enemies of the Kingdom, doing so until harvest time. The mustard seed and leaven parables describe the small beginnings of the Kingdom, its hidden transforming action, and the wonders of its future growth. The parables of the treasure and the pearl confirm that some men and women will sacrifice everything for the joy of living in the Kingdom. Finally, the parable of the net reminds that not until the end of the world will we know who has met God's standards for life in the Kingdom of Heaven.[2]

These parables of the weeds (Mt 13:24-30, 34-43) and net (Mt 13:47-50), along with the later parable of the ten virgins

(Mt 25:1-13), point out that the Kingdom will fully come at the end of the world (Mt 13:41; 24:30; 25:31). It is already "at hand" in the preaching of John the Baptist (Mt 3:2), and in the proclamation of Jesus (Mt 4:17, 23; 9:35) and the apostles (Mt 10:7). By his healing ministry, Jesus even anticipates the blessings that will come when it is fully established (Mt 12:28). Other signs of its imminent or actual arrival are the disciples' experience of its blessings (Mt 6:33), the attempts already by some to enter it (Mt 11:12; 21:31), the realization of former hopes (Mt 13:17), the fact that Peter possesses the keys of the Kingdom (Mt 16:19), and the statement of the Lord that some will see it realized before their death (Mt 16:28).

Kingdom and Church.   The final glorious return of the Son of Man inaugurates the Kingdom (Mt 13:41; 24:3; 25:31). However, as we have seen, Matthew presents Jesus returning in glory to his Church (Mt 28:16-20). Moreover, the parable of the wedding banquet, offered as a description of the Kingdom (Mt 22:1-14), is modified by Matthew to describe the Kingdom as the marriage of his Son, an image used consistently for the Church. Those who receive the message of the Son are "the citizens of the kingdom" (Mt 13:38), and those who reject him as king (Mt 27:41) will have the Kingdom taken away from them (Mt 8:11-12; 21:43).

Disciples who hear "the message about God's reign" (Mt 13:19), who receive "a knowledge of the mysteries of the reign of God" (Mt 13:11), and who truly "seek first his kingship" over them (Mt 6:33), are, in Matthew's understanding, those who inherit the Kingdom (Mt 5:3, 10; 25:34). They replace those to whom it had formerly been pledged (Mt 21:43). Their task is to pray for the spread of the Kingdom (Mt 6:10) and to preach it to the ends of the earth (Mt 10:7; 24:14; 28:20).

While the Kingdom is really part of afterlife (Mt 25:31-46), Jesus' preaching about it gave rise to the Church, his Church (Mt 16:18). This new period of history and the resulting life of the Church is never identified with the Kingdom, but certainly anticipates or foreshadows it. "Jesus knew that the Kingdom was beginning in his own work, and so the Church and the early stages of the Kingdom overlap."[3] While the disciples are now described as "citizens of the kingdom," the ones who produce the fruits of righteousness (Mt 21:43), the Kingdom "still transcends the church and remains an object of hope for the future."[4]

However, Matthew's focus regarding the inauguration of the Kingdom is not primarily the Church, but Christ. The Kingdom comes in him who now has full authority to reign (Mt 28:16-20). Insofar as the Kingdom is the embodiment of the Old Testament's hopes, it is now Jesus who fulfills these hopes. The Church is the prolongation of Jesus' call and teachings. If Matthew understands the establishing of the Church as part of God's plan, it is simply because it is Christ's Church, the assembly of those who take his yoke and learn from him (Mt 11:28-30). Matthew's ecclesiology is highly developed precisely because his christology is. He can stress the life of the Church (Mt ch. 18) because Jesus, like the *shekinah*, is present to it (Mt 18:20); in fact, he is greater than the temple itself (Mt 12:6), always present to the disciples (Mt 28:20).

Matthew sees Jesus as fulfilling the Old Testament hopes regarding the reign of God. Jesus first proclaims his message to the Jewish people, many of whom are potentially his future Church. Unfortunately, their leaders imply a rejection of Jesus (Mt chs. 1-10) which then becomes explicit (Mt chs. 11-13), in evidence to the end. By their rejection of Jesus the Pharisees actually "shut the doors of the kingdom in men's faces" (Mt 23:13). Their disregard of the words of Jesus lead to the collapse of their leadership and complete ruin for their followers (Mt 7:24-27). Although originally Matthew had probably seen continuity between Christianity and Judaism, he ends by presenting the Church as Israel's replacement. The predominantly Gentile Church is imaged in the ritually unclean leaven that will facilitate the entry of the masses into the Kingdom.[5]

The whole of Book III begins with the question: "Are you 'He who is to come' or do we look for another?" (Mt 11:3). The section goes on to portray Jesus' rejection by his opponents, a rejection implying rejection of the Kingdom as well (Mt 12:28). Those who know the answer to John's question (Mt 11:3) believe, become disciples (Mt 12:46-50), and have the Kingdom explained to them (Mt 13:11). The explanation implies that while the Kingdom is future, its blessings are anticipated in the Church.

Characteristics Of Life For The Kingdom

Matthew deals at length with the requisite conditions for entry into the Kingdom. He integrates all six sayings provided by his sources (Mt 8:11; 11:12; 18:3, 8-9; 19:23; 23:13); he modifies his sources twice to further stress the requirements for entering the

Kingdom (Mt 7:13-14, 21); and introduces three additional sayings not found in his sources (Mt 5:20; 13:41-43; 21:31).[6] Given the struggles of his community, the theme is obviously important, weaving its way through all the discourses.[7] Matthew believes that entering the Kingdom is difficult (Mt 7:13-14), that many will not achieve it, including those who thought they would (Mt 13:41-43; 21:31); it will require commitment greater than that demanded by the Pharisees (Mt 5:20). For Matthew, those who wish to enter the Kingdom need to take a totally new direction in life.

A new direction in life. When a rich young man asks Jesus what he must do to enter the Kingdom and possess eternal life, Jesus' answer is firm: "Follow me."[8] Jesus alone knows the Kingdom, teaches it to others, guides people toward it, and judges their suitability for entrance. Those who follow Jesus are guaranteed greatness in the Kingdom (Mt 11:11). This is the essential requirement, a new direction centered on Jesus. In fact, "a comparison of parallel accounts indicates that the expressions "for my sake" (5:11; 10:39; 16:25; 19:29), and "for the sake of God's reign" (19:12) are used synonymously by Matthew, and indicate that "one's attitude toward Jesus is his attitude toward the kingdom."[9] To those who seek life in the Kingdom Jesus says: "Come to me...I will refresh you. Take my yoke... learn from me Your souls will find rest" (Mt 11:28-30).

The blessings of the Kingdom are experienced in Jesus, the crucial condition for entry into the joy of the Lord (Mt 25:21, 23) being an exclusive commitment to follow Jesus (Mt 4:19; 8:22; 9:9; 16:24; 19:21). This following has two steps to it: "Reform your lives" (Mt 3:2), and become the "little ones who believe in me" (Mt 18:6). Before launching out in this new direction, those who wish to enter the Kingdom must first turn away from their former lives and values. This call to repentance, an essential part of Jesus' ministry (Mt 4:17), not only implies a turning from sin (Mt 11:20-24; 3:7-10), an observance of the commandments (Mt 19:16-19), and an inner sincerity of life (Mt 12:33-37), but also a detachment from anything that might diminish the exlusiveness of Jesus' claim to our commitment (Mt 16:21-26).

Repentance and reform of life lead to faith in Jesus, and Jesus himself insists that this is an essential requirement, distinguishing those who will enter the Kingdom from those who will be cast out (Mt 8:10-12). In fact, those who believe in Jesus already experience the blessings of the Kingdom (Mt 8:13; 9:29; 15:28). This

faith, the basis of the new direction in life, is faith in Jesus
(Mt 18:6; 27:42), and requires that those wishing to enter the
Kingdom build on his word (Mt 7:24-27), and publicly manifest
their faith in him (Mt 10:32-33).

New attitudes.   Mathew's community discourse begins with
Jesus pointing out that the Kingdom belongs to those who
"become like little children" (Mt 18:3). Matthew's Jesus then
goes on to specify that childlikeness means humility (Mt 18:4).
Since Jesus is the only teacher of the Kingdom, "Whoever exalts
himself shall be humbled, but whoever humbles himself shall be
exalted" (Mt 23:12). Conscious awareness of the Lordship of
Jesus makes one not only humble, but also healthily dependent
and trusting in the Lord (Mt 6:24-34). Those who wish to enter
the Kingdom should not be anxious about the future. Provided
they are singlemindedly committed to the Kingdom (Mt 6:24),
they can trust that all their needs will be met (Mt 6:32-34).

This trusting simplicity and humility of the child is combined
with the prudence of the mature, who train themselves to read
the signs of the times (Mt 16:2-3; 24:32-33). Such prudence leads
to a life of preparedness for the ever-expected return of the Lord
(Mt 24:36-51; 25:1-13, 31-46). To those who seek to enter the
Kingdom Jesus says: "Keep your eyes open, for you know not the
day or the hour" (Mt 25:13). This lack of knowledge concerning
the time of the end challenges those who wish to "inherit the
Kingdom" to live in such a way that they are always ready to
enter into the joy of the Lord (Mt 25: 21, 23).

Genuine humility and vigilance lead to the new attitudes of
compassion toward others and the communal vigilance of
avoiding scandal. True humility helps those who seek the
Kingdom to avoid condemning others, showing mercy instead
(Mt 9:13; 12:7). This spirit of compassion is greater than sacrifice,
leading to efforts to avoid all scandal and its evil effects (Mt 13:41;
18:6). Those who seek the Kingdom do not condemn but, aware
of their own sin, seek out wanderers to bring them back to a
merciful and forgiving God (Mt 18:21-35).

A new lifestyle.   The new direction in life and the new attitudes
of those who seek the Kingdom lead to a style of living more
committed than that taught by the scribes and Pharisees. In
Matthew, Jesus explicitly links this higher righteousness with
entrance into the Kingdom (Mt 5:20), and affirms that the absence
of such righteousness in life assures loss of the Kingdom. This

lifestyle is not built on observance of laws, even though laws are not repudiated. Rather, the new ethic is based on a personal relationship with Jesus (Mt 7:24; 18:6). This implies obedience to the teachings of Jesus (Mt 7:21-23), which place us in contact with the saving will of God (Mt 6:10; 11:27) which alone brings us to life (Mt 12:50). Those who seek the eternal life of the Kingdom must "hunger and thirst for holiness" (Mt 5:6), make it their prime interest (Mt 6:33), and accept even persecution in order to maintain it (Mt 5:10). Matthew sees this higher righteousness as so essential for life in the Kingdom that he can refer to those who enter the Kingdom simply as "the saints," or the righteous (Mt 13:43, 49; 25:37, 46). In fact, for Matthew, "The kingdom of God becomes a reality upon earth whenever and wherever the will of God is performed."[10]

This obedience to the call of the Kingdom implies responsibility to ease the entrance of others (Mt 23:13). Not only the leaders, but all the community are called to this endeavor (Mt 16:19; 18:18). Having described those to whom the Kingdom belongs, Jesus reminds them that they have the responsibility of being salt and light to the world (Mt 5:13-16). He then goes on to interpret responsibilities toward the commands, piety, and spirit of the Law for those entering the Kingdom (Mt 5:17 - 7:28). Later, still in the context of Kingdom, Jesus returns to the theme of responsibility, affirming that the reliable servant shares his master's joy (Mt 25:23). In the story of the last judgment, people gain or lose the Kingdom according to their measure of responsibility for others (Mt 25:45-46).

This new lifestyle, required for the Kingdom, implies an obedience and a sense of responsibility that prove themselves by their fruits (Mt 12:33). In talking to his disciples of the Kingdom, Jesus said that they who accepted the message would yield fruit (Mt 13:23), and further calls this fertile seed "the citizens of the kingdom" (Mt 13:38).

While constantly maintaining a distinction between Church and Kingdom, Matthew sees that qualities in the former are necessary for entrance into the latter Among the requirements for entrance into the Kingdom, Matthew stresses the need for a new direction in life based on a genuine conversion to follow Jesus, implying repentance and faithful confession of the Lord. This new direction calls for new attitudes of humility and trust, vigilance and compassion. Finally, those called to the Kingdom are characterized by a holiness of life based on obedience to the will of God and manifested in responsibility for the community.

Community Life In The Church

Matthew shows his followers how the Church is linked to the Kingdom. He also shows how Jesus' call to reform because the Kingdom was at hand could now be answered by living in the Church. For Matthew, the Church is a community of ongoing conversion, in constant formation, a community that lives reconciliation and forgiveness, that shares during its common pilgrimage.

A community of ongoing conversion. The Church is the community of the called (Mt 22:14), who have responded to Jesus' personal invitation (Mt 4:18-22; 9:9-13). They are his personal followers (Mt 19:27), who have accepted the implications of their choice (Mt 8:18-22) and can now be referred to as his family (Mt 12:46-50). They have followed him into his boat (Mt 8:23-27), been taught by him in his home (Mt 13:36): both possible images of the Church. Jesus is with them always (Mt 1:23; 28:20), protecting them (Mt 14:22-33), teaching them the mysteries of the Kingdom (Mt 13:11), unfolding to them the will of the Father (Mt 11:25-27), and revealing to them individually what the prophets and saints had longed to hear (Mt 13:17). His Church is free of outside pressures (Mt 17:26), confesses his Lordship (Mt 14:33; 16:16), builds on his word (Mt 7:24-27), obeys his commands (Mt 28:18-20), and becomes salt and light to the world in his name (Mt 5:13-16).

This community, blessed by its Lord, is made up of "the little ones" who have been reborn in him (Mt 18:6).[11] Some of them are outcasts of society (Mt 21:14), despised sinners (Mt 9:11; 21:31), and Gentiles (Mt 28:19). His Church is called to be the wise (Mt 25:2), the blessed (Mt 25:34), the righteous (Mt 13:43, 49; 25:37, 46), and the chosen (Mt 22:14; 24:22, 24, 31), but is actually a mixed community of good and bad (Mt 13:24-30, 47-50). Some are not as dedicated as they ought to be (Mt 25:14-23), and others have not lived up to their commitment (Mt 22:11-14). Some easily lose their faith (Mt 13:19) or give mere lip service to Jesus (Mt 7:21-23). Some cause other disciples to lose faith (Mt 18:6), and still others create an atmosphere of division and hate (Mt 24:10-12). It is a community misled by false prophets (Mt 7:15-20; 24:11), tempted to lawlessness (Mt 5:17-20), and threatened by persecution (Mt 5:10, 44; 10:23; 24:9). Matthew presents Jesus' temptations as a reliving of the chosen people's temptations (Mt 4:1-11), for Matthew sees his own community tempted. He reminds believers that they have followed Jesus into his boat, and though storm-tossed, they will be saved if they maintain their faith in him (Mt 8:18-26).

His gospel is punctuated with reminders to his community that they are called to an ongoing conversion. He reminds them of the power of prayer (Mt 7:7-11), the value of the golden rule of life (Mt 7:12), the need to enter through the narrow gate (Mt 7:13-14), and the call to produce good fruit (Mt 7:15-20). He challenges them to a genuine personal religion uniting confession and action (Mt 7:21-27).

While stressing the blessings of a life committed to the Lord, Matthew, throughout his work, repeats the need to be aware that the disciples will also face judgment; he constantly reminds them that some will be found worthy and others will not (Mt 13:24-30, 36-40, 47-50; 24:45-51; 25:1-30).

To the description of the banquet of the Kingdom Matthew adds the short parable on the invited but unsuitably dressed guest. This Matthean addition is a further admonition to the members of his own community that being in the Church is not enough; they must continue their ongoing conversion to the Lord (Mt 22:11-14). He adds the episode of the destruction of Jerusalem (Mt 22:7) to remind the disciples of the dire consequences of infidelity.

We have already seen Matthew's bitter attacks on the Pharisees (Mt 23:1-39). The only redeeming feature of these attacks is that Matthew has interspersed applications to his own community and its leaders. The speech thus becomes a warning, a renewed call to his own community.

Matthew sees his Church as called and blessed, but also in need of constant conversion. He reminds them that, under daily judgment, they need to walk the hard road, constantly prepared to meet the Lord.

A community in constant formation.   We saw in Chapter Two that Matthew's was a community in transition. Aware of the need to build on a solid foundation (Mt 7:24-27), Matthew used his pastoral sensitivity to collect for his people material that could help the community's discipline and formation in this time of change.

Although the disciples of Jesus had only a loose organization during his lifetime, there are clear organizational needs by the time of this gospel. Matthew can refer to the community as "Church" on levels both universal (Mt 16:18) and local (Mt 18:17). In his discourse on the Kingdom he uses a series of parables to help his community understand themselves as Church. However, it is in Book IV (Mt 14:1 - 19:1) that Matthew particularly presents material for the discipline and formation of the community. The narrative describes the disciples' growing acknowledgement of Jesus, while the discourse on the Church is a manual of pastoral directives, a construction of Matthew based on material from Mark (Mk 9:33-50) and Q (Lk 9:46-48; 15:3-7; 17:3-4). Its focus is the community's self-discipling, rather than guidelines for superiors. The discourse can be divided into two parts: the first (Mt 18:1-14) deals with the general spiritual climate of mutual concern and upbuilding that should permeate the community; the second (Mt 18:15-35) with the need of challenge, correction, and forgiveness for the strengthening of the life of the Church.

The disciples are called to live the childlike quality of humility in their relationships with each other. We have seen how Jesus insisted that there be no squabbling over rank and title in his Church (Mt 23:8-10). Now he calls all to "change and become like," implying a true conversion in the way we treat other members of the community. If all live in genuine humility, there will be true community in the Church.

However, the peaceful growth of the community is seriously damaged by scandal (Mt 18:5-9). Matthew is aware of the inevitability of scandal, but reminds all of the seriousness of this harmful crime against another's growth. Members of the community should respect the faith of others, welcoming them as they would Jesus, and ready to endure suffering rather than stunt a brother's or sister's growth.

Jesus came to call sinners to repentance (Mt 9:13). The "little ones" that he loves and that his Father protects stray at times. The protective love of God wants no one to be lost, and this divine attitude ought to be the basis for ecclesial relationships. Jesus did not come for the self-righteous, but for the poor, sorrowing, lowly, hungry, and persecuted (Mt 5:3-12).

The community is strongly challenged to create an atmosphere of humility, to constantly strengthen mutual growth by the absence of scandal, to be perennially sensitive to the possibility of weakness, and to consistently and lovingly recall those who stray.

The willingness of Matthew's community to correct the sinful brother or sister clearly shows both the commitment necessary and the reality of sin in the New Testament communities. The willingness to call back, correct, and forgive (Mt 18:15-18) indicates a Church unwilling to let the growth of all be fatally threatened by a hardened sinner. The Church makes no claim to be perfect. Matthew prescribes a person-to-person correction, to be followed by a challenge from a representative group of the community. If these personal challenges to change are unfruitful, they are to be followed by a full community confrontation, even excommunication, of the sinner. The community's discerned judgment is given the support of the Lord.

There follows a saying on the power of united prayer, which is either a digression or is placed here to indicate the community's responsibility to pray for erring members (Mt 18:19-20).

The discourse ends with a parable on the need of limitless forgiveness. Even the directives on excommunication are placed between two sections on forgiveness and love. Forgiveness from the heart, general compassion, and love, are for Matthew the underpinnings of all community life and discipline.

A community of reconciliation and forgiveness. Although Matthew's Church faces persecution from outside and mediocrity from within, the most hurtful experience seems to be the attacks of fellow Christians. We have already seen the conflicts between the various groups in Matthew's Church. In addition, people who have been close in their common commitment to the Lord now experience betrayal and hate from each other (Mt 10:21-22).

Matthew worked to unite his community, to give it independence from Judaism and a sense of mission to the Gentiles. As he did so, he called his people to a reconciliation without which their community could not grow. In addition to the community discourse, the theme of reconciliation and forgiveness echoes through the entire gospel.

God himself is presented as merciful (Mt 9:13; 12:7) and forgiving (Mt 18:26-28), and the disciples are not only urged to imitate his compassion, but are threatened if they do not (Mt 6:15; 12:36-37; 18:35).

In the first great sermon, Jesus declares: "Blest are they who show mercy; mercy shall be theirs" (Mt 5:7). When Jesus compares his teaching with those of the past, the first contrast is between anger and Christ's call to a sense of concern that avoids even abusive language (Mt 5:21-22). Matthew adds two reflections to the Lord's: reconciliation is a condition for authentic prayer and sacrifice (Mt 5:23-24), and reconciliation must be attained before final judgment (Mt 5:25-26). Jesus revokes the law of retaliation in the fifth antithesis, calling the community not to resist the evildoer, but to show benevolence to all (Mt 5:38-42). He then reminds Matthew's community to love their enemies and pray for their persecutors, in imitation of a perfect and merciful God (Mt 5:43-48).

Later, when the disciples ask Jesus to teach them to pray, he offers a prayer in which the only contribution the disciples make to God is reconciliation with those who have offended them (Mt 6:12). Matthew alone adds this harsh reminder: "If you do not forgive others, neither will your Father forgive you" (Mt 6:15).

In a divided community such as Matthew's, the commentary that begins chapter seven seems again appropriate. "If you want to avoid judgment, stop passing judgment. Your verdict on others will be the verdict passed on you" (Mt 7:1-2). There follows the story of the speck in another's eye, with the call to avoid hypocrisy, to understand and forgive.

We have seen in the last section the calls for concern, reconciliation, and forgiveness found in the discourse on the Church. The need to accept others (Mt 15:23; 18:14), forgiving them when weak in their faith (Mt 18:21), was an experience the apostles themselves had when they first entered Jesus' boat (Mt 8:23-27; 14:22-33). However, Jesus now abolishes all restrictions on Christian forgiveness; in a parable found exclusively in Matthew, he states that forgiveness must be limitless (Mt 18:21-22).[12] This call to the community to practice forgiveness is further stressed by the parable of the unforgiving servant (Mt 18:23-35), an allegory of humankind's incalculable debt to God. God not only frees us, but writes off our debt altogether; we should treat others in the same way (Mt 18:35).[13]

Matthew calls his Church to reconciliation and forgiveness. He points out that their spirit of reconciliation is grounded in divine mercy. He suggests they imitate in their community life the impartial and universally forgiving God.

A community of sharing.   Matthew calls his community to share with the world the blessings they have received from the Lord (Mt 28:18-20). As Jesus shared his authority with the Church, so the Church goes out now in his name to bring the good news. In fact, Matthew compiles a discourse of directions for the missionaries of the early Church (Mt ch. 10). He has shown how he values the roots of Christianity in the Old Testament, stressed continuity in obedience and a rejection of lawlessness (Mt 5:17; 7:12; 11:13; 15:6; 22:36, 40; 23:23), and focuses on the responsibility to share with others the call of the Lord (Mt 25:14-30).

The community not only shares the teachings of the Lord, but common prayer as well, whether it be community expression of praise and request to the Father (Mt 6:9-13), or the discernment and petition of a united community (Mt 18:19-20). Their common prayer climaxes in the ritual celebration of the Eucharist. We have seen that the two modifications introduced into Matthew's presentation of the Lord's supper reflect rituals in his own community and confirm their practice. This eucharistic concern of Matthew also leads him to adapt the second feeding story to support eucharistic symbolism. "That the Church saw in the feeding miracles the prototype of the Lord's Supper and their own Eucharistic celebrations is certain."[14] It has also been suggested that "Matthew weaved into this gospel fabric eucharistic threads which are colored with mercy." When criticized for the people he ate with, Jesus quotes Hosea's preference for mercy, not sacrifice, showing thereby "the inner dispositions needed for true covenantal sharing of the sacrifice."[15]

We have seen that Matthew's community was probably wealthy; and there are traces of the materialism that damages faith (Mt 6:19, 24; 13:12; 19:23-26). He calls his Christians to a true spirit of poverty (Mt 5:3), and a sense of detachment and confidence in the Lord (Mt 6:26-34). He offers the community the models of the apostles who abandoned their possessions to follow the Lord (Mt 4:18-22; 9:9-13); reminds them of the detachment of Jesus (Mt 8:18-22); and calls them to share their goods as part of their faith in Jesus (Mt 19:16-22).

In its common pilgrimage to the Lord, the community receives from Jesus the authority to teach, preach, and heal. They now have the shared responsibility to build this community and minister to the world. This shared ministry must produce results (Mt 21:43-44) and be carried out with responsibility (Mt 25:14-30). In fact, fruitfulness is a sign of the genuine conversion of the Church (Mt 7:16; 13:23).

Matthew complements these characteristics for entrance into

the Kingdom with a description of the comunity life of the Church. He sees the Church as constantly in need of ongoing conversion, discipline, and formation, and urges his fellow Christians to practice reconciliation, forgiveness, and sharing as they pilgrimage to the Lord. To those anticipating an apocalyptic return of the Lord, to those still expecting the reconstruction of Israel, Matthew's message is that Jesus is present in their community: in its faith, life, love, and hope.

Leadership And Authority In The Church

We have seen how Matthew is influenced by the reaction to Jamnian Pharisaism, by the need to unify a divided community, and by the desire to create a sense of independence and mission in his people. Underlying each of these issues is the importance of legitimate authority. In addition, several of Matthew's interests and motifs, such as his portrait of Jesus, his use of the Old Testament, and his arrangement of the discourses, have authority as underlying concerns. It can even be said that the whole gospel climaxes in 28:18-20, the proclamation of Jesus' authority and the grounding of ecclesiastical authority.

Early Christian communities anxiously faced the question of where the Lord's authority could be found. John speaks of Jesus' departure and the coming of the Paraclete to reveal to us his teaching. Luke presents the ascension, followed by a variety of ways in which Jesus continues his powerful presence through his Spirit. For Matthew, Jesus never departs, continuing to exercise his preaching, healing, and teaching authority in his Church.

Authority in the Church. Matthew's Jesus is the authoritative teacher: all ten uses of "authority" highlight his exclusive claims.[16] He is a person of power whom all approach with reverence; he teaches with authority (Mt 7:29; 21:23), heals with authority (Mt 8:8-9), forgives sin with authority (Mt 9:6), and even has authority to share his power (Mt 9:8; 10:1; 28:18). His authority comes from his Father (Mt 11:25-27), validated by the Law and the prophets (Mt 5:17-18), and vindicated in confrontation with his opponents (Mt 22:15-40). His authority is not rooted in visions or miracles, but in his word (Mt 7:24-29). Even after his resurrection, when Jesus returns in power, he commissions his followers to teach what he had taught them during his ministry (Mt 28:18-20).

Jesus shares his authority with his Church. The Twelve, who are generally referred to as disciples, except on one occasion when called "apostles," receive from Jesus the authority to heal (Mt 10:1) and preach (Mt 10:7), and, after the resurrection, to teach (Mt 28:20). There are also charismatic leaders in the community (Mt 23:34), "and such a college of prophets and teachers (alias scribes or wisemen) seems to form the leadership in the Antioch of Matthew's day."[17] In places, the community as a whole has authority to impose sanctions (Mt 18:17) and give directions (Mt 18:19-20).[18]

For Matthew, authority is now centered in the Church. While Mark's Jesus has compassion on the crowds by teaching them (Mk 6:34), Matthew's sees them as sheep without a shepherd and appoints the Twelve to share in his ministry (Mt 9:36 - 10:1). Matthew's concern is not "how Jesus exercised his authority in the past, but that he is now making it available through the Church."[19] Because of his concern to center authority in the Church, Matthew excludes the story of the exorcist exercising power without being in union with the Church (Mk 9:38-40).

Even though Matthew is concerned with authority in the Church, convinced that authority has been given to the Church (Mt 9:8; 28:20), and details disciplinary involvement by the Church (Mt 18:1 - 19:1), there is still no clear structural organization in his community: no special positions, no presiding officers, and no signs of a hierarchical structure like that of Qumran. Most religions end up with an elitist governing class that mimics civic structures, but there is no such sign in Matthew's community. Nevertheless, while burdensome worldly structures are absent (Mt 20:25), and the seeking of position is condemned (Mt 23:8-10), the Twelve do have prominence (Mt 10:1-42), the teachers and people do have roles (Mt 23:34), the community engages in disciplinary activity (Mt ch. 18), false leaders are controlled (Mt 7:15; 24:11), and some charismatic activity possibly rejected (Mt 7:22). The Matthean community unquestionably experiences and prolongs the authority of Jesus.

Rather than identify the structures of authority, Matthew is more concerned to address the question of leadership style and the requisite conditions for the authentic exercise of Christian authority. He had criticized the irresponsible leadership of the Pharisees, and he likewise challenges those Christian leaders who "lord it over" others and "make their importance felt" (Mt 20:25-27). He presents exclusively to the disciples the parable of the faithful and unfaithful servants (Mt 24:45-51), and the parable of the lost sheep (Lk 15:3-7) becomes in Matthew a teaching on the responsible shepherding of the people (Mt 18:10-14).

Matthew's is an authority of compassion. Mercy is greater than sacrifice or obedience (Mt 9:13; 12:7; also 1 Samuel 15:22), and all law is summed up in charity (Mt 7:12; 22:39). Jesus came as the Servant (Mt 12:18-21), and the community's authority is a participation in Jesus' (Mt 9:8; 10:1-25). Anyone who exercises authority in his name will need his attitude of the humble servant (Mt 18:1-4), respect for the freedom of the community (Mt 17:26) and its own rights to self-discipline (Mt ch. 18). Those in positions of authority must never mislead others (Mt 5:19), scandalize (Mt 17:24-27; 18:5-9), or alienate them (Mt 18:10-14). Rather they must be people of faith (Mt 8:26; 14:31; 17:19-20), love (Mt 22:37-39), and followership (Mt 8:22-23).

Jesus' three temptations include the struggle with the nature of authentic power, and what are the genuine, and unchristian worldly means, of achieving one's mission (Mt 4:1-11). Matthew's Church, like the Church of every age, faces similar temptations of confusing Christ's authority with human authority. We must all listen to the Church (Mt 18:17), rejoice that such authority has been given to us (Mt 9:8), but also continually evaluate means and structures that claim to channel it.

Peter the rock. In dealing with the issue of authority in the Church, no text has received so much attention as Matthew's presentation of Peter's confession of Jesus at Caesarea Philippi, and Jesus' endowing of Peter with special authority to bind and loose (Mt 16:13-20). Mark gives a strong presentation of Peter's leadership role in the community. Matthew uses ten of Mark's references and omits five others, but without notable change in Peter's position. With the aid of Mark's material, Matthew shows Peter as the leading figure among the apostles: he is called first (Mt 4:18) and referred to as the first (Mt 10:2); Jesus works a miracle for him (Mt 8:14), and takes him on Tabor and in Gethsemane (Mt 17:1; 26:37); Peter is a spokesperson for the twelve (Mt 16:16; 17:4; 19:27; 26:33-35) and follows Jesus during the trial (Mt 26:69). Matthew also adds two references to Peter which are not found in the parallel sections of Mark and Luke (Mt 15:15; 18:21-22). In these, Peter asks Jesus to explain a parable and to specify the extent of Christian forgiveness. Matthew also has three references to Peter not found elsewhere in the New Testament. In the first, Jesus saves Peter as he tries to walk on the water (Mt 14:28-31). In the second, Jesus confers a special authority on him, which has come to be known as the "primacy of Peter" (Mt 16:16-19). In the third, Jesus asks Peter about the suitability of paying the temple tax, then works a miracle to pay it for him (Mt 17:24-27).[20]

Although Peter receives his special nickname in 16:18, Matthew calls him "Peter" from the beginning (Mt 4:18), for he always sees him as the rock or foundation of the Church. In fact, Matthew's portrait of Peter is more consistent than that of Mark or Luke: Peter is the sole apostolic spokesperson, the first in importance, the center of special episodes (Mt 8:14-15; 14:28-31; 17:24-27; 26:57-75), and the proclaimer of the Church's faith (Mt 16:16). At times, Peter is the model for the early Church's faith (Mt 16:16; 17:4; 19:27; 26:33-35), and also for its weaknesses (Mt 14:29-31; 16:22-23; 26:69-75). Jesus calls Peter the "rock" on which he will build his Church (Mt 16:18), but he is also a stumbling block in his rejection of the passion (Mt 16:23).

The passage dealing with the role of Peter (Mt 16:13-20) is a key part of Matthew's gospel. Many non-Roman Catholic scholars either see this passage as presenting Peter as a model for the community without conferring special privileges, or question the very genuineness of the saying as coming from Jesus.[21] In support of the former, they emphasize that the powers given to Peter were also given to the community (Mt 18:18). In the latter, they see the Matthean saying as midrash: a pious reflection on Mark's text concerning Peter and the meaning of his name.

The episode at Caesarea Philippi comes at a turning point in Matthew's christology and ecclesiology. It is most likely that Peter was already dead when this was written, and that Matthew is more interested in authority in the Church than Peter's historical place.

The episode comes from a semitic background: "bar" (meaning "son of"), "flesh and blood," "gates of Hades," and "keys of the Kingdom" are all Aramaic phrases, possibly indicating the primitive character of the story.[22] Moreover, the play on words "Peter" and "rock" can be seen only in Aramaic. The story seems to parallel the conferring of power on Eliakim to become the viceroy of Judah (Isaiah 22:19-23). Peter is portrayed as having complete authority, delegated from Jesus. Eliakim was made prime-minister in place of Shebna, who was unworthy of office, and, possibly, leadership is presented to Peter instead of to the scribes and Pharisees (Mt 23:13-14).

Peter is given the authority to "bind" and "loose", which means power to interpret the value of actions in the light of Jesus' teaching. Like the rabbis who gave decisions on conduct, Peter can bind in the light of Jesus' teachings.[23] This episode deals specifically with Peter, not with his faith, or himself as an expression of the community. He is the first, or firstborn, of the new community; the rock of the new community, as Abraham was of the old (Isaiah 51:1-2).

Peter embodies not only the authority of Jesus, but also "the ugly side of church leadership."[24] The episode we have just seen comes between Peter's lack of faith (Mt 14:22-33) and his rejection of Jesus' passion (Mt 16:21-23). From Caesarea onward, Peter's leadership has a ring of scandal to it: when talk is cheap, Peter is outspoken (Mt 26:33-35); when faith is tested, he rejects Jesus and denies his own discipleship (Mt 26:69-75). He is presented in strength and in weakness, but also in his willingness to repent (Mt 26:75).

Peter's authority is complemented by the community's (Mt 18:18). He is the basis for the community's authority: no successor is referred to, even after his death. The authority conferred on Peter is passed on to the community.[25]

Ecclesial Spirituality Of Matthew

In this chapter we have considered Matthew's understanding of the nature of the Kingdom and its relation to the Church. We have examined what he considers to be the characteristics of life in the Kingdom and community life in the Church. We have reflected on his broad-based community authority and his understanding of specific authority in Peter.

Although Matthew gives us only the first stages in a systematic ecclesiology, he is still notable among the evangelists for his concern with the Church. His interest is not primarily with structures or legalism but with spirituality. He is convinced that God comes to dwell among us in Christ (Mt 1:23); that Christ the Lord founds and builds his Church (Mt 16:18); and that all men and women will make their home in it (Mt 13:32). Matthew's christology is the basis for his ecclesiology, and his ecclesiology is the basis for his spirituality. He gives us an ecclesial spirituality centered on Christ, based on the Word, and lived in community.

Centered on Christ.   Matthew does not distinguish between the pre-resurrection and post-resurrection Jesus, but consistently presents Jesus as the Lord of the Church from the beginning of the gospel. Jesus' ministry becomes a ministry to Matthew's Church: Jesus continues to be present in the life and activity of the Church. When the Church's faith in and commitment to Jesus are firm, it will not only face the storms of life (Mt 8:26) but everything will be possible (Mt 17:20).

Matthew calls his Church to root its life in Jesus alone, to reject all other guides and teachers (Mt 23:10). Its spirituality is life based on the revelation of Jesus (Mt 11:25-27) and empowered with his presence (Mt 28:20).

Based on the Word.   Jesus fulfills the Law and interprets it anew in the light of love (Mt 22:37-38). This fidelity to the past and interpretation of it for the future is also part of Matthew's ministry. The very last words of Jesus that he records annul one of his previous directives (Mt 28:19 and 10:5b). The directives are not fixed, but need to change to manifest the same love in new circumstances. Matthew himself hands on the teachings, interpreting them for his community's new needs. His interpretation is valuable for his community, but the fact that he sees the very need to interpret is valuable for ours. The Word of Jesus, the Church's only secure foundation (Mt 7:24-27), is a living and lifegiving Word, good news for every generation. The exhortations of the first gospel are not to legalism, but to appreciation that everything must be measured by the Word of the Lord, at times unchanging, but ever new (Mt 13:52). This kind of commitment to the Word is a struggle, and, as we have seen, even Matthew admits to its strains.

As new circumstances arise, Peter and the community have authority to discern, interpret, direct, and bind regarding the lifegiving meaning of the Word. They are commissioned to bring this Word to all nations, that all may build on the firm foundation of the Lord's living revelation.

Lived in community.   The ecclesial spirituality to which Matthew calls us is centered on Jesus, based on the Word, and also lived in community. This community is called to ongoing conversion, constant formation, reconciliation, and sharing. It is not a restricted nationalistic group but a universal inclusive community. Its members are from all shades of Jewish and Gentile backgrounds, and Matthew calls them to work through their differences in light of the centrality of Jesus and his Word.

The inclusiveness of Matthew's community is seen not only in its membership, but also in its authorities. There are charismatic prophets, scribes, teachers, apostles, and disciples. There are collegial structures in the twelve and in the community, and there is Peter. Matthew gives no explanation of their interrelationship, presenting all as part of the community of the Lord. He sees their varied ministries as building up their common life.

Commitment to living together as Church is the first step towards the Kingdom. The disciples repent, reform their lives, and together commit themselves in faith to follow Jesus. This new direction in life implies new attitudes of humility and trust, prudence and vigilance. Their new lifestyle is the common pursuing of their own "greater righteousness," and its facilitation in others. Church is Matthew's spirituality: a Christ-centered community life based on the ever vital Word of God.

Chapter Six
DISCIPLESHIP

*Then extending his hand toward his disciples, he
said, "There are my mother and my brothers.
Whoever does the will of my heavenly Father is
brother and sister and mother to me" (Mt 12:49-50).*

We have seen something of Matthew himself, his community,
his purpose, his portrait of God, and his vision of Church. In each
case, his challenge for disciples comes through clearly. Matthew,
in his own life of dedication, calls disciples to a ministry of prophetic challenge, wisdom, and teaching. He calls disciples to in-
teract with their world: to face the internal crises of growth, to
confront the problems and pressures of life, and to be a leaven in
affluent urban life. He reminds those committed to Jesus to
value the roots of their faith, but also to interpret it creatively so
that it can perennially give life to themselves and to others. He
directs disciples to radicalize their commitment in faithful obedience to the will of God, as revealed in Jesus and witnessed by
the Spirit. He stresses the need of a deep personal relationship
with Jesus: our hope, healer, teacher, unifier, mediator, and
Lord. Furthermore, he calls disciples to enter the reign of God
through repentance and a faithful confession of the Lord, in
humility, vigilance and compassion, manifested in obedience and
community responsibility. He goes on to insist that the disciples'
call to the Lord be lived out in a community of ongoing conversion, constant formation, reconciliation, and sharing. This communal life under God should be centered on Christ, based on the
Word, and lived in community.

This chapter is not a complete synthesis on discipleship. It
deals with material complementary to that already presented.
We will examine the nature of discipleship in Matthew, the new

attitudes to which disciples are called by Jesus' Sermon on the
Mount, the new vision identifiable in Matthew's call to greater
righteousness or deeper holiness, and the components of radical
commitment to the Lord. This chapter on discipleship is further
enriched by the final chapter on the disciples' need of and
dedication to the mission of ministry to others.

The Nature of Discipleship

In Chapter Three, we have seen that many approach Jesus with
a ceremonial reverence born of faith. Crowds follow him in faith
and expectancy (Mt 4:25; 14:13; 21:8). At times, even the word
"disciple" is used in the broad sense of the many who meet with
Jesus (Mt 8:21; 10:42; 12:49; 27:57), and Matthew sometimes
changes his sources to refer specifically to disciples where the
sources do not (Mt 9:19 and Mk 5:24 or Lk 8:42; Mt 12:49 and Mk
3:34; Mt 23:1 and Mk 12:37 or Lk 20:45). On other occasions,
Matthew introduces disciples where no other gospel mentions
them (Mt 13:36; 15:12, 23; 19:10; 26:1). However, the word "disciple"
in Matthew is generally reserved for the Twelve, and in twenty-
one cases the word explicitly or implicitly refers to the Twelve.[1]

In addition to the word "disciple" and its rather restricted use,
other images portray commitment to Jesus. We have already
referred to the crowds that follow Jesus, and who seem to anticipate the people of Matthew's Church. There are also those faith-
filled people who seek his healing power (Mt 8:1-13; 9:1-8, 18-34;
15:21-31; 17:14-18), those who serve him (Mt 8:14-15), and those
who confess their belief in him (Mt 9:22, 29; 15:28).[2]

Call.   Out of many who follow and believe, there is the smaller
group of disciples whom Jesus personally calls. They become the
"remnant" or basis for his Church. The first gospel describes the
call of the first disicples (Mt 4:18-22), the call of Matthew (Mt 9:9-
13), and the call and missioning of the Twelve (Mt ch.10). One call,
that of the rich young man, is rejected (Mt 19:16-22). On three
occasions we read the general requirements of the call to discipleship (Mt 8:18-22; 12:46-50; 16:24-28; 19:23-30).

The call of the first disciples shows Jesus' initiative in it, the
close connection between call and mission, the need for detachment, and that the result of the call is the following of Jesus. The
call of Matthew follows the healing of the paralytic and the forgiveness of sin, and becomes an example of Jesus' call of sinners

to his service. In Chapter Ten, the discipleship of the Twelve is shown in ministry.

The backdrop for these personal calls is the constant challenge of Jesus to disciples to repent (Mt 3:1; 4:17), detach (Mt 8:18-22; 19:23-30), dedicate themselves to him in obedience to the Father (Mt 12:46-50), and accept the cross (Mt 16:24-28).

The disciples who listen to his call, build on his word, and bear fruit, become like brothers and sisters to Jesus (Mt 12:48-50).[3] Discipleship implies a close relationship with the Lord, and Matthew often refers to the disciples as those who are "with Jesus."[4] Jesus is the presence of God to the people (Mt 1:23; 18:20; 28:20), and they are disciples who allow this presence to transform their lives.

Jesus' call to discipleship is for all, but many will not listen: "the learned and the clever" (Mt 11:25), those who are attached to their wealth (Mt 19:22), the scribes and Pharisees (Mt 23:33-34), and the city of Jerusalem (Mt 23:37-39). Those who listen include outcasts of society (Mt 11:5), helpless children (Mt 11:25), those "who are weary and find life burdensome" (Mt 11:28), and the Gentiles (Mt 12:21).

Those who hear the call must face a moment of crisis and decision (Mt 13:9, 43), and with the simple enthusiasm of the child and the singlemindedness of the true learner, joyfully give up everything to secure life with Jesus (Mt 13:44-46).

Those who make such a decision to follow Jesus are called to witness fearlessly to the risen Lord (Mt 28:19-20), and, as Matthew's addition to the Transfiguration shows, the fallen and fearful disciples are raised up when Jesus comes to be with them.[5] Jesus' followers, sometimes referred to as disciples, sometimes as people of little faith (Mt 14:31; 16:8; 17:20), are learners; by means of the miracles (Mt 8:1, 10, 14-15, 23-27; 9:22, 25, 27-31; 15:28), some of which are witnessed only by the disciples (Mt 8:14-15, 23-27; 14:22-33), Jesus continues their training in commitment to him.[6]

"Disciple" comes from the Latin "discere," meaning "to learn." Discipleship in Matthew means to be called to personally learn from Jesus. The call is itself efficacious: it gives to the disciple the power and ability to follow and to minister. Discipleship means to have received the special protection of the Father and his revelation in Jesus. The call to Jesus is attained through the acceptance of the cross and lived out in ministry for others.

Response.   Jesus' call is historically to a mixed community. This is especially so in Matthew's Church: there are good Christians, "citizens of the kingdom" (Mt 13:38), and bad Christians, apostasizers and evildoers (Mt 13:41). The latter have lived like Christians, even worked miracles and prophesied in Jesus' name (Mt 7:22), and yet the Lord in judgment says to them: "I never knew you. Out of my sight, you evildoers!" (7:23). Even the committed disciples at times have doubt (Mt 14:31; 28:17), little faith (Mt 6:30; 8:26; 14:31; 16:8), fear (Mt 14:26, 30), cowardice (Mt 8:26), or indignation (Mt 20:24; 26:8).[7] Jesus refers to Peter as a scandal (Mt 16:23); calms the disciples' squabbles over privilege (Mt 20:20-28); bears the betrayal of a friend (Mt 26:69-75); and lives through desertion by all (Mt 26:56).

Matthew's parable discourse deals with response to the Lord's call. If this discourse was composed for Matthew's community, as it surely was, then we are dealing with the quality of acceptance of the call. Jesus sows the seed of his call but is realistic regarding response. Some will reject the call, and of those who seem to accept it, some will fail under persecution or their own attachment. Even those who fully accept the call will respond in various ways yielding "a hundred- or sixty- or thirty-fold" (Mt 13:23). In four parables exclusive to him, Matthew points out that only the disciples who see the call as a pearl or treasure (Mt 13:44-46) can respond in an evil world (Mt 13:24-30, 47-50).

Response to the Lord's call is shown by repentance (Mt 3:8), which in Matthew "is no longer a precondition for grace, but the response to it."[8] This response implies the rejection of temptations (Mt 4:1-11), painful choices (Mt 10:32-39), confession of the Lord (Mt 10:32; 14:33), and commitment to a holiness beyond that of the scribes and Pharisees (Mt 5:20). The response is also communal (Mt ch. 18), for the disciples are called to welcome and treat everyone as if Jesus himself (Mt 10:40-42; 18:5, 10).

Response is manifested in public witness to the Lord (Mt 5:14-15). Disciples are to be lights to the world, standards to follow, prophetic voices in a corrupt world (Mt 5:12; 23:34). This prophetic witness is to be manifested not only in confession and words, but in deeds as well (Mt 7:21, 24; 12:33; 21:28; 23:3).

Moreover, once made, the response must be maintained so that the disciples become salt to the world (Mt 5:13). This perseverance will be through hardships similar to those of Jesus (Mt 10:16-23), and may even include sharing in his cup of sorrow (Mt 20:22).

Blessings.   The Lord's call is complemented by the persevering response of the disciples. Those who respond are granted the blessings of God. The Father, rejoicing in their response, protects them with his angels (Mt 18:10-14) and reveals to them the inner-most secrets of life (Mt 11:25-27). Disciples have access to God: his life, protection, teaching, and joy (Mt 25:21, 34).

Disciples are also blessed with the privilege of Jesus' company. They journey "with Jesus," rewarded with his constant presence (Mt 18:20; 28:20). The disciples are like brothers and sisters to Jesus (Mt 12:49-50), but acknowledge and worship who he is (Mt 14:33).

This close personal relationship leads to further blessings of discipleship. Jesus assures his followers of abundant blessings in eternity (Mt 19:29), but even now they are blessed with insight, enlightenment, and understanding. Given special attention by Jesus,[9] the mysteries of the Kingdom are explained to them, which they alone understand (Mt 13:11).[10] They are given access to the revelation of the Father (Mt 11:27-28); they are taught and obey his will (Mt 12:49-50) Blessed with authority to preach, heal, and teach (Mt 10:7-8; 28:20), they are commissioned by the Lord to minister and make disciples in his name (Mt 28:19). They are, in fact, immersed in the reality of Father, Son, and Holy Spirit (Mt 28:19).

Disciples who respond to the call of the Lord are blessed with a new existence made up of relationship with the Trinity, commit-ment to Jesus, a life directed exclusively by the teachings of the Lord, and a mission sustained by his effective presence.[11]

Discipleship calls for changes in attitudes, vision, and lifestyle, as we shall see in the remainder of the chapter. Our first glance at Matthew's understanding of the nature of discipleship reveals various levels of commitment to the following of Jesus. However, Matthew is realistic in acknowledging the weaknesses of even the disciples. The quality of their response, together with the mystery of the grace of God, lead to varied yields in their commitment.

Jesus takes the initiative in every call: disciples are chosen by the Lord regardless of their background. If they respond to his call with perseverance, there results a deep relationship with God, the Church, and with others, and a transformation of their own lives.

The New Attitudes Of The Sermon On The Mount

Sermon on the Mount (Mt 5:1 - 7:29).   This masterpiece of compositional and theological synthesis, though a collection of Jesus' teachings no doubt given over an extended period of his ministry, is, from Matthew's introduction and conclusion, clearly intended to be viewed as a unity (Mt 5:1; 7:28). Not only has Matthew created the sermon and located it on the mountain, in remembrance of Moses' reception of the Law on Sinai, he has also identified the audience as the disciples, though others crowd around.[12]

The sermon commands reflection and attention, summarizing for the disciples the nature of their call to holiness. Matthew, having composed the speech and selected the audience, indicates his intention of addressing the message of the Lord to the disciples of his own time. It is the new revelation of what life under God ought to be. Matthew concludes the sermon (Mt 7:29) with a statement on the authority of Jesus' teaching. The crowds do not listen to Jesus because he has authority, but are convinced of his authority after hearing his words. Matthew's community, too, is called to build its life on the authoritative word of Jesus.

The sermon is offered to the disciples in the hearing of the crowds, just as Jesus' word today is given to the disciples while the world looks on. The sermon is given from the mountain top, the traditional place of divine revelation, and presents the disciples with the new attitudes to life which ought to be theirs as a result of their commitment to the Lord. These new attitudes will result from Matthew's work of theological interpretation. The sermon's major function is "to provide the disciple of Jesus with the necessary tools for becoming a Jesus theologian ...the enabling of the disciple to theologize creatively along the lines of the theology of the master."[13] It is a call to an evolving spirituality which includes creative interpretation (its hermeneutical dimension) and the exploration of new ways of living (its heuristic dimension).

The sermon indicates those attitudes which will make the disciple happy (Mt 5:3-12), and an initial indication that these attitudes lived by the disciple will be salt and light for the whole world (Mt 5:13-16). It then presents new approaches to former religious practices and laws, and how Jesus' coming has changed them (Mt 5:17-48). From basic attitudes to life and laws the sermon moves to deal with authenticity in such religious devotions as almsgiving, prayer, and fasting (Mt 6:1-18). Disciples must realize how much God's providential care is placed over them, and this should lead to a new attitude toward wealth and possessions (Mt 6:19-34). Since God's love is for all, disciples ought to avoid judgment of others, pray for them, and treat them as they would wish to be treated (Mt 7:1-12). The sermon moves toward its conclusion by calling the Church to an awareness that they must live prudently, walk the narrow and rough road, be on their guard, and bear fruit (Mt 7:13-23). The sermon ends with a powerful statement on the need for disciples to build their lives on the foundation of the authoritative word of Jesus (Mt 7:24-29).

Various interpretations have been suggested for the Sermon on the Mount. We have already seen that some commentators see it as a replacement of the Mosaic Law by the new moral code of the beatitudes; others believe that it was a way of life which Jesus expected to be followed literally in anticipation of the imminent end of the world. Others, feeling the goals set by the sermon unattainable by sinful men and women, see it as a way of preparing people to be ready for gratuitous salvation.[14]

When we examine the sermon, we see that Jesus calls for an authentic fidelity to the spirit of the Law and the covenant. He does not call for obedience to Law, but a life in conformity with the will of God as discerned in the Law. The sermon challenges legalism of both society and religion, and call us to accept God's grace, not his demands. The whole sermon culminates in love, the norm by which every law is measured. The sermon affirms the spiritual value of people in themselves, not of their accumulation of obedience to outward laws. Matthew ends this section by stating: "When he came down from the mountain, great crowds followed him" (Mt 8:1); an indication that facilitating the following of Jesus was the sermon's purpose.

The Beatitudes (Mt 5:3-12).   Matthew begins the sermon on Jesus' call to holiness with the beatitudes, paralleling the presentation of the ten commandments which began the Law of Moses (Exodus 20:1-17). Moses' commandments tell people of punishment if they do not live in certain ways, whereas Jesus' beatitudes tell them how happy they will be if their attitudes are his own.

As we have them now, there are nine beatitudes. The ninth was probably a postscript to an original eight. Of the basic eight, only three are common with Luke's list: the first, fourth, and fifth. It is likely that Matthew's source Q provided him with the same three beatitudes as Luke, to which he added four more, giving us the symbolic number seven. He then added verse 5, on the lowly, to give two groups of four, equal even in the number of words used. The postscript was then added.[15]

Beatitudes, common proverbial forms of speech in the Old Testament, are also found in the New, where they take on a christocentric characteristic. Happiness is promised because of a life in relation with Christ; it is eternal, experienced even in this world in the midst of life and its hardships.[16] Happiness comes to the disciple who lives these spiritual attitudes.

The beatitudes themselves are not radically new, since they are found in Isaiah 61, but the fact that Matthew gathers them together strategically at the head of this great sermon shows his intention of presenting a beatitudinal spirituality. We are not dealing with eight different groups of people, but eight inward attitudes which need to be part of every disciple's life. Matthew's position is that Jesus' words are meant to "place their stamp on the entire lives of those who hear."[17] He gives us a spirituality which is not based on law or cult but on a conversion of attitudes to those of beatitudinal living.

The first component of conversion is to become spiritually poor. In Jesus' time "the poor" had become "a kind of title of honor for the righteous."[18] To be poor in spirit was a sign of righteous acceptance of one's condition in life. Matthew has been accused of watering down Luke's emphasis on material poverty, possibly because Matthew's was a wealthy community. It is more likely that Matthew has gone to the heart of religion, calling disciples to an awareness of the poverty of all human effort and a realization of need for God. The spiritually poor are told the Kingdom of heaven belongs to them already. Only this beatitude, the eighth, and the ninth are in the present tense and could describe present challenges to Matthew's own community.

"Blest are the sorrowing; they shall be consoled." Here, all those who undergo life's hardships and live through oppression, domination, and abuse of their rights are assured that God will be their consolation and support. "So much of our lives...points to a kind of listless spirit and depression. This listlessness and sense of alienation are other words for mourning."[19]

"Blest are the lowly; they shall inherit the land." Lowliness is not a weak, but a strong characteristic. It is the attitude of one who accepts life under God without complaint; one completely in tune with God's plan. Such a person can live in our oppressive world in hope; can creatively confront the abuse of power, wealth, and sex, and remain committed to God's plan in spite of the dominance of evil. Such disciples are promised a new earth.

"Blest are they who hunger and thirst for holiness; they shall have their fill." Matthew has added "for holiness." The seeking of holiness in a life fully conformed to the will of God is so basic to the disciple that it becomes like food and drink. Such an attitude of commitment assures personal fulfillment and satisfaction.

"Blest are they who show mercy; mercy shall be theirs." This beatitude is tailored for Matthew's own community, which, we have seen, needs a spirit of compassion. In fact, this beatitude like the ones that follow, are more appropriate to the early community than to the times of Jesus.

"Blest are the singlehearted, for they shall see God." Those who are singleminded, in complete loyalty to God, are promised that God will be active in their lives.

"Blest too the peacemakers; they shall be called sons of God." This is the only use of the word "peacemakers" in the Bible. Blest are those who are not only peaceful, but work for peace, bringing it about through their active commitment. They are guaranteed a share in the divine life. The peacemaker is so like God that he or she is referred to as a child of God.

"Blest those persecuted for holiness' sake; the reign of God is theirs." The use of the present tense may again indicate an attitude particularly needed in Matthew's community, which is persecuted for its interpretation of holiness. However, fidelity to its Christ-based interpretation assures entrance to the Kingdom of God.

The last beatitude, which expands on the ideas of the eighth, changes to the second person. It seems to presume that persecution is being undergone by those to whom it is addressed.

These attitudes are presented to the disciples as the synthesis of the Christian way of life. Disciples ought to be permeated with these approaches to life: salt to a valueless world and light to its darkness.

The "antitheses."   After a statement on the values of the old law and the new, Jesus considers six commands of the scribal tradition, contrasting each of them with the new approaches required by commitment to him. In these contrasts, or antitheses, Jesus gets to the heart of the religious value which the law was intended to protect. Jesus strengthens fidelity to the first two, which belong to the decalogue; the others are regulations from the Old Testament, or Pharisaic interpretations of them, and Jesus revokes the force of prior regulation, calling for new attitudes to each issue. Again we see a spirituality based on human dignity, where commitment implies the commitment of a person's inner values, attitudes, and intentions. In these antitheses, we see yet again the centrality of Jesus and his teachings, since each contrast leads to the statement "what I say to you is this."[20] Jesus' teaching replaces prior interpretations. He is the only teacher now, and he certainly approaches life under God in a new way. The antitheses read like "Jesus' total overthrow of legalistic thinking."[21]

In the form in which we now have them, Matthew not only exclusively challenges Pharisaic interpretations, but adds to each antithesis some applications to his own community.

The first antithesis recalls the commandment against murder, but goes on to call for reconciliation, wholeness, and authenticity in our dealings with others. Matthew adds two reflections of his own, insisting on the need for forgiveness and reconciliation to assure authentic worship and prepare for judgment. Instead of presenting what must be avoided, so that the worst does not happen, Jesus calls for attitudes which positively construct human relationships.

The second antithesis not only reaffirms the commandment against adultery, but goes on to create a respectful, chaste approach to life in thought and desire, as well as in action. By avoiding a minimalistic approach, Jesus protects the rights and dignity of women. Matthew's appendices to this antithesis stress the theme of avoidance of scandal.

Jesus revokes the old divorce law, calling for fidelity; again, a forceful insistence on the dignity and growth potential of human relationships

In the fourth antithesis, Jesus again revokes a previous regulation. This is hardly to be taken as the forbidding of all oaths, but rather their misuse to manipulate God; or their overuse, which shows lack of religious respect. It is a call to truthfulness and authenticity. Matthew adds several applications appropriate to his Greek-speaking community.

The fifth antithesis, which "supplies us with the clearest example of revocation,"[22] forbids any kind of retaliation, including that prescribed in the Torah. Jesus' call is for the peace and reconciliation that build up relationships under God. This challenge to the love and compassion of God reflects the very attitudes of the suffering Jesus. Again, Matthew adds pastoral directives for his own community.

All five antitheses are summed up in the great call for universal love. Prior regulations restricting love are passed over, and Jesus insists that the disciples' love be impartial and unrestricted.

The antitheses end with the call to imitate the perfection, or wholeness and integrity, of God. If disciples live the new attitudes proposed by the Lord, they will move toward a wholistic and integrated spirituality.

The Vision of Greater Holiness

Holiness. A correct understanding of holiness is of special concern to Matthew. The word "holiness," sometimes translated "righteousness," occurs seven times in Matthew, all of them being his own insertions (Mt 3:15; 5:6, 10, 20; 6:1, 33; 21:32). Jesus himself wanted to fulfill all the requirements of holiness (Mt 3:15). In his first sermon, he proclaims blest those who hunger and thirst for holiness (Mt 5:6), and are willing to undergo persecution for the sake of holiness (Mt 5:10). He insists that the holiness of his followers surpass that of the scribes and Pharisees (Mt 5:20), and goes on to condemn showiness in outward practices of holiness (Mt 6:1). He wants his disciples to seek God's way of holiness before anything else (Mt 6:33). Finally, toward the end of his ministry, he condemns those who were not open to the holiness called for by the Baptist (Mt 21:32).

The holiness of the Pharisees was based on obedience to the Law, while other groups in Judaism also stressed obedience to the cult. For Matthew, neither obedience to laws and regulations (Mt 23:23), nor faithful obedience to ritual (Mt 3:8) are acceptable, unless there is genuine reform and a turning back to the God of the covenant. For Matthew, it is not obedience to laws that leads to holiness, but conversion to a way of holiness that leads to the bearing of good fruit (Mt 7:18-22).

This holiness is preceded by repentance (Mt 3:2, 8, 11; 4:17; 11:20; 12:41), but its real starting point is an awareness of a new relationship between God and the disciples. God is the Father who protects his little ones (Mt 18:14), revealing his will exclusively through Jesus (Mt 11: 25-27). Holiness is the faithful living of the

will of God, revealed by Jesus and discerned in his teachings (Mt
7:21; 12:50). Moreover, disciples are called to holiness of life
through the personal initiative of Jesus (Mt 11:28-30).[23] The
disciples' journey is hard (Mt 7:13-14), and their faithful obedience to the will of God leads them to build a new world in faith
(Mt 24:1-34), live in vigilant hope (Mt 24:35 - 25:30), and be
always ready to be judged on their charity (Mt 25:31-46).[24]

The holiness of Christ's disciples is not encumbered with anxiety,
scrupulosity, or legalism (Mt 6:33-34; 15:1-20; 23:23), but is the
perfection of commitment to the will of the Father. "The ideal is
the integrated and uncomplicated personality wholly consecrated to the service of God."[25] The disciples strive for perfection; a wholistic commitment to a covenantal relationship with
God (Mt 5:48; 19:21; 22:37). The relationship leads to holiness of
life, shown in good works and justice (Mt 6:1-18), authentic relationships in matters of wealth and sex (Mt ch. 19), and the pro-
ducing of good fruits (Mt 7:16-21; 12:33; 13:23; 21:43).

Holiness is the result of the transforming relationship with
Jesus. It is a commitment to the Father's will encountered in
Jesus. It leads to a new level of existence, new attitudes to life,
and a new way of being present to the Lord and to each other.

Faith.   Holiness is based on faith in Jesus. Those who seek cures
are challenged to faith (Mt 8:13; 9:2, 29; 15:28), and when Jesus
sees even the preliminary signs of faith, he is moved to establish
a deeper relationship. The powerful involvement of Jesus in
peoples' lives follows on their faith in him. Disciples who are
specially called are explicitly described as those "little ones who
believe in me" (Mt 18:6). Their holiness is conditioned by their
recognition of Jesus as their Lord who heals, saves, and teaches
them. They become children of God because of their relationship
to Jesus.

Matthew writes of the apostles' experience of Jesus as Lord
(Mt 11:1-6), and consistently shows his own community how
Jesus fulfills scripture and so ought to be the object of their faith.
This is important to Matthew, since understanding is a prereq-
uisite for faith. Having understood who Jesus is, the disciple
commits his or her whole person to Jesus.

The faith of the disciple is in Jesus as Lord, and as the one in
whom we encounter God. It implies both adhesion to his word
and imitation of his life of suffering (Mt 10:17-22; 16:24-26),
poverty (Mt 6:19-21; 19:23-26), humility (Mt 18:1-4), charity

(Mt 25:31-46), and service (Mt 20:24-28).[26] This holy life, based on fidelity to Jesus' word and imitation of his lifestyle, allows Jesus to recognize his disciples (Mt 7:21-23).

The fundamental redirection of one's life to Jesus by faith in him is only the beginning of an ongoing life of faith with its ups and downs. Even the disciples are criticized for their deficient faith (Mt 6:30; 14:31; 16:8; 17:20; 21:21; 28:17). This deficient faith does not mean unbelief, but a commitment which has not reached its full potential. The disciples are referred to as weak in faith when they doubt or show lack of confidence and trust. This lack of trust is not the same as denial of Jesus, for the episodes often conclude with Jesus presenting himself again as their ultimate reassurance and support.[27]

Disciples have made a commitment in faith, but that faith needs to grow. Sometimes their faith seems less than that shown by passing acquaintances of Jesus (Mt 17:14-20). On other occasions, disciples proclaim a faith that they cannot live out (Mt 14:28-31; 26:31-35). In fact, their faith seems to fail precisely when it should have been demonstrated (Mt 8:26; 14:31; 16:8; 17:20). There is even the serious issue of the factual apostasy of some of the disciples (Mt 24:12). In addition to the disciples' weak faith, Matthew also suggests that people who do not know Jesus can still show genuine faith in him, even though it is incomplete (Mt 25:31-46).

Some people never commit themselves to Jesus as disciples, but show faith in him by acknowledging his power. Others never become disciples, but show their faith by living a lifestyle based on Jesus' teachings. Disciples are the ones who totally redirect their lives to faith in Jesus. Once this commitment is made, it can grow or weaken, for the disciple is a constant learner.

Love.   A commitment to holiness by faith in Jesus is expressed in love (Mt 5:44-48; 7:12; 22:37-39). This had been Jesus' own way of fidelity to his Father's will. His whole public ministry was a concrete manifestation of service, concern, and love.

In his teachings, Jesus placed love of others in the list of the ten commandments (Mt 19:19); in fact, he made it equal to the love of God (Mt 22:39). When discussing the emphasis on regulations or worship as means to show holiness, he concluded both times by saying he preferred a loving compassion before either of them (Mt 9:13; 12:7). In the latter case, he places love above even the sabbath commandment.

Jesus understands love not only as greater than individual commands or practices, but as the embodiment of the spirit of all. He says the greatest command of the law is love of God and neighbor (Mt 22:36), adding: "On these two commandments the whole law is based, and the prophets as well" (Mt 22:40). Toward the end of the Sermon on the Mount, he summed up his teachings: "Treat others the way you would have them treat you: this sums up the law and the prophets" (Mt 7:12).

When speaking of the final judgment, he reminds his disciples that their talent must not be hoarded, but lovingly used for others (Mt 25:14-30); they must live in reconciliation with all (Mt 18:21-35), because the judgment itself will be based on love (Mt 25:31-46).[28] When Jesus speaks of the world's rejection of his message, he says: "The love of most will grow cold" (Mt 24:12).

We have seen elsewhere how Jesus centers his teachings on love in the Sermon on the Mount and the community discourse, how he insisted that forgiveness and reconciliation be limitless among his disciples. Moreover, the love he called for was qualitatively different than that shown by his predecessors (Mt 5:43-48).

The greatest holiness to which the disciples are called is a life of faith in Jesus, manifested by love for others. All laws are secondary to and must be interpreted in light of this commandment of love. Love is the perfection of the Father; it is exemplified in the life of Jesus; it transcends all religious legalism; it directs us to God.

The Radical Demands Of The Disciples' Life

Hardships. Disciples are called to self-denial (M16:24-26), detachment (Mt 8:18-22), commitment to others (Mt ch. 18), persecution in their ministry (Mt ch. 10), and a wholehearted striving for the perfection of God (Mt 5:48). They must enter life through the narrow gate and walk the rough road (Mt 7:13-14). If their response to the call of Jesus leads to new attitudes to life and a new vision of holiness, it also implies a new asceticism of radical self-gift. They are called to live poverty of spirit, to undergo life's hard experiences, to accept life under God without complaint, to ceaselessly pursue holiness, to be compassionate, to be singleminded in loyalty to God, to work for peace, and to endure persecution (Mt 5:3-12).

While faith and love are the motivations of disciples, they lead to the fruitfulness of obedience to the ethical demands of the Lord — demands that touch the very heart of human need and the source of sin (Mt 5:21-48). The cultivation of reconciliation, respect for others, chaste living, truthfulness, forgiveness, and universal love calls for a conversion unparalleled in religious traditions.

Disciples called to preach, teach, and heal in Jesus' name are also called to prolong his ministry of suffering. Disciples need to realize that their lives will include opposition to sin (Mt 6:13; 13:19), detachment from their possessions (Mt 4:20-22), homelessness (Mt 8:19-20), and the lack of a supportive family (Mt 8:21-22; 10:37-39). Discipleship includes a sense of joy where others see no reason for joy (Mt 9:14-17), prudence and vigilance in a rejecting world (Mt 10:16). Disciples will be called to imitate the redemptive suffering of Jesus, even as they are persecuted and put to death (Mt 10:17-23). Discipleship means confidently entrusting oneself to the providential Father (Mt 10:28-39) in spite of the experience of constant rejection (Mt 10:24-27).

This participation in suffering with Jesus requires a spirit of poverty (Mt 6:19-21; 19:23-26), an attitude of humility (Mt 18:1-4), and the motivation of constant love (Mt 22:37-39; 25:31-46).

The narrow entrance that few wish to take, the rough road that few wish to follow (Mt 7:13-14), are the beginnings of a journey that leads to the cross. "If a man wishes to come after me, he must deny his very self, take up his cross, and begin to follow in my footsteps" (Mt 16:24). This acceptance of the cross is the only way to life (Mt 16:25-26), the ultimate measure of one's commitment to Jesus (Mt 10:38-39). Moreover, it is a journey that each one must make for him- or herself. No one can substitute, and no one can loan that which is necessary to welcome the Lord (Mt 25:8-9).

Discipleship implies an appreciation of the paradoxes of life. It is the detachment, self-denial, humility, rejection, and even death that lead to life. Jesus sums this up: "Whoever would save his life will lose it, but whoever loses his life for my sake will find it" (Mt 16:25). Disciples are called to willingly accept the hardships of life as a way to share in the sufferings of Jesus, and then, with him, to experience new life.

Good works.   Faith in Jesus and commitment to him are manifested in bearing the good fruit of works on behalf of others. The Sermon on the Mount presents the three good works of almsgiving, prayer, and fasting, and gives directions on the value and genuine-

ness of each. The core of these three sayings probably goes back
to Jesus, but tneir present form has several typically Matthean
characteristics and is undoubtedly from Matthew's hand.[29]

Jesus criticized those who do not practice what they preach
(Mt 23:4), or who proclaim him as Lord but do not do the will of
the Father (Mt 7:21). He also gave two parables that stressed the
need to do the will of the Father (Mt 21:28-32; 25:31-46), and
taught his disciples to pray: "Our Father... your will de done"
(Mt 6:10).

The Baptist criticized the lack of fruitfulness (Mt 3:10), as did
Jesus himself (Mt 7:18-20; 11:20-24; 21:33-43). In fact, Jesus
claimed that although lives may look the same, when difficulties
come only those will remain secure which are built on the practical living out of his word (Mt 7:26-27). Elsewhere, he stresses
that the profession of Christianity is not enough, disciples must
live out that faith in recognizable forms (Mt 5:16; 22:11-14). The
three good works that Matthew refers to were also the three
major forms of Jewish piety: almsgiving, prayer, and fasting.
These are offered as three examples of how to live out the higher
righteousness described in the sermon.

In dealing with almsgiving (Mt 6:1-4), Jesus encourages hidden-
ness in the disciples and condemns any sign of ostentation. This
good work should be a sign that the disciples live in hope, not a
gesture that seeks present recognition. After all, Jesus assured
them of reward for even a cup of cold water given in his name
(Mt 10:42). Almsgiving is a way of showing trust in the Lord (Mt
6:19-34) and commitment to Jesus (Mt 19:21). However, there are
values greater than alsmgiving: namely, the generous service and
worship of the Lord (Mt 26:6-13).

The second good work is personal prayer, and, again, the contrast is between ostentatious display and the quiet simplicity and
humility that aid one to accept one's emptiness before God (Mt
6:5-14). Prayer is a total self-gift to God, as a needy child before a
Father. This personal prayer complements community prayer (Mt
18:19-20).

Jesus himself often goes on his own to pray (Mt 14:23-24), and
encourages his disciples to do likewise (Mt 6:6-8). He teaches
them to pray to God as their Father (Mt 6:6, 9; 7:11) as he has
done (Mt 11:25; 26:39, 42), for confident prayer to the Father will
be fruitful (Mt 7:7-8).

Matthew uses this context to introduce his version of the Lord's prayer (Mt 6:9-13). It is longer than Luke's version; is divided into seven petitions; has a more Jewish flavor to it, especially in the first three petitions; and seems more of a liturgical elaboration than a private prayer. The first three petitions are in the passive tense and deal with the action of God in the world: sanctifying his name, spreading his Kingdom, and effecting his will. The remaining four petitions deal with God's care of his Church. The disciples pledge to do but one thing: to be reconciled among themselves.

Fasting is the third good work, again presented as something to be done in quiet simplicity without outward show. Moreover, it should be done with joy (Mt 6:16-18). Later, the Pharisees criticize the disciples for not observing the public fasts of Jewish groups. While fasting is praised as a sign of penance, Jesus reminds the Pharisees that his coming is a reason for joy, not sadness (Mt 9:14-17).

These good works are signs of faith in Jesus, and of the totality of commitment to the Lord.

Selfless service. The radical commitment of disciples is seen in the way they live out their discipleship in the concrete circumstances of their life and ministry. Jesus challenges specific groups of people with radical demands.

Jesus criticizes false prophets and condemns irresponsible leadership (Mt ch. 23). He speaks against seeking positions and titles (Mt 23:8-12), rebuking even the disciples (Mt 20:20-28). He gives an example of the ministry of leadership, and reminds his disciples of their pastoral responsibilities (Mt 18:10-14). To all his disciples he says: "The gift you have received, give as a gift" (Mt 10:8). He calls those whose gift is leadership to a genuine conversion in their leadership styles, so that they do not imitate this world's leaders, but rather commit themselves to serving their followers, as he has served his (Mt 20:25-26).

Matthew's Church is a wealthy community, and Jesus' radical demands include the Christian use of wealth. We have seen that the disciples were presented as examples of detachment. Moreover, Jesus' call to share with the poor is firm and clear (Mt 19:21), even though he acknowledges that the special grace of God is necessary to overcome attachment to wealth (Mt 19:26).

We have seen that Jesus lays the foundation for stronger attitudes of commitment in marriage (Mt 5:27-30). When, in his ministry, Jesus is questioned as to whether he supports liberal divorce or restricted divorce, he answers that he rejects all

divorce (Mt 5:31-32; 19:3-9).[30] Matthew adds an exception (Mt
5:32; 19:9) which seems to refer to marriage within prohibited
degrees of kinship. In such cases, he claims, divorce is not only
permitted but necessary. Even the exception clause serves the
same purpose as Jesus' statement, namely, the protection of the
dignity of marriage and the challenge to live faithfully.[31] When
listing possible interferences to following God's call, Matthew
omits "wife" where Luke inserts it twice (Lk 14:20, 26). Matthew
does not seem to think that marriage in any way interferes with
the demands of discipleship.

Having spoken on marriage, Jesus next speaks of those who
accept celibacy for the Kingdom. This statement is only in
Matthew, but the majority of scholars consider it original to
Jesus.[32] Those who are celibate "for the Kingdom" are proclaimed
blest by the Lord, for they offer themselves totally to his reign.
While celibates are considered positively here by Matthew, he
will not go so far as to introduce degrees of commitment based
on celibacy, as Luke seems to have done (Lk 20:27-40).[33]

Discipleship includes the hardships and sufferings of a life and
ministry committed to Jesus. These are a sharing of the Lord's
cross. One's totality of commitment is shown by the fruits of one's
conversion, including the good works of almsgiving, prayer, and
fasting. Moreover, for each disciple the specific conditions of
their own life bring further demands and challenges that also
need to be integrated into one's commitment to Jesus.

Matthew's gospel can be read as a manual on discipleship. No
matter which sermon or which period of Jesus' ministry he
presents, the constant focus is Jesus' call to the disciples of
Matthew's own Church.

Matthew has a layered approach to commitment to Jesus,
stretching from those who never knew him but lived the love he
called for, to those personally called to the deeper commitment
of discipleship and mission. The latter are those who live and
journey "with Jesus," and with whom Jesus is always present.
They are called to develop new attitudes; a new vision of deeper
holiness, based on faith in Jesus and the extension of God's love
to the world. The life of the disciple is a prolongation of the Servant life of Jesus, lived through hardship and the cross, and shown
in the fruits of good works and selfless service in each one's life.

Jesus' first words of invitation were: "Come after me and I will make you fishers of men" (Mt 4:19). For Matthew, there is always a close connection between call and mission. The Matthean Jesus is like the rabbis, who gathered around them followers to learn their interpretation of life and spread it to others. Matthew restricts the concept of discipleship to the Twelve in Jesus' lifetime, but by the time he writes, he sees the whole Church membership as disciples of Jesus' word and ministers to the world. The gospel describes Jesus' training of the foundational leadership of the Church, but it is written neither for them nor for their successors. The gospel in its present form is a broad challenge to all followers of Jesus for a deepening of their response to the call of the Lord.

Chapter Seven
MISSION AND MINISTRY IN MATTHEW

*"Full authority has been given to me both in heaven
and on earth; go, therefore, and make disciples of
all the nations" (Mt 28:18-19).*

The entire gospel of Matthew is written in light of the Lord's final
commission. Coming to his Church in glory, the risen Lord claims
universal authority and shares that authority with his Church. In
view of this call to mission and ministry, Matthew has arranged
his retelling of Jesus' life story such that it becomes a manual for
the formation and education of the Church to the Lord's mission.

A sense of the Church's calling and an awareness of its universal mission permeate the gospel. Matthew's community had
broken with Judaism and was consolidating its independence
through a common mission. Matthew's gospel fosters this
awareness and growth, alternating between the developmental
stages of Jesus' ministry, and discourses on the continuing formation of the missionary Church. The gospel presents Jesus as
preparing himself for ministry by baptism, the conquest of evil,
the commitment to reform, and a calling of others to share his
ministry (Mt 3:1-4:25). The early ministry of the Lord is described
as that of healing and welcoming to life and growth. This period
also includes the call of others to commitment, to personal and
corporate ministry (Mt 8:1 - 9:38). Book III presents the crowd's
growing rejection of the ministry of Jesus and the realization
that a shift in ministry is inevitable (Mt 11:2 - 12:50). After the
death of John the Baptist, Jesus' ministry is focused more on the
disciples. He is acknowledged as the healing and compassionate
Servant who is also Messiah and obedient Son (Mt 14:1 - 17:27).
However, Jesus' ministry continues to include confrontation

with opponents in a final attempt to call them to a new way of life (Mt 19:2 - 22:46). Unfortunately, this fails, and the prophetic challenges of the Lord's life and ministry inevitably lead to his death.

The five discourses interspersed throughout the ministry call the disciples to commit themselves to holiness of life (Mt 5:1 - 7:27); a mission of outreach to others (Mt 10:1-42); an awareness of what it means to be a Church on mission (Mt 13:1-50); the ministry of the upbuilding of one's own community (Mt 18:1-35); a realization of the judgment awaiting everyone (Mt 23:1 - 25:46).

The gospel gives the impression of moving through the ministry of Jesus to the climax of his final appearance. On reflection, it can readily be seen that the glorious final appearance and commission are not the climax, but the starting point for the whole gospel. The full identify of Jesus and his call to his Church, become the motivation for both the writing of the gospel and the ongoing call of disciples. The risen Lord, reigning over his Kingdom, calls his Church to be a Church on mission.

In this final chapter, we will examine Matthew's concepts of mission and ministry, study the discourse on mission, identify Matthew's understanding of the universal mission of the Church, and conclude with a reflection on the prophetical vocation of the Church.

Mission And Ministry In Matthew

Mission and ministry are closely connected. Mission refers to the reasons why people exist or "are sent." Ministry refers to services accomplished because of mission. Mission is visionary; ministry is functional. The vision of mission manifests itself concretely in a variety of ministries; the latter then become clear indications of one's sense of mission. In this first part of our last chapter, we will examine Matthew's understanding of mission as rooted in the Father's plan, centered in the life of Jesus, and extended to the Church. We will then review some of the characteristics of ministry in Matthew, focusing on his concept of all ministry as Christ-centered, liberational, integrated, and ecclesial.

Mission. The Father gives content and direction to mission; it is his plan which is gradually unfolded through salvation history (Mt 18:14). To carry out this plan, the Father directs the history of the chosen people, gives them his inspiring and guiding word through the prophets (Mt 1:22), and through the great leaders of the nation, is their constant protection (Mt 22:31-32). It is part of the Father's plan that Mary "was found with child through the power of the Holy Spirit" (Mt 1:18, 20). The Father missions Mary, Joseph, the magi, and John the Baptist: all are sent to contribute to the unfolding of God's plan.

Jesus himself is sent by the Father, his mission to reveal the Father to the world (Mt 11:27) in the work for universal salvation (Mt 18:14).

Although Jesus is sent in the Father's name, the Father continues to be the prime actor in this vision of salvation. He knows the world's needs (Mt 6:8), and nothing happens without his consent (Mt 10:29). The mission comes to fruition only if the Father himself has directed it (Mt 15:13), and will continue until the Father ends it (Mt 24:36).

Jesus is the embodiment of mission, constantly fulfilling the requirements of scriptures, totally dedicated to the Father who sent him (Mt 26:39, 42). He is Emmanuel, "God is with us" (Mt 1:23), twice confirmed in his mission from the Father (Mt 3:17; 17:5). He is the channel of the Father's will (Mt 11:25-27) and the faithful Servant of the Lord (Mt 12:18-21), carrying out his mission in spite of suffering and death (Mt 26:39, 42; 27:46).

As part of his mission to the world, Jesus focuses attention on the Father's constant care (Mt 6:8; 10:29), limitless forgiveness (Mt 18:21-35), impartiality toward all (Mt 5:45), and perfect love (Mt 5:48).

With mission comes authority, and Jesus, endowed with authority from the Father (Mt 3:17; 11:27; 17:5), is the sole authoritative teacher (Mt 7:28-29; 28:20), the healer from God, (Mt 9:8), and the preacher of a new life (Mt 4:17). His mission of revealing the Father's love and will to the world is achieved in the three-fold office of preacher, healer, and teacher.

Jesus carries out his mission totally obedient to the Father's plan (Mt 26:42). This obedience guarantees the fruitfulness of the seeds the Father has sown (Mt 7:21; 13:23).

Jesus' mission is now the mission of the Church (Mt 28:20). Disciples faithfully carry it on when they too are obedient to the design of God (Mt 7:21; 12:50). The mission remains demanding, but disciples need not fear because the Father actively pursues his plan through them (Mt 10:20). He is their source of success

(Mt 15:13), support (Mt 18:19), and recognition (Mt 5:16).

The Church continues, or prolongs, the mission of Jesus. The Lord shares his authority (Mt 10:1; 28:18-20), challenging his disciples to build on the foundation he laid (Mt 7:24-27). But all is to be to the glory of the Father (Mt 5:16), for this alone guarantees entrance into the Kingdom (Mt 7:21-23).

Jesus is still present and active among his disciples (Mt 1:23; 18:20; 28:20), whose responsibility is now to proclaim Jesus' message to the world personally (Mt 10:32-33; 28:20) and as community (Mt 5:45; 18:10, 35). This challenges the disciples to face the hardships and sufferings Jesus himself endured (Mt 16:24-25; 20:23).

Ministry.   The ministries of the Church manifest its sense of mission. These ministries, fostered by the Lord and based on his example, have four characteristics: they are Christ-centered, liberational, integrated, and ecclesial.

The ministry of the Church is centered on Christ. The anointing of Jesus in Bethany is described as "a good deed she has done for me" (Mt 26:10), just as Peter's mother-in-law, when cured, "got up at once and began to wait on him" (Mt 8:15). In the second example, Matthew even changes his source from "them" to "him." Ministry is always a service to Jesus, as the great judgment scene also clearly affirms. "I assure you, as often as you did it for one of my least brothers, you did it for me" (Mt 25:40). Moreover, the Church's ministry is not only to Christ present in others, but also a ministry done in Christ's name for the good of others (Mt 10:40; 18:20; 28:19). The disciples' faith in Jesus leads them to minister in his name, and, with his authority, even to perform miracles in his name (Mt 21:21-22).

Ministry in the name of Jesus is also liberational. He cures the blind, dumb, crippled, and diseased. He heals the hurts of life: hunger (Mt 14:13-21), loss (Mt 8:5-13), fear of the unknown (Mt 8:23-27), and alienation (Mt 15:29-31). He raises the dead (Mt 9:23-26), those bound by Satan (Mt 8:28-34), and those in sin (Mt 9:1-7). In his ministry, Jesus is moved to compassion for the crowds, and as a result shared his ministry with others (Mt 9:36 - 10:1). They are called now to extend this integral liberation to others: the liberation of body, mind, heart, and soul. However, the disciples quickly learn that to continue this healing ministry of the Lord they need constant trust in his active presence to them (Mt 17:19-20). They have received his healing gift and must share it with others: "Cure the sick, raise the dead, heal the leprous, expel demons" (Mt 10:8). Ministry in Jesus' name brings integral, wholistic well-being to all people and nations.

The Church's ministry in Jesus' name is as his: an integrated ministry of world salvation and human growth. The mission is visionary and global, the ministry concrete and local.

The harvest is great (Mt 9:37); in fact, it is the whole world (Mt 28:20). All peoples will eventually be brought before the Son of Man for their final judgment (Mt 25:31). Did they know his message and build on it? (Mt 7:21-27); acknowledge the Lord or reject him? (Mt 10:32-33) Furthermore, the end will only come when ministry in his name has been extended to all nations of the world (Mt 24:14).

The mission of integral world dedication is visionary, but effected locally, often in very small ways (Mt 10:42). Ministry in Jesus' name means not scandalizing those with whom you live, looking after those who stray or fall, praying for each other, and living in forgiveness and reconciliation (Mt ch. 18). It means giving food, drink, clothing, and comfort to the needy (Mt 25:31-40), and responding to the hurts of life we encounter each day (Mt 9:1-8, 18-34).

Finally, all ministry in Jesus' name is ecclesial: the ministry of the whole Church in its members. Jesus shares his authority with his foundational leadership (Mt 16:19) and with his whole Church (Mt 18:18). He challenges the Twelve to responsible ministry (Mt ch. 10) and elsewhere suggests the same to all disciples (Mt 25:14-30). While we have seen something of the institutionalized ministry of the Twelve and the charismatic ministry of the prophets, the personal calls to ministry and communal calls to corporate ministry are also strongly commended.

All disciples are called to become "fishers of men," mediators of the Lord's message to others. The two feeding stories (Mt 14:15-21; 15:32-38) are modified by Matthew to heighten the disciples' mediating roles: they recognize the people's need, aware of their own responsibility to them. They take the initiative in service, and through their response show the power of the Lord to others. By a careful piece of editing, Matthew demonstrates the responsibility of the Church to take initiative in responding to the needs of the world.[1]

Matthew presents us with an understanding of mission as centered in the Son who obediently carries out the vision and

plan of the Father. This mission is now extended to the whole
Church, effected through Christ's ministries in the Church;
ministries which are Christ-centered, liberational, integrated,
and ecclesial.

The Discourse On Mission

A theology of mission.   Jesus' early ministry, described in
chapters 1-9, was successful. He had given the great Sermon on
the Mount, worked miracles, and received the enthusiastic support of the crowds. He toured the towns and villages teaching,
preaching, and healing. As his followers increased, "his heart
was moved with pity. They were. . . like sheep without a
shepherd" (Mt 9:36). It is in this context of expanded ministry
that Matthew locates the second of his great discourses, the sermon on mission. In response to an increased demand for his
preaching and healing ministries, Jesus calls forth the Twelve to
share in his ministry, and gives them instructions on how to
minister in his name.

This second discourse of Jesus, like the other four, is compiled
by Matthew from material scattered throughout his sources (Mk
3:16-19; 6:6-11; 8:34-38; 9:37, 41; 13:9-13). Luke, who also used
Mark, deals with similar topics but in different places (Lk
6:12-16; 9:1-6). Matthew not only combines episodes on call and
mission, but adds material on steadfast confession and en-
durance drawn from the apocalyptic discourse in Mark. Matthew
also uses several references from Q which Luke places among
comments made to disciples during Jesus' final journey (Lk
12:3-6). Matthew insightfully places these same comments in the
missionary discourse (Mt 10:27-29).

The missionary discourse is a deliberate editing by Matthew,
who wishes to address the missionary work of the whole Church.
The commissioning of the Twelve is merely the occasion for Matthew to cultivate mission and ministry in disciples of all times. In
fact, the speech in its present form shows Jesus sending out the
Twelve, but Matthew "says not a word about what they did, or
where they went, nor does he even mention that they return-
ed."[2] Once he has used the episode as a starting point, he is no
longer interested in the history of the ministry of the Twelve, but
rather his concern is the theology of mission and ministry in the
universal Church. He has molded his sources into a speech of
final testament and succession not unlike that which Jacob gave

to the Twelve patriarchs (Genesis 49:1-33).[3]

The discourse can be divided into two parts: the missionary call and the work itself (Mt 10:1-23), and the minister who goes in Christ's name (Mt 10:24-42).

The call and work of the missionary. The discourse opens solemnly, as do all the discourses, and Matthew immediately summarizes the purpose of the whole speech: the description of the summoning and commissioning of the whole Church (Mt 10:1). Matthew has never mentioned the Twelve before, but introduces them here in dealing with the empowering of the new Israel. Matthew identifies immediately the major characteristic of authentic Christian ministry: its source in Jesus, through sharing in his own ministry and authority.

Matthew goes on to list the names of the Twelve in this passage, whom he calls "apostles" for the only time. His list refers to Peter as the first, and speaks of Matthew as the tax collector (Mt 9:9-13), whose call had already been described with Mark's call of Levi (Mk 2:13-17). Since Matthew's gospel comes after Mark's, and after considerable developments in the early Church, he can introduce the Twelve as abruptly as he does, presuming that his audience is well acquainted with them. It is these Twelve who Jesus commissions for the early missionary work of the Church.

Matthew then inserts instructions from Jesus: a program of action with accompanying pastoral directives. The statement that restricts the mission to Israel probably goes back to one of the early missionary ventures of the disciples. This will be changed by Jesus' final commission (Mt 28:19).

The message of the missioners is the same as that of John the Baptist (Mt 3:2) and Jesus (Mt 4:17): a challenge to reform because the reign of God is close at hand. In addition to the mandate to preach, the apostles, for a second time (Mt 10:1, 8), are commissioned to heal.

There follows a call to simple detachment and selfless generosity in the missioners. They are reminded that they have received the call of the Lord freely, and so should minister freely to others. They do not need to take provisions with them because, though they minister freely, they can be assured of provision with food and lodging.

The missioners are told to stay in one place for the duration of their ministry, and to stay with a worthy person: one likely to receive both messenger and message. Welcomed in Jesus' name, the missioners' greeting will be effective for the household. Rejection of the missioners is no light matter—it is described with the same condemnation that Jesus uttered against the cities which rejected him (Mt 11:20-24).

Jesus now gives a series of warnings on the dangers in ministry. What Mark describes as the hardships of the end times (Mk 13:9-13) are transferred by Matthew to describe the hardships of ministry. The sufferings described refer to persecutions by both Jews and Gentiles. These persecutions are probably from Matthew's time, but are still a reflection of what Jesus has foretold (Mt 16:24-28). In their sufferings disciples are reminded to have confidence in the presence of the Spirit, who continues to work through them.

Ministering in Christ's name.   The disciples who go on mission represent the Lord and can expect no better treatment than Jesus received Rejection is a part of ministry; not even Jesus avoided it (Mt 12:22-32). The apostles ought not to be oppressed by fear of rejection or persecution. They speak for Christ and should do so courageously. The missioners have the support of the Lord throughout their suffering; three times he tells them not to be afraid in their ministry (Mt 10:26, 28, 31).

Not only do the missioners prolong the words of Jesus, they also prolong his sufferings. This, too, is part of the hardship of a disciple's life, and cannot be avoided without serious consequences (Mt 10:28). Rather, the disciples should trust in the provident and caring Father, knowing that public proclamation of the Lord will lead to the Lord's recognition and acceptance of them.

The Lord's support needs to be in the forefront of the missioners' lives, encouraging them to fearless commitment through all the persecutions and hard choices of discipleship. "He who will not take up his cross and come after me is not worthy of me. . . he who brings himself to nought for me discovers who he is" (Mt 10:38-39). Selfless commitment to ministry brings with it self-fulfilment and self-discovery. The missioners will need to recall this as they face the trials of family division resulting from commitment to Jesus. The hardships and pain of family division are often more difficult to bear than external persecution. However, faithful dedication to Christ's mission makes the disciples integral parts of Jesus' own family (Mt 12:46-50).

These verses on fearless commitment to Jesus in spite of persecution go well beyond what the apostles could have expected to face during Jesus' lifetime, and are further indications that this discourse is an address designed to cultivate a sense of mission in Matthew's Church.

The discourse ends with a return to the theme of the missioners representing Christ, and to judgment of others because of the quality of welcome and hospitality they show to the travelling missionaries.

A missioner is referred to in four ways: "you," "a prophet," "a holy man," and "one of these little ones." These descriptions of the disciples are indicative of the qualities Jesus hoped to find in his missioners: prophetical commitment, holiness of life, and a spirit of humility.

The discourse concludes with Jesus' assurance of blessings on those who welcome the missioners of his Church.

Spirituality and ministry. This discourse is based on a historical episode which actually ended very successfully (Lk 9:10-17; Mk 6:30-44). However, Matthew is not interested in a single historical occurrence, but in the universal Church's missionary mandate.

Authentic ministry comes from the commission and authority of Jesus (Mt 10:1). A responsibility of the whole Church (Mt 10:2-5), it should be prudently planned according to pastoral needs (Mt 10:5b-6). The essential dimension of all ministry is evangelization and proclamation of the good news (Mt 10:7). This is good news for those who receive it, since it has healing effects in each one's life (Mt 10:8).

The minister must live simply, grateful for the redemptive gift received, but also as a sign of the credibility of the Church, which simply passes on to others what is freely given by the Lord. Even Matthew's community, which seems quite wealthy (Mt 10:9), is challenged to detachment.

As a further gesture to encourage credibility, ministers should associate with worthy people and give clear signs of rejection of the evil standards of the day (Mt 10:11-14). Ministry in every generation requires, in addition to simplicity and detachment, prudence, common sense, and sensitivity to the environment (Mt 10:16-18).

Since ministry is an extension of the life of Jesus, the minister must be ready for persecution, abandonment, rejection, and loss

of family affection (Mt 10:19-27). However, the work must go on.
It is interesting that this discourse is given to people with very
little background or knowledge of their faith! A minister is
treated like Jesus was, and life is filled with a tension between
feelings of rejection and appreciation of God's providential care
(Mt 10:27-39).

Ministry is indispensible for the Church. It is for each person
committed to ministry, the way of living discipleship and the
cross; for many, it is the only way of hearing the good news of the
Lord.

The Universal Mission Of The Church

Mission to the Gentiles.   One of the major problems faced by
all early Christian communities was the mission of Christianity.
Did Christ come to gather the faithful ones from among the
Jewish nation and prepare them for the end? Or did his coming
mean the end of traditional Judaism and the founding of a new
assembly of God's people? How long would the new situation
last? Were Christ's followers expected to work only with Jews, or
with Gentiles as well? If so, were Gentiles intended to first
become Jews, as part of their initiation into the chosen group?

These were difficult questions which became even more com-
plicated with the passing of time. In fact, a majority of Jews did
not accept Jesus, and their leadership almost unanimously condemned him. Early missions to the Jews were largely failures,
and the Gentiles who became followers saw no point in first
becoming Jews. Although the temple and city were destroyed,
Judaism reinterpreted its former way of life and reconsolidated
its organization at Jamnia.

What was supposed to be the relationship between Christianity
and the Gentiles? There was no easy answer, and the prolonged
debate of the early Church shows clearly that Jesus had given no
final word on the problem, for if he had done so, the debate
would hardly have been so bitterly extended.

In Matthew's gospel, Jesus sees his mission and that of his
Church as directed exclusively to the Jews (Mt 10:5, 23; 15:24). In
places, there are also abusive remarks concerning the Gentiles
(Mt 5:47; 7:6; 15:26), and intolerance of them even from the
disciples (Mt 15:23).

However, Matthew also underlines events that herald the
future direction of the Church: four Gentiles contribute to the

genealogy of the Messiah; the Gentile magi welcome him at his birth; and he inaugurates his ministry in Galilee of the Gentiles (Mt 4:15). Jesus works miracles for faith-filled Gentiles (Mt 8:10; 15:28), is acclaimed by them (Mt 27:54), and anticipates the proclamation of his messge to them (Mt 10:18).

Jesus' own attitude to the Gentiles shows signs of a break with traditional Judaism. He visits Gentile country (Mt 4:24; 8:28-34), meets with Gentiles (Mt 8:5-13; 15:21-28), and suggests the Kingdom will be given to them instead of to the Jews (Mt 21:28-43). When he describes the final judgment, he says "all the nations will be assembled before him" (Mt 25:32).

Some of Matthew's community problems are unquestionably read back into Jesus' life. The debates concerning the entry of the Gentiles are more likely to have originated in Matthew's Church, where the struggle seems to have been bitter. Jesus worked with the Jews, as did the early Church. Even in the first gospel, "The Gentile mission . . . is the mission in order to introduce the Gentiles into the Israel-Christian community."[4]

Only after the events surrounding the Jewish war of 70 and the polemics of the late 80s and early 90s does Christianity's commitment to the Gentile mission become a real possibility. Matthew is writing at this time, and although his gospel shows signs of Jesus' own historical practice, and indications of community conflict, Matthew has given the gospel a distinct overlay of commitment to the Gentile mission.[5] This can only be seen as the insightful reinterpretation of a creative theologian and pastor.

Mission to the rejected.   While Jesus' own historical mission was primarily, if not exclusively, to the Jews, additional episodes help the early Church appreciate its mission, and redirect it for the future based and rooted in Jesus' attitudes.

Matthew tells us that everyone is affected by Jesus' coming (Mt 21:10). Crowds follow Jesus everywhere (Mt 8:1), at times so large that Jesus teaches from a boat (Mt 13:2). He preaches to them all, leaving them spellbound at his message (Mt 7:28). Moreover, he cures all who come to him for healing and wholeness (Mt 4:24; 8:16; 14:36; 15:29), and feeds all whose hunger moves him to compassion (Mt 14:21; 15:38).

Matthew summarizes Jesus' ministry as one of teaching, preaching, and healing all who come to him (Mt 9:35). Jesus' concern for all is most clearly shown in his fully lived conviction that every life is precious, and that all laws must be secondary to compassion and love (Mt 12:12). Jesus proves these convictions by his constant attention to society's rejected.

Jesus cures the leper whom society and religion reject (Mt 8:1-4). He heals the son of a centurion associated with the hated occupying forces (Mt 8:5-13). He exorcizes the Gadarene demoniacs condemned to the graveyards (Mt 8:28-34). He heals the ritually unclean woman with the hemorrhage (Mt 9:20-22).

He calls a tax collector (Mt 9:9-13) and a Zealot (Mt 10:4) to share his mission; shows concern for children (Mt 18:1-6), especially the sick (Mt 9:18-26); and welcomes the blind and the dumb (Mt 9:27-34).

The book of Leviticus (21:18) excluded the blind and crippled from public ministry, and King David cursed them (2 Samuel 5:8), but Jesus welcomed them into the temple area (Mt 21:14).

He ate with people whom others considered sinners (Mt 9:10); was explicitly called a friend of "those outside the law" (Mt 11:19);[6] and proclaimed that prostitutes and sinners believed in the Baptist and would enter the Kingdom (Mt 21:31-32).

Although his coming was for all, Jesus showed special concern for the underprivileged and outcast. He called his chosen "the little ones," reminded all who heard him that they would be judged on their attitudes of welcoming the needy and distressed, wherever they encountered them (Mt 25:31-46).[7] He speaks of blessings for those who were never thought to have them (Mt 21:33-43; 22:1-10), for those who refused grace and later changed their mind (Mt 21:28-32), and for those who seemingly come to God at the last minute (Mt 20:1-16).

Historically, Jesus may not have extended his own mission outside of the Jews. However, his whole ministry was permeated with concern for the rejected of society and religion. He is the Servant who never crushes the bruised reed, or quenches the smouldering wick (Mt 12:20). His attitudes were of openness and compassion, universal love and understanding. Matthew can apply scripture to Jesus: "In his name, the Gentiles will find hope" (Mt 12:21).

Mission to the world.   A new sense of mission was necessary for the Church in the 80s and 90s. Matthew's gospel ends with the final commission of Jesus to evangelize the world.[8] This mandate of the glorified Lord colors the message of the entire first gospel.

This solemn final word of the Lord is similar to Moses' final ad-

dress in Deuteronomy (5:30-33),[9] and takes on characteristics of
Jesus' final wish, will, and testament. It is hardly likely that
Jesus actually gave this solemn command; had he done so, it is
most improbable that Paul would have had to struggle so much to
gain the apostles' acceptance for something Jesus had commanded. Rather, "it must be presumed that the Church, having learned
and experienced the universality of the Christian message,
assigned that knowledge to a direct command of the living
Lord."[10] Matthew could do this, based on the general attitudes of
Jesus to the rejected and the broad proclamation of universal
salvation.

Matthew does not see the practice of Jesus and his new
pastoral directives as inconsistent. He considers each appropriate in a given period of history. In this new period, the Church
needs to face the possibility of reinterpreting Jesus' message based
on his known attitudes and values. This is truly a courageous
move on Matthew's part.

By the time this conclusion is written, the exclusive mission to
Israel is finished, and, for all practical purposes, the Church is
committed to a universal mission. Jesus says: "Make disciples of
all the nations" (Mt 28:19).

The mandate is a late addition, as its theological and liturgical
language indicate. No doubt it took the Church considerable time
to work through the debate on mission, but by the time Matthew
writes, the new direction is clear.

The universal mission of the Church is actually discerned by
the Church, not commanded by Jesus. In fact, Jesus' practice
could lead to restricted interpretations. Matthew, the Christian
theologian, is seen at his best here, in his willingness to reread
Jesus' life and attitudes and apply them to new circumstances
with a resulting redirection in Church teachings and practice.

A Prophetic Church

Prophetic ministry.   Matthew challenges his Church to public
witness to the Lord and his teachings, and the mission discourse
can be seen as an education to prophetic ministry. A prophet is
someone who speaks on behalf of God, conveying to a community the teachings of God and his denunciation, consolation, or
challenge to rebuild.[11] The prophet forthtells the word of God
rather than foretells it. Matthew sees his community's task as
one of proclaiming the word to all nations. He calls the disciples

to bear fruit (Mt 7:17), be salt to their environment (Mt 5:13), and light to the world (Mt 5:14).

Matthew's community includes prophets, as his denunciation of false prophets presumes (Mt 7:15; 24:11, 24). In fact, Jesus promised to send prophets to guide and minister to his community (Mt 23:34). However, the concept of prophet, while used in a special way for a few, is also applied broadly to the ministering disciples. At the end of the mission discourse, Jesus blesses those who welcome his followers as the prophets they are (Mt 10:41). Earlier, when presenting the beatitudes, Jesus commented that the sufferings of disciples' lives are a result of their prophetic ministry (Mt 5:12).

In Matthew, it is the community that exercises the prophetic ministry to the world. When outlining the life of disciples in the Sermon on the Mount, Jesus speaks of the disciples in relation to "the prophets before you" (Mt 5:12). Later, he will equate his "little ones" with "prophets" (Mt 10:41). Rather than speak of individual prophets in Matthew's community, it would be more accurate to speak of his community as a prophetic one. The charismatic gifts of Jesus are now lived out in the community as a whole (Mt 10:1).

When speaking of false prophets, Matthew describes them as "performing signs and wonders so great as to mislead even the chosen if that were possible" (Mt 24:24). They come to the community "in sheep's clothing but underneath are wolves on the prowl" (Mt 7:15). These comments give us some indication regarding the qualities of authentic prophecy. To participate in Christ's prophetic ministry, now lived out in the communal experience of the Church, it is not necessary to perform great deeds or make spectacular predictions. Rather, the Lord's prophetic ministry of his Church is built on fidelity to his word (Mt 7:24-27; 28:20) and lived in love of God and neighbor (Mt 22:37-40). It is manifested through evangelization in a ministry of selfless sacrifice for others (Mt 10:5-39). Furthermore, the prophetic voice of the Lord rings out to the world in the quality of holiness of his disciples' lives (Mt 5:3-12); a quality that restores values to a tasteless world, light to its darkness (Mt 5:13-16).

The prophetic word of Jesus is now heard in the life of his Church, and so he can say that whoever welcomes any one of his little ones as a prophet will receive God's blessing and reward.

Persecution in evangelization. Mark's gospel presents the great persecutions of the Church as part of the events of the end of the world (Mk 13:9-13). Matthew sees these persecutions as part of the daily life of a missionary Church. After all, Jesus was not persecuted because he healed and exorcized the needy, but because his words were prophetic in their call for personal, communal, and institutional changes. The disiciples' missionary work too will provoke division (Mt 10:34), and, like the prophets before them, they will be flogged, hunted down, and killed (Mt 23:34).

The very quality of their prophetic message leads to persecution. By including persecution material in his missionary discourse, Matthew suggests that persecution is brought about by the prophetic ministry of the Church. Mark, who placed persecution among the beginning calamities of the end times, saw persecution as an occasion for witnessing to the Lord. Matthew sees persecution as directly linked to the missionary proclamation of the Church: persecution is a result of witnessing.[12] The contemporary prophecy of the Church will be persecuted, just as prophetic challenge has always been (Mt 23:33-36).

It is in this context of persecution because of prophetic ministry that Jesus three times consoles and encourages his disciples (Mt 10:26, 28, 31). He goes on to call for maturity in their faith as they publicly proclaim him (Mt 10:32-33). Whenever the Church is storm-tossed, its members afraid, there is the need of intensifying and maturing faith (Mt 8:23-27).

Persecution is not to be viewed as abnormal in the context of the Church's mission. Disciples are encouraged to take it in stride. If audiences reject them, their blessings will return to themselves (Mt 10:13). When people do not listen, they should go elsewhere (Mt 10:14). If missioners are brought to trial, it is a further chance to bear witness to the Lord (Mt 10:18). When accused, they will become mouthpieces for the Holy Spirit (Mt 10:20). When persecuted in one town, they should flee to the next (Mt 10:23).

In all efforts to proclaim the message of the Lord, the disciples are told: "Be on your guard with respect to others" (Mt 10:17); "Do not let them intimidate you" (Mt 10:26); "Do not be afraid of anything" (Mt 10:31). "You will be given what you are to say" (Mt 10:19); "Speak in the light" (Mt 10:27); "Proclaim from the housetops" (Mt 10:27). Jesus appeals to all his disciples: acknowledge me, take up your cross, come after me (Mt 10:32-39).

Matthew's prophetic Church appreciates that hardships and hurt are a part of the disciples' lives (Mt 8:18-22; 16:24-26) and a natural component of their ministry to the word of the Lord (Mt 10:5-39). These sufferings, or negative asceticism, complement their own positive asceticism of detachment, prayer, faith, and love. They minister in the Lord's name (Mt 10:40-41), and realize they will be treated like he was (Mt 10:24-25). Called to be prophets (Mt 23:34), they need to produce the fruits of prophetic witness (Mt 7:16-18), and to accept the essential suffering that goes with this task (Mt 5:12b). They can also be peaceful and happy, since they will not only find self-fulfillment in this service (Mt 10:39), but also the blessings of the Lord: "Be glad and rejoice, for your reward is great in heaven" (Mt 5:12).

A city set on a hill.   The final commission of the exalted Lord challenges his Church to proclaim his message to the ends of the earth. Jesus shares his authority and mission with his Church, and Matthew arranges his material to help train his community to be a Church in mission. The Church's service to the Lord and in the Lord's name is the broad prophetic ministry of evangelization. Jesus says to his disciples: "You are the light of the world. A city set on a hill cannot be hidden" (Mt 5:14). In Matthew's vision, the Church now replaces the city built on a hill, namely Jerusalem and the Old Testament message. The Church is now the channel of God's revelation and challenge.

Matthew's community sees itself as a prophetic Church, proclaiming that humanity, restored to wholeness in Jesus, is called to a life centered on love, not law; on faith in Jesus alone, and trust and hope in his word.

In the second great discourse, Matthew gives us a theology of mission that details the call and work of the Christian disciple, emphasizing how each disciple now ministers in Jesus' name. In fact, the very spirituality of Matthew's Church is a spirituality of ministry.

This ministry to which every member of the Church is called is part of the ongoing universal mission of the Church. Jesus came, directing his Church to be concerned with all nations and every individual. His message, love, and call are for everyone.

At a crucial turning point in the history of the early Church, when his community is consolidating its own independence from

Judaism, Matthew calls all the disciples to a realization that
Jesus is still present (Mt 28:20), working in them and through
them (Mt 10:40-42). His mission is now their mission: to reveal
the Father's will to the world (Mt 11:27) as it is found in the words
of Jesus (Mt 7:24-27; 28:20). He calls them to be the city set on a
hill for everyone to see: a prophetic presence to the world.

Conclusion
MATTHEW AND CHRISTIAN LIFE
IN THE 1980s AND 1990s

Matthew was a model pastor, an exceptional religious leader: the
kind of person needed in every period of transition. He knew
how to challenge his people with the best of the new and the old.
He handled crises creatively, able to make the difficult period of
his Church an era of wonderful growth.

Matthew was a gifted disciple who used all his talents in the
service of the Lord. He was one of the prophets, wisepeople, and
teachers that the Lord had anticipated his community would
need. A brilliant theologian, he was highly educated in Judaism
and singularly committed to the continuing universal value of
Christianity. He had a love for the sources of his faith and an
openness to the times ahead, which led him to retell the story of
Jesus with sensitivity to both the past and the future. His biblical
spirituality is a rich synthesis of Jesus' foundational teachings
and of his own inspired interpretation of them.

Matthew was a community leader whose people lived through
a major crisis of history. He encouraged and supported his community through threatening world events, destructive internal
division, bitter theological warfare, and the usual social and
religious pressures of urban life. His community lived at a turning
point in Christianity, having to make decisions that brought them
even greater hardships. Matthew's servant leadership called the
community to reconciliation, renewal, and a corporate sense of
mission, and succeeded in giving it an identity independent from
its Jewish roots.

Matthew was an insightful theologian. While committed to the
past, he shows no fear of losing its values. Open to the future, he
seems unthreatened by it. Rather, he exemplifies a calm confidence and courageous freedom in giving new meanings to old
teachings, or, more correctly, in articulating new ways of living
enduringly significant teachings. Matthew does not manage the
past for a present generation, but rather leads the present
generation to embody past values in new, relevant ways. He interprets faith and discovers new ways of living it.

Matthew was a disciple whose whole life, vision, and value system were centered on Jesus Christ. The Lord became his hope; his healer, teacher, and reason for building his community; the way to God, the all-powerful Lord and judge. Matthew's reverence and awe for the Lord, however, did not restrict his willingness to suggest how the Lord might handle, in the present, situations which he had never to handle before. Matthew brought Jesus' vision to bear on new circumstances. The vision was dynamic, not static; it was a catalyst for change in every generation, not limited by the past.

Matthew was a person of the Church, who through hard times had acquired more skill in building community than had most of his contemporaries. His gospel is not only shaped by Church interests, but was more influential in the early Church than any other New Testament writing. He called the Church to become the Kingdom, but never equated the two. He saw his community as always in preparation for the reign of God, constantly called to ongoing conversion, formation, reconciliation, and faith-sharing. For Matthew, commitment to live as Church is the first step towards the Kingdom. He challenges his people to center their lives on Christ, measure all by his word, and live as his community.

Matthew was a spiritual director for the early Christians, calling them to quality self-gift in discipleship. He writes his gospel in such a way that Jesus addresses Matthew's Church rather than the crowds in Palestine. The first gospel becomes a handbook on discipleship for Matthew's community in the 80s and 90s. He calls for new attitudes to life, a new vision of holiness, and a new willingness to integrate the hardships of life with commitment to the Lord.

Matthew was a missionary with a world vision, and his vision motivates his Church. The mandate to convert the world comes in Jesus' words, but from Matthew's experience and appreciation of what Jesus would have done. He directs his Church to be the Lord's prophetic voice in every generation and nation of the world. Each disciple is called to the work of evangelization, ministering in Christ's name and power. The vision is for a world given to Christ; the ministry is to every person, in their giftedness or their rejection. The Lord's prophetic call is for everyone, and his love knows no distinctions. Unfortunately, Matthew was not always consistent in pursuing his goal of worldwide missionary endeavor. Matthew not only calls humankind to share the Lord's love, but also reminds humankind of its weakness, sinfulness, and natural tendency to mutual recrimination, bitterness, polemical attitudes, and partisanship. His approach to the Pharisees is not objective, but reflects the angry responses of one recently engaged in divisive theological debate. He challenges us to imitate his strengths and avoid his weaknesses.

Matthew is a model pastor, a gifted disciple, a community leader, an insightful theologian, a convert to Christ, a person of the Church, a spiritual director, a missionary with a world vision for the Church. His gifts are exceptional, his commitment profound and his ministry far-reaching. The effects of his interpretation of Jesus' teaching greatly influence the Church and are still with us today.

We can imitate his dedication, apply his responses to our own community needs, reproduce his willingness to interpret the message, follow his focus on Christ, be enthused by his commitment to Church, respond to his call for discipleship, and appreciate his vision and sense of mission.

Matthew's teachings and attitudes seem appropriate to our world and Church of the 1980s and 1990s. Our problems and needs are not unlike those of his own community, and his creative responses to his problems can be valuble to us.

All genuine Christian life must be rooted in the saving events of Jesus, and Matthew is diligent in identifying these sources and establishing them as the foundation for faith. But Christian life does not merely repeat a literalist and fundamentalist version of Jesus' life. Authentic Christian commitment requires living and lifegiving interpretation of those historical events in every generation. Only such rooting and interpreting guarantee the genuineness of faith. Matthew is an outstanding example of both approaches, integrating and elevating the past to a present way of life and spirituality.

In these post-Vatican II years of division and debate, Matthew's fidelity to the lifegiving past and openness to a promising future can be a basis for mutual appreciation, true community, and a new sense of mission for us all.

NOTES

CHAPTER ONE

[1] See Sean Kealy, "The Modern Approach to Matthew," *Biblical Theology Bulletin*, 9 (1979), p. 165.

[2] See Alexander Jones, *The Gospel according to St. Matthew* (New York: Sheed and Ward, 1965), p. 27: "The allusions of Clement of Rome (I Ep. ad Cor., 95 A.D.) of the Epistle of Barnabas (100-130 A.D.), of Ignatius of Antioch (d. 115 A.D), of the Didache (c. 100 A.D.), clearly reflect the text of the first Gospel. Nor are these reflexions confined to the discourses (logia) of our Lord (e.g. Ignatius, Ep. ad Smyrn. 1:1; cf. Mt 3:15). The authority of Mt's text is even underlined by the phrase 'as it is written', which is technical for the canonical writings of the O.T. (Ep. Barn, 4:14, alluding to Mt 22:14)."

[3] See Floyd V. Filson, *A Commentary on The Gospel according to St. Matthew* (London: Adam and Charles Black, 1971), p. 16: "It finds repeated and explicit statement in important ancient writers: Irenaeus (*Against Heresies*, iii. I.I), Pantaenus (quoted by Eusebius, *Ch. Hist.* v. 10. 3), Tertullian (*Against Marcion*, iv. 2), Origen (quoted by Eusebius, *Ch. Hist.* vi. 25. 4), Eusebius (*Ch. Hist.* vi. 25. 3), and many others."

[4] See Rev. C. Stewart Petrie, "The Authorship of 'The Gospel According to Matthew': a Reconsideration of the External Evidence," *New Testament Studies*, 14 (1967-68), pp. 15-32; also the summary by Robert H. Gundry, *Matthew: A Commentary on His Literary and Theological Art* (Grand Rapids, Michigan: William B. Eerdmans Publishing Co., 1982), pp. 610-611, 620.

[5] See W. F. Albright and C. S. Mann, *Matthew*, Anchor Bible Series (New York: Doubleday and Co., Inc., 1971), p. CLXXVIII.

[6] For a more detailed presentation of these developments in biblical criticism, see the Appendix in my book *Luke: The Perennial Spirituality* (Santa Fe: Bear & Company, 1982, 1985).

[7] On this point, see John P. Meier, *The Vision of Matthew: Christ, Church, and Morality in the First Gospel* (New York: Paulist Press, 1979), pp. 17-18, who notes "His Jewishness was variously conceived. Some thought of him as a conservative legalist (B. Bacon), a converted Pharisee and rabbi (E. von Dobschutz), or a provincial Jewish-Christian schoolmaster (M. Goulder). Others saw something of a 'Hellenistic' coloration in Matthew's Jewishness (Kilpatrick, Stendahl, Hare, and A. Kretzer)."

[8] Some of these authors and their views are presented by Meier, *Vision*, pp. 18-19.

[9] For the quantitative relationship of these three sources, see Beda Rigaux, *The Testimony of St. Matthew* (Chicago: Franciscan Herald Press, 1968), p. 19.

[10] See "Source Criticism," in *Luke: The Perennial Spirituality*, pp.285-288; see also Rigaux, pp. 13-14, 114.

[11] See B. C. Butler, *The Originality of St. Matthew (Cambridge: University Press, 1951);* Bernard Orchard, *Matthew, Luke and Mark*, 2nd ed. (Manchester, England: Koinonia Press, 2nd edition, 1977).

[12] See John McKenzie, "The Gospel According to Matthew," *The Jerome Biblical Commentary* (London: Geoffrey Chapman, 1970), p. 65.

[14] See Howard Clark Kee, *Jesus in History*, 2nd ed. (New York: Harcourt Brace Jovanovich, Inc., 1977), pp. 76-120: Chapter 3, "Jesus as God's Eschatological Messenger: The Q Document."

[14] See Petrie, p. 32: " 'Q', which might well stand for 'quirk', should be wholly forgotten and promptly despatched into the limbo of forlorn hypotheses"; Albright and Mann, *Matthew*, p. XL: "It cannot be too strongly emphasized that this theory is not the assured result of critical scholarship, and some recent critics have pleaded for the priority of Matthew's gospel . . . Moreover, it is only necessary to posit that Luke read Matthew before compiling his gospel...to dispense with the mysterious 'Q' altogether"; also John Pairman Brown, "The Form of 'Q' known to Matthew," *New Testament Studies*, 8 (1961-62), p. 33; Rev. R. T. Simpson, "The Major Agreements of Matthew and Luke against Mark," *New Testament Studies*, 12 (1965-66), p. 275.

[15] See Albright and Mann, *Matthew*, p. XL; Dr. E. P. Sanders, "The Argument from Order and the Relationship between Matthew and Luke," *New Testament Studies*, 15 (1968-69), p. 261: "We must then become more open to the possibility that there was more contact between Matthew and Luke than their independent employment of the same two sources. The simplest explanation is that one knew the other; evidence not discussed here makes it likely that Luke used Matthew." Butler, *Originality*, p. 170: "Luke's direct dependence on Matthew is not only an adequate, but the only adequate, explanation of the data."

[16] For supportive presentations of "Q", see Dr. E. L. Abel, "Who wrote Matthew?" *New Testament Studies*, 17 (1970-71), pp. 138-139; Francis Wright Beare, *The Gospel according to Matthew* (San Francisco: Harper and Row Publishers, 1981), p. 49; Eduard Schweizer, *The Good News according to Matthew* (Atlanta: John Knox Press, 1975), p. 70.

[17] See Raymond E. Brown, and John P. Meier, *Antioch and Rome* (New York: Paulist Press, 1982), p. 53.

[18] Abel, pp. 138, 142.

[19] This technique of abbreviation has been well documented by Heinz Joachim Held, "Matthew as Interpreter of the Miracle Stories," in

Gunther Bornkamm, Gerhard Barth, Heinz Joachim Held, *Tradition and Interpretation in Matthew* (Philadelphia: The Westminster Press, 1963), pp. 165-299.

[20] For a fine synthesis of current discussion, see Beare, *Matthew*, pp. 44-49.

[21] For details of Matthew's vocabulary, see Rigaux, p.19.

[22] See David Hill, *The Gospel of Matthew* (London: Oliphants, 1972), p. 89.

[23] Rigaux, p. 178, gives the following list of citations by formula: 1:23 = Is 7:14; 2:6 = Mi 5:1; 2:15 = Ho 11:1; 2:18 = Jr 31:15; 2:23 = ?; 4:15-16 = Is 8:23 and 9:1; 8:17 = Is 53:4; 12:18-21 = Is 42:1-4; 13:35 = Ps 78:2; 21:5 = Is 62:11 and Zc 9:9; 27:9-10 = Zc 11:12-13 and Jr 32:6-9.

[24] See William G. Thompson, *Matthew's Advice to a Divided Community* (Rome: Biblical Institute Press, 1970), p. 101.

[25] McKenzie, *Matthew*, p. 62.

[26] See Charles H. Lohr, "Oral Techniques in the Gospel of Matthew," *Catholic Biblical Quarterly*, 23 (1961), pp. 419-427.

[27] See O. Lamar Cope, *Matthew: A Scribe Trained for the Kingdom of Heaven* (Catholic Biblical Quarterly Monograph Series, 5, Washington, D. C. 1976), p. 65.

[28] See H. Benedict Green, *The Gospel According to Matthew* (Oxford: University Press, 1975), pp. 20-21.

[29] Rigaux, p. 21.

[30] Lohr, p. 407.

[31] For reviews of Matthean studies, see Kealy, "Modern Approach," pp. 165-178; Daniel Harrington, "Matthew Studies since Joachim Rhode," *Heythrop Journal*, 16 (1975), pp. 375-388; C. F. D. Moule, "St. Matthew; some neglected features," in *Essays in New Testament Interpretation* (New York: Cambridge University Press, 1982), pp. 67-74.

[32] See Butler, *Originality*, and Orchard, *Matthew*.

[33] See for example the article by Petrie; also The Rev. David G. Deeks, "Papias Revisited," *Expository Times*, 88 (1977-78), pp. 296-301, and 324-329; The Rev. A. C. Perumali, "Are not Papias and Irenaeus competent to report on the gospels?" *Expository Times*, 91 (1979-80), pp. 332-337.

[34] See Jerome Murphy-O'Connor, "The Structure of Matthew XIV-XVII," *Revue Biblique*, 82 (1975), p. 361; John A. T. Robinson, *Redating the New Testament* (Philadelphia: The Westminster Press, 1976), p. 9; Albright and Mann, *Matthew*, p. XLVIII.

[35] See for example Abel, pp. 138-152.

[36] See note 33. For a different understanding of "Q", see Pairman Brown, pp. 27-42.

[37] For a good overview of the question of sources, see Beare, *Matthew*, pp. 44-49.

[38] See B. W. Bacon, "The Five Books of Matthew against the Jews," *Expositor*, 15 (1918), pp. 56-66; *Studies in Matthew* (New York: Holt, 1930).

[39] See the summary of these positions in Kealy, pp. 170, 173-174.

[40] See Cope, *Matthew: A Scribe*; Robert H. Gundry, *The Use of the Old Testament in St. Matthew's Gospel* (Leiden: Brill, 1967); *Literary and Theological Art*.

[41] For a general description of this trend, see J. J. Collins, "The Rediscovery of the Biblical Narrative," *Chicago Studies*, 21 (1982), pp. 45-58; regarding Matthew, see James Reese, "How Matthew Portrays the Communication of Christ's Authority," *Biblical Theology Bulletin*, 7 (1977), pp. 139-144; Philip L. Shuler, *A Genre for the Gospels: The Biographical Character of Matthew* (Philadelphia: Fortress Press, 1982).

[42] See Kealy, "Modern Approach," pp. 170-171; Filson, pp. 20-24.

[43] See G. D. Kilpartrick, *The Origin of the Gospel According to St. Matthew* (Oxford: The Clarendon Press, 1946), p. 139; Cope, *Matthew: A Scribe*, pp. 10, 130.

[44] See Bornkamm, Barth and Held, *Tradition*; Schweizer, *Matthew*; Jack Dean Kingsbury, *Matthew: Structure, Christology, Kingdom* (Philadelphia: Fortress Press, 1975); *Matthew*, Proclamation Commentaries (Philadelphia: Fortress Press, 1977).

[45] See Thompson, *Matthew's Advice*.

[46] See Meier, *Vision*; Brown and Meier, *Antioch*.

[47] These commentaries of the 1980s would include: John P. Meier, *Matthew* (Wilmington, Delaware: Michael Glazier, Inc., 1980); Beare, *Matthew*; Gundry, *Literary and Theological Art*.

[48] Rigaux, p. v.

[49] See Eugen Biser, "Wisdom," *Sacramentum Mundi*, Karl Rahner, Cornelius Ernst and Kevin Smyth, eds. (New York: Herder and Herder, 1970), Vol. VI, pp. 359-362.

CHAPTER TWO

[1] See Paul Hinnebusch, *St. Matthew's Earthquake* (Ann Arbor, Michigan: Servant Books, 1980), pp. ix, 1-12.

[2] See Hinnebusch, p. 8.

[3] For a good overview of historical developments in Palestine leading upto New Testament times, see Norman Perrin and Dennis C. Duling, *The New Testament: An Introduction*, 2nd ed. (New York: Harcourt Brace Jovanovich, Inc., 1982), pp. 3-15.

[4] For further information on the groups within Judaism, see Bruce M. Metzger, *The New Testament: Its background, growth, and content* (Nashville: Abingdon Press, 1965), pp. 34-60.

[5] See Beare, *Matthew*, pp. 11-12.

[6] C. F. D. Moule, *The Birth of the New Testament* (1962; rpt. London:

Adam and Charles Black, 1973), p. 172, considers that the first gospel "reflects a variety of community ideals some charismatic, some constitutional, some acceptable to the Evangelist himself, others alien to his outlook."

[7] Rigaux, p. 88.

[8] Schweizer, *Matthew*, p. 398.

[9] James P. Martin, "The Church in Matthew," *Interpretation*, 29 (1975), p. 44.

[10] R. G. Hamerton-Kelly, "Gospel of Matthew," *Interpreter's Dictionary of the Bible*, Suppl. Vol. (Nashville: Abingdon Press, 1976), p. 580.

[11] See Brown and Meier, *Antioch*, pp. 2-8.

[12] See Eugene A. LaVerdiere and William G. Thompson, "New Testament Communities in Transition," *Theological Studies*, 37 (1976), pp. 578-580.

[13] George T. Montague, *The Holy Spirit* (New York: Paulist Press, 1976), p. 303.

[14] LaVerdiere and Thompson, pp. 574-575.

[15] See Perrin and Duling, pp. 73-74.

[16] Matthew's only independent reference to the Sadducees is his example of the disagreements the Pharisees and Sadducees had regarding the bible (Mt 22:23-33).

[17] See Green, *Matthew*, p. 188.

[18] See Kilpatrick, p. 128.

[19] Douglas R. A. Hare, in *The Theme of Jewish Persecution of Christians in the Gospel According to St. Matthew* (Cambridge: University Press, 1967), p. 104, states: "In each of nine references to synagogues Matthew adds 'autos' 'their' (Matt. 4:23; 9:35; 10:17; 12:9; 13:54) whenever the context fails to indicate that the synagogue is an institution belonging to 'the hypocrites' (Matt. 6:2, 5; 23:6, 34)."

[20] See Kilpatrick, p. 115.

[21] See Cope, *Matthew: A Scribe*, p. 126; Beare, *Matthew*, p. 282.

[22] Hare, *Jewish Persecution*, p. 3.

[23] See William G. Thompson, *Matthew's Advice to a Divided Community* (Rome: Biblical Institute Press, 1970), p. 68.

[24] Beare, *Matthew*, p. 14.

[25] Some authors point out how the seven woes are the reverse of seven of the beatitudes (2-8). See J. C. Fenton, *Saint Matthew* (Harmondsworth, England: Penguin Books, 1963), p. 368.

[26] See LaVerdiere and Thompson, pp. 576-578.

[27] Matthew's condemnations should be put in perspective. Beare, pp. 448-449, comments: "As a blanket indictment of 'the scribes and the Pharisees', the charge is grossly unjust. There would be sanctimonious hypocrites among them, but most of them were scrupulous in the observance of the Law. Matthew puts them in the worst possible light, with

168

no suggestion that they have any good features."

[28] See Kingsbury, *Structure*, p. 153.

[29] Rigaux, p. 87.

[30] Beare, *Matthew*, p. 452, comments: "This is beyond question a masterpiece of vituperation. Over the centuries, among Christians, it has stigmatized the Pharisees, and with them the scribes, as consummate hyprocrites, so that the very term 'Pharisee' has become a byword. Among our Jewish friends, this is not so. Among them the Pharisees are held in honor, as they were in the time of Jesus."

[31] Bornkamm, Barth, Held, *Tradition*, p. 88.

[32] Hare, *Jewish Persecution*, pp. 151-152.

[33] See Robinson, *Redating*, p. 352, who dates Matthew's gospel c.40-60.

[34] See Abel, p. 145, who suggests that the topic of the temple tax in 17:26 must date the first draft of Matthew before 70. However, see also Kilpatrick, p. 129, who suggests that the abolition of the poll tax suggests a date after 97.

[35] See Albright and Mann, *Matthew*, p. 286, who consider that "the increasingly explosive situation in Palestine in the decades before A.D. 64, could have easily led Jesus to speak of the fall of Jerusalem without this being an "extraordinary feat of prescience." They then conclude that "to write off the saying in 24:2 as prophecy after the event is wholly unjustified." See also Gundry, *Literary and Theological Art*, p. 600, for similar positions to Albright and Mann.

[36] .Gundry, *Literary and Theological Art*, p. 606-607, thinks that Matthew's community is persecuted not by the Pharisees, but by Nero c. 64 or 65.

[37] Another reason for not dating the gospel late is that it shows no knowledge of the Pauline letters, which were circulating around 100. We shall see that Pauline positions are present in Matthew's community.

[38] See Kilpatrick, p. 124; Beare, *Matthew*, p. 10.

[39] Kingsbury, *Matthew*, p. 97.

[40] See B. T. Viviano, "Where Was the Gospel According to St. Matthew Written?" *Catholic Biblical Quarterly*, 41 (1979), pp. 533-546; Kilpatrick, p. 134; Howard Clark Kee, *Understanding the New Testament*, 4th ed. (Englewood Cliffs, New Jersey: Prentice-Hall, Inc., 1983), p. 130.

[41] See Kingsbury, *Matthew*, pp. 97-98.

[42] Meier, *Vision*, p. 14.

[43] D. S. Wallace-Hadrill, *Christian Antioch* (New York: Cambridge Univ. Press, 1982), pp. 14-15.

[44] Hare, *Jewish Persecution*, p. 168; see also Wallace-Hadrill, p. 4.

[45] Brown and Meier, *Antioch*, pp. 1-8; see also Raymond E. Brown, "Not Jewish Christianity and Gentile Christianity but Types of Jewish/Gentile Christianity," *Catholic Biblical Quarterly*, 45 (1983), pp. 74-79.

CHAPTER THREE

[1] See Prof. Kenzo Tagawa, "People and Community in the Gospel of Matthew," *New Testament Studies*, 16 (1969-70), p. 151.

[2] Fenton, p. 26.

[3] Kingsbury, *Matthew*, pp. 24, 28.

[4] See Kealy's remarks on Trilling, "Modern Approach," p. 170.

[5] See Peter F. Ellis, *Matthew: His Mind and His Message* (Collegeville, Minnesota: The Liturgical Press, 1974), pp. 22-24.

[6] See Gundry, *Literary and Theological Art*, p. 9.

[7] Schweizer, p. 542.

[8] See LaVerdiere and Thompson, p. 573.

[9] See Kilpatrick, *Origins*, p. 135-137.

[10] See K. Stendahl, *The School of St. Matthew*, 2nd ed. (Philadelphia: Fortress Press, 1968), pp. 24-29.

[11] Filson, pp. 20-21.

[12] Beare, *Matthew*, p. 5; see also Hill, *Matthew*, p. 43; Bacon, "Five Books."

[13] Hill, *Matthew*, p. 43.

[14] Meier, *Vision*, pp. 263-264.

[15] Matthew begins with a genealogy and ends with a commission, echoing the structure of the Books of Chronicles. See Donald Senior, "The Ministry of Continuity," *Bible Today*, 14 (1976), p. 672: "The purposes of Matthew and the Chronicler are strikingly similar: both seek to reinterpret history in order to gain perspective for their people."

[16] See Kingsbury, *Structure*, p. 35.

[17] See Meier, *Vision*, pp. 33-36.

[18] See Meier, *Vision*, pp. 37-39.

[19] See John P. Meier, "Salvation History in Matthew: In Search of a Starting Point," *Catholic Biblical Quarterly*, 37 (1975), pp. 207, 213; also Brown and Meier, *Antioch*, pp. 60-63.

[20] See Brown and Meier, *Antioch*, p. 61.

[21] See Philippe Rolland, "From the Genesis to the End of the World: the Plan of Matthew's Gospel," *Biblical Theology Bulletin*, 2 (1972), pp. 155-176.

[22] See Meier, *Vision*, pp. 33-35.

[23] Meier, *Vision*, p. 26.

[24] See Kilpatrick, *Origins*, p. 76.

[25] See Filson, p. 4.

[26] 1:22; 2:5, 15, 17, 23; 4:14; 8:17; 12:17; 13:35; 21:4; 27:9-10. See also F. C. Grant, "Gospel of Matthew," *Interpreter's Dictionary of the Bible*, Vol. III (Nashville: Abingdon Press, 1962), pp. 307-310, where the author lists sixty-one Old Testament quotes used in Matthew.

[27] See Cope, p. 121.

[28] Ellis, p. 15. The whole section on pages 13-16, dealing with the function of the discourses, is excellent.

170

[29] Joachim Jeremias, *The Parables of Jesus* (London: SCM., Press, Ltd., 1972), p. 247.

[30] See Jeremias, p. 11.

[31] For additional reading on the parables, see Jeremias' excellent work; also R. I. Dillon, "Towards a Tradition-History of the Parables of the True Israel (Matthew 21,33 - 22,14)," *Biblica*, 47 (1966), pp. 1-42; Margaret Pamment, "The Kingdom of Heaven According to the First Gospel," *New Testament Studies*, 27 (1980-81), pp. 211-232; M. Goulder, "Characteristics of the Parables in the Several Gospels," *Journal of Theological Studies*, 19 (1968), pp. 51-70.

[32] Kingsbury, *Matthew*, p. 48.

[33] See Held, "Matthew as Interpreter of the Miracle Stories," pp. 165-299

[34] Kingsbury, *Structure*, p. 128.

[35] See Rigaux, pp. 137-138: "Mt, like the other Synoptics, used two noble words to disignate his people: 'Isreal,' 11 times, 'the people,' 9 times. True, he used the expression 'the Jews' 5 times, but in 4 of these the designation is attributed to pagans (2,2:27,11,29,37). Only once did Mt speak of 'the Jews' (28,15) and it was his own personal reflection after the Resurrection: 'To this day that is the story among the Jews.' The expression takes on a tone of scorn."

[36] See Ellis, pp. 10-13.

[37] See Kingsbury, *Structure*, p. 25.

[38] See Thompson, *Matthew's Advice*, pp. 14-15; Beare, *Matthew*, p. 29; Lohr, pp. 427-430; Terence J. Keegan, "Introductory Formulae for Matthean Discourses," *Catholic Biblical Quarterly*, 44 (1982), pp. 415-430; David L. Barr, "The drama of Matthew's Gospel: a reconsideration of its structure and purpose," *Theology Digest*, 24 (1976), pp. 349-359.

[39] Brown and Meier, *Antioch*, p. 51.

[40] Brown and Meier, *Antioch*, p. 57.

[41] Beare, *Matthew*, p. 317.

CHAPTER FOUR

[1] See Beare, *Matthew*, p. 38.

[2] For "father," see 11:25, 26, 27; 24:36; 28:19; for "my father," see 7:21; 10:32, 33; 11:27; 12:50; 15:13; 16:17; 18:10, 19, 35; 20:23; 25:34; 26:29, 39, 42, 53; "your father," see 5:16, 45, 48; 6:1, 6, 8, 14, 15, 26, 32; 7:11; 10:20, 29; 18:14; 23:9.

[3] Matthew distinguishes between Jesus' relationship to his Father and the disciples' relationship to the Father. "My Father" and "your Father" never become "our Father". The only "our Father" (Mt 6:9) is when the disciples pray together. Moreover, Matthew "restricts the application of God's Fatherhood to disciples; it is not a universal Fatherhood of all men." Green, p. 90.

[4] Beare, *Matthew*, p. 43.

[5] Kingsbury, *Matthew*, p. 45.

[6] See Raymond E. Brown, *The Birth of the Messiah* (New York: Doubleday and Co., Inc., 1979), p. 141: "Conception christology and pre-existence christology were two different answers to adoptionism." Hill, *Matthew*, p. 77 says: "Mt. 1-2... are unlikely to have been designed to combat Jewish calumny of Jesus' origins, since those calumnies belong to a date later than Matthew's gospel."

[7] Schweizer, *Matthew*, p. 32; also Brown, *Birth*, p. 189.

[8] Fenton, p. 35.

[9] The main quotes are from Micah 5:1, Hosea 11:1, Jeremiah 31:15, and a fourth source, unknown. See The Rev. M. J. Down, "The Matthean Birth Narratives," *Expository Times*, 90 (1978), pp. 51-52, who says: "It is as rum a collection of verses from the Old Testament as you could make, and includes one 'prophecy' not from the Old Testament at all, or any other known source . . . We must conclude that the evangelist did not start with prophecy and invent a story; he started with a story and slipped in certain prophecies, in some cases not too cleverly."

[10] Midrash is a reflective process that leads to the creation of a story to teach more clearly the scripture texts. Matthew's infancy narratives are technically not midrash. As Brown says, *Birth*, p. 561: "The birth stories were composed, not to make the Old Testament Scriptures more intelligible, but to make Jesus more intelligible." However, the technique Matthew uses could be broadly described as midrashic.

[11] Gundry, *Literary and Theological Art*, p. 13.

[12] See Aaron Milavec, "Matthew's Integration of Sexual and Divine Begetting," *Biblical Theology Bulletin, 8* (1978), *p. 112.*

[13] See Fenton, p. 41; Brown, *Birth*, p. 91; Helen Milton, "The Structure of the Prologue to St. Matthew's Gospel," *Journal of Biblical Literature*, 81 (1962), p. 177.

[14] See Milavec, p. 113; Brown, *Birth*, p. 73.

[15] Schweizer, *Matthew*, p. 29.

[16] See A. Tostato, "Joseph, Being a Just Man (Matt 1:19)," *Catholic Biblical Quarterly*, 41 (1979), pp. 547-551; Otto A. Piper, "The Virgin Birth: The Meaning of the Gospel Accounts," *Interpretation*, 18 (1964), pp. 131-148.

[17] See J. Edgar Burns, "The Magi Episode in Matthew 2," *Catholic Biblical Quarterly*, 23 (1961), p. 53; Albright and Mann, *Matthew*, p. 14.

[18] See Brown, *Birth*, p. 112.

[19] See Milavec, p. 115.

[20] Commenting on Mt 23:37 Schweizer, *Matthew*, p. 444, says: "The Old Testament speaks of God in the imagery of a bird protecting its young (Deut. 32:11; Isa. 31:5; Ps. 36:7). Converts to Judaism were also described as having been taken 'under the wings of the Shekinah (=the presence of God).' Jesus thus comes to occupy the place of God himself."

²¹ Fenton, p. 407, suggests the following: "The greater part of these three chapters describes events which happened on a Wednesday (26:1-16), Thursday (26:17-75), Friday (27:1-61), Saturday (27:62-66), and Sunday (28:1-15)."

²² See J. D. M. Derrett, "Haggadah and the Account of the Passion," *Downside Review*, 97 (1979), pp. 308-315. Judah sells Joseph for 20-30 pieces of silver. The twelve patriarchs then have a meal, but Joseph does not partake. He is placed in a pit for three days and three nights. The payment is seen as blood money. Eventually the wife of Potiphar enters the story. In the New Testament, Judas sells Jesus for 30 pieces of silver. The twelve apostles then have a meal, but Jesus does not partake. He is buried for three days. The payment is viewed as blood money. Finally the wife of Pilate enters the scene.

²³ Notice too how "Judas, who has betrayed the Son of David, hangs himself like Ahithophel, who betrayed David (2 Sam. 17:23)." Schweizer, p. 505.

²⁴ Hill, *Matthew*, p. 344, says that Matthew is "determined to make the Jews responsible for the execution of their Messiah." Beare, *Matthew*, p. 539, comments on Mt 27:62-66: "Surely one of the most extravagant of inventions. Nothing like it is found in any of the other Gospels. The Pharisees appear for the first time in the entire Passion story."

²⁵ The following are references to Messiah: Mt 1:1, 16, 17, 18; 2:4; 11:2; 16:16, 20; 22:42; 23:10; 26:63, 68; 27:17, 22.

²⁶ See Mt 1:1; 9:27; 12:23; 15:22; 20:30-31; 21:9, 15.

²⁷ See W. R. G. Loader, "Son of David, Blindness, Possession, and Duality in Matthew," *Catholic Biblical Quarterly*, 44 (1982), pp. 570-585.

²⁸ See Mt 8:19; 12:38; 19:16; 22:16, 24, 36 and their parallels in Mark and Luke.

²⁹ Among those commentators who interpret Matthew as presenting Jesus as Wisdom, see: M. Jack Suggs, *Wisdom, Christology, and Law in Matthew's Gospel*, Cambridge, Mass.: Harvard University Press, 1970), especially pp. 31, 58; Schweizer, *Matthew*, p. 447; Beare, *Matthew*, p. 267. For opposing positions, see: G. N. Stanton, "Salvation Proclaimed: X. Matthew 11:28-30: Comfortable Words?" *Expository Times*, 94 (1982), pp. 3-9; Green, p. 118.

³⁰ See Kingsbury, *Structure*, p. 87: "Whereas Matthew brings the term "Shepherd" (*poimen*) only three times and the verb "to herd" (*poimaino*) but once, the word "sheep" (*probaton*) occurs in his Gospel no fewer than eleven times."

³¹ See Mt 2:2; 21:5; 25: 34, 40; 26:28; 27:11, 29, 37, 42.

³² See Beare, *Matthew*, p. 102, who says: "It is not impossible that there is an overtone here, in the words of the voice from heaven, of the sacrifice of the only, the beloved Son of God-a hint that in the baptism

he is being called not only to kingship, but to death."

[33] D. Hill, in "Son and Servant: An essay on Matthean Christology," *Journal for the Study of the New Testament*, 6 (1980), pp. 2-16, reacts to Kingsbury's consistently expressed position that Son of God is the central concept which integrates all others in Matthew. Hill suggests that the Servant theme gives meaning even to the Son of God christology of Matthew.

[34] See Kingsbury, *Structure*, p. 42: "And that the term Son of God has not become a mere vacuous appellation for Jesus, simply appropriated by Matthew from the tradition, is apparent from the circumstance that of the twenty-three times it occurs in the first Gospel, eleven times it is redactional in nature."

[35] Kingsbury, *Structure*, p. xi.

[36] Kingsbury, *Matthew*, p. 55: "Thus, in any number of passages the disciples and people of faith who address Jesus as 'Lord' are in reality calling upon him in his capacity as the Messiah, the Son of God (cf. 8:2, 6, 8, 21, 25; 14:28, 30; 16:22; 17:4, 15; 18:21; 22:43-45; 26:22). In other passages, he is called 'Lord' in his capacity as the Son of David (cf. 9:28; 15:22, 25, 27; 20:30-31, 33; 21:3). And in still others he is 'Lord' in his capacity as the Son of Man (cf. 7:21-22; 12:8; 24:42; 25:37, 44).

[37] See Beare, *Matthew*, p. 108.

[38] See Ellis, p. 112: "Mark's dependence for the title upon Dn 7:13ff seems more than obvious. In Matthew the dependence upon Dn 7:13ff is certain. He uses the title 30 times, uses it in the context of the whole Daniel episode, and makes additional references to Daniel confirming his designation of Jesus as Daniel's authoritative Son of Man."

[39] See Herman C. Waetjen, "The Genealogy as the Key to the Gospel according to Matthew," *Journal of Biblical Literature*, 95 (1976), p. 222.

[40] George T. Montague, *The Holy Spirit*, (New York: Paulist Press, 1976), p. 310.

CHAPTER FIVE

[1] Some commentators have tried to distinguish the specific meaning of each of these concepts. Some identify "kingdom of God" and "kingdom of heaven," seeing the former as more suited to the Gentiles, the latter more appropriate for Christians of Jewish origin. Others are more specific, considering that "kingdom of heaven" refers to a reality totally future, to be experienced after the end of this world. They understand "kingdom of God" to refer to God's present sovereignty on earth, as established through the covenant. Some writers see "the kingdom of the Son of Man" as referring to the Church, while others, acknowledging that it is always future (Mt 16:28; 20:21), identify it with the kingdom of God. See Pamment, pp. 211-232; and for the opposite opinion see Albright and Mann, *Matthew*, p. 155.

See Dr. B. Gerhardsson, "The Seven Parables in Matthew xiii," *New Testament Studies*, 19 (1972-73), pp. 16-37.

Filson, p. 43.

Mark Sheridan, "Disciples and Discipleship in Matthew and Luke," *Biblical Theology Bulletin*, 3 (1973), p. 242.

See Schweizer, *Matthew*, pp. 306-307.

See G. Todd Wison, "Conditions for Entering the Kingdom," *Perspectives in Religious Studies*, 5 (1978), p. 42.

See Alexander Jones, *The Gospel According to St. Matthew* (New York: Sheed and Ward, 1965), pp. 24-25: "His first discourse describes the true subjects of the kingdom and their spirit; his second instructs its missionaries; the third illustrates its hidden but irresistible power; the fourth the mutual obligations of its citizens; the fifth its establishment in power on the ruins of Judaism."

For synonyms for entering the kingdom, see Wison, p. 42.

Wilson, p. 43.

[10] Pamment, p. 229.

[11] Schweizer, *Matthew*, p. 361, says: "The metaphor of becoming a child in time came to be associated with baptism, as similarly in 1 Peter 2:1 ff., and was interpreted by the community in the light of their doctrine of baptism as referring to birth through water and the Spirit."

[12] Schweizer, *Matthew*, p. 377 compares "seventy times seven" with Lamech's song of revenge (Genesis 4:23-24), and sees the world's restoration to wholeness through the forgiveness of the disciples.

[13] The debt in the parable is enormous, ten thousand talents. Albright and Mann, *Matthew*, p. 223, write: "The talent was equivalent to six thousand denarii. Two denarii would provide a man and his family with adequate living for one day."

[14] Hill, *Matthew*, p. 256.

[15] Michael Crosby, *Spirituality of the Beatitudes: Matthew's Challenge for First World Christians* (New York: Orbis Books, 1981), p. 146.

[16] See 7:29; 8:9; 9:6, 8; 10:1; 21:23, 24, 27; 28:18.

[17] Brown and Meier, *Antioch*, p. 70.

[18] See J. D. M. Derett, " 'Where two or three are convened in my name...' a sad misunderstanding," *Expository Times*, 91 (1979), pp. 83-86, who sees Mt 18:19-20 as referring to a legal dispute, not prayer.

[19] Reese, p. 141.

[20] For a more thorough commentary on the relevant passages see *Peter in the New Testament*, Raymond Brown, Karl P. Donfried, John Reumann eds. (New York: Macmillan Co., 1974), pp. 75-107.

[21] Hill, *Matthew*, p. 258 summarizes opinions; Gundry, *Literary and Theological Art*, p. 9, sees Peter as a representative disciple; Albright and Mann, *Matthew*, p. 195, say: "It is hard to know what kind of thinking, other than confessional presupposition, justifies the tendency of

some commentators to dismiss this verse (xvi:18) as not authentic."

22 See Schweizer, *Matthew*, p. 336.

23 Brown and Meier, *Antioch*, pp. 64-66, comment on Peter's power to make "halakic" decisions, and repeat Streeter's famous phrase about Peter being "the supreme Rabbi" of the Church.

24 Meier, *Vision*, p. 187.

25 For a presentation of recent developments in the understanding of Peter in Matthew's gospel, see Jack Dean Kingsbury, "The Figure of Peter in Matthew's Gospel as a Theological Problem," *Journal of Biblical Literature*, 98 (1979), pp. 67-83.

CHAPTER SIX

1 See Sheridan, p. 237.

2 For a comparison with Luke's approach to discipleship, see Doohan, *Luke*, chapter six.

3 See Beare, *Matthew*, p. 285, for the interesting insertion of "sister" in Mt 12:50.

4 See Kingsbury, *Matthew*, pp. 56 and 80-81.

5 See Schweizer, *Matthew*, p. 350.

6 For Matthew's use of the miracle stories at the service of his concept of discipleship, see Kingsbury, *Matthew*, p. 48.

7 See Kingsbury, *Matthew*, p. 33.

8 T. Hartley Hall, "An Exposition of Matthew 4:21-23," *Interpretation*, 29 (1975), p. 65.

9 See Albert Kirk and Robert E. Obach, *A Commentary on the Gospel of Matthew* (New York: Paulist Press, 1978), p. 161.

10 Disciples in Matthew understand everything. See Mt 13:10-17; and Matthew's omission of references to misunderstanding in Mark: Mt 14:33 and Mk 6:52; Mt. 16:9 and Mk. 8:17; Mt 17:4 and Mk 9:6; Mt. 17:9 and Mk 9:10; Mt 17:23 and Mk 9:32; see also Murphy-O'Connor, "Matthew XIV-XVII," p. 378.

11 See Meier, *Vision*, pp. 215-216.

12 Luke's great sermon is on the plain, offered to all the crowd. See "Charter Sermon" in Doohan, *Luke*, pp. 240-247.

13 H. D. Betz, "The Sermon on the Mount: Its Literary Genre and Function," *Journal of Religion*, 59 (1979), p. 296.

14 See Schweizer, *Matthew*, pp. 195 and 203; Hill, *Matthew*, p. 109.

15 Some commentators suggest that the original seven were 1st, 2nd, 4th, 5th, 6th, 7th, and 9th. The third was added for balance, then the 8th for theological reasons and to form an "inclusion" with the first. The 9th was a postscript. See Beare, *Matthew*, p. 128; Schweizer, *Matthew*, pp. 78-98; Neil J. McEleney, "The Beatitudes of the Sermon on the Mount/Plain," *Catholic Biblical Quarterly*, 43 (1981), pp. 1-13.

16 See Hill, *Matthew*, pp. 109-110.

17 Schweizer, *Matthew*, p. 98.

176

[18] Schweizer, *Matthew*, p. 86.

[19] Crosby, p. 74.

[20] See Schweizer, *Matthew*, p. 118.

[21] Schweizer, *Matthew*, p. 136.

[22] Meier, *Vision*, p. 260.

[23] See J. P. Burchill, "Discipleship is Perfection. Discipleship in Matthew," *Review for Religious*, 39 (1980), pp. 36-42.

[24] See A. Feuillet, "Le caractère universel du jugement et la charité sans frontière en Mt 25,31-46," *Nouvelle Revue Théologique*, 102 (1980), p. 195.

[25] Green, p. 77, quoting Gerhardsson, p. 48.

[26] See Rigaux, p. 164.

[27] See Charles H. Giblin, "A Note on Doubt and Reasssurance in Mt 28:16-20," *Catholic Biblical Quarterly*, 37 (1975), p. 75.

[28] See Thomas Deidun, "The Parable of the Unmerciful Servant (Mt 18:23-35)," *Biblical Theology Bulletin*, 6 (1976), p. 211; Robert A. Guelich, "The Matthean Beatitudes: 'Entrance Requirements' or Eschatological Blessing?" *Journal of Biblical Literature*, 95 (1976), pp. 414-434.

[29] See Schweizer, *Matthew*, pp. 138-159.

[30] See Meier, *Vision*, pp. 248-257.

[31] See J. J. Kilgallen, "To what are the Matthean Exception-Texts (5,32 and 19,9) an Exception?" *Biblica*, 61 (1980), pp. 102-105.

[32] See Jerome Kodel, "The Celibacy Logion in Matthew 19:12," *Biblical Theology Bulletin*, 8 (1978), p. 19.

[33] Jacques Dupont considers that the celibacy logion refers to the separated partners of a marriage contracted between near relatives. In support of this see Quentin Quesnell, "'Made Themselves Eunuchs for the Kingdom of Heaven' (Mt 19,12)," *Catholic Biblical Quarterly*, 30 (1968), pp. 335-358.

CHAPTER SEVEN

[1] See, Held, pp. 181-187.

[2] Francis Wright Beare, "The Mission of the Disciples and the Mission Charge: Matthew 10 and Parallels," *Journal of Biblical Literature*, 89 (1970), p. 3.

[3] See Joseph A. Grassi, "The Last Testament-Succession Literary Background of Matthew 9:35-11:1 and its Significance," *Biblical Theology Bulletin*, 7 (1977), pp. 172-175.

[4] Prof. Kenzo Tagawa, "People and Community in the Gospel of Matthew," *New Testament Studies*, 16 (1969-70), p. 162.

[5] See S. Brown, "The Matthean Community and the Gentile Mission," *Novum Testamentum*, 22 (1980), pp. 193-221.

[6] See Feuillet, pp. 179-196; also Hill, *Matthew*, p. 174.

[7] See Feuillet, pp. 186-187.

[8] See Douglas R. A. Hare and Daniel J. Harrington, " 'Make Disciples of All the Gentiles' (Matthew 28:19)," *Catholic Biblical Quarterly*, 37 (1975), pp. 359-369, who interpret 28:19 as referring only to the Gentiles; also John P. Meier, "Nations or Gentiles in Matthew 28:19?" *Catholic Biblical Quarterly*, 39 (1977), pp. 94-102, who responds to Hare and Harrington and claims that 28:19 refers to all nations, Jews and Gentiles.

[9] See Ellis, p. 136.

[10] Hill, *Matthew*, p. 362.

[11] For definitions on prophecy, see David Hill, *New Testament Prophecy* (Atlanta: John Knox Press, 1979), p. 7.

[12] See Hare, *Jewish Persecution*, p. 100.

Bibliography

Abel, Dr. E. L. "Who Wrote Matthew?" *New Testament Studies*, 17 (1970-71), pp. 138-152.

Albright, W. F. and C. S. Mann. *Matthew*. New York: Doubleday and Co., Inc., 1971.

Bacon, B. W. "The Five Books of Matthew against the Jews." *Expositor*, 15 (1918), pp. 56-66.

Studies in Matthew. New York: Holt, 1930.

Barr, David L. "The drama of Matthew's Gospel: a reconsideration of its structure and purpose." *Theology Digest*, 24 (1976), pp. 349-359.

Beare, Francis Wright. "The Mission of the Disciples and the Mission Charge: Matthew 10 and Parallels." *Journal of Biblical Literature*, 89(1970), pp. 1-13.

--- *The Gospel according to Matthew*. San Francisco: Harper and Row, Publishers, 1981.

Betz, H. D. "The Sermon on the Mount: Its Literary Genre and Function." *Journal of Religion*, 59 (1979), pp. 285-297.

Biser, Eugen. "Wisdom." *Sacramentum Mundi*. Karl Rahner, Cornelius Ernst and Kevin Smyth, eds. New York: Herder and Herder, 1970, Vol. VI, pp. 359-362.

Bornkamm, Gunther, Gerhard Barth, Heinz Joachim Held. *Tradition and Interpretation in Matthew*. Philadelphia: The Westminster Press, 1963.

Brown, John Pairman. "The Form of 'Q' Known to Matthew." *New Testament Studies*, 8 (1961-62), pp. 27-42.

Brown, Raymond E. *The Birth of the Messiah*. New York: Doubleday and Co., Inc. 1979.

--- "Not Jewish Christianity and Gentile Christianity but Types of Jewish/Gentile Christianity." *Catholic Biblical Quarterly*, 45 (1983), pp. 74-79.

Brown, Raymond E. and John P. Meier. *Antioch and Rome*. New York: Paulist Press, 1982.

Brown, Raymond E., Karl P. Donfried, John Reumann, eds. *Peter in the New Testament*. New York: Macmillan Co., 1974.

Brown, S. "The Matthean Community and the Gentile Mission." *Novum Testamentum*, 22 (1980), pp. 193-221.

Burchill, J. P. "Discipleship is Perfection. Discipleship in Matthew." *Review for Religious*, 39 (1980), pp. 36-42.

180

Burns, J. Edgar. "The Magi Episode in Matthew 2." *Catholic Biblical Quarterly*, 23 (1961), pp. 51-54.

Butler, B. C. *The Originality of St. Matthew*. Cambridge: University Press, 1951.

Cope, 0. Lamar. *Matthew: A Scribe trained for the Kingdom of Heaven*. Washington: Catholic Biblical Quarterly Monograph Series 5, 1976.

Collins, J. J. "The Rediscovery of the Biblical Narrative." *Chicago Studies*, 21 (1982), pp. 45-58.

Crosby, Michael. *Spirituality of the Beatitudes: Matthew's Challenge for First World Christians*. New York: Orbis Books, 1981.

Deeks, The Rev. David G. "Papias Revisited." *Expository Times*, 88 (1977-78), pp. 296-301, and 324-329.

Deidun, Thomas. "The Parable of the Unmerciful Servant (Mt 18:23-35)." *Biblical Theology Bulletin*, 6 (1976), pp. 203-224.

Derrett, J. D. M. "Haggadah and the Account of the Passion." *Downside Review*, 97 (1979), pp. 308-315.

--- " 'Where two or three are convened in my name...': a sad misunderstanding." *Expository Times*, 91 (1979), pp. 83-86.

Dillon, R. I. "Towards a Tradition-History of the Parables of the True Israel (Matthew 21,33 - 22,14)." *Biblica*, 47 (1966), pp. 1-42.

Doohan, Leonard. *Luke: The Perennial Spirituality*. Santa Fe: Bear and Co., 1982.

Down, The Rev. M. J. "The Matthean Birth Narratives." *Expository Times*, 90 (1978), pp. 51-52.

Ellis, Peter F. *Matthew: His Mind and His Message*. Collegeville, Minnesota: The Liturgical Press, 1974.

Fenton, J. C. *Saint Matthew*. Harmondsworth, England: Penguin Books, 1963.

Feuillet, A. "Le caractère universel du jugement et la charité sans frontière en Mt 25, 31-46." *Nouvelle Revue Théologique*, 102 (1980), pp. 179-196.

Filson, Floyd V. *A Commentary on The Gospel according to St. Matthew*. London: Adam and Charles Black, 1971.

Gerhardsson, Dr. B. "The Seven Parables in Matthew xiii." *New Testament Studies*, 19 (1972-73), pp. 16-37.

Giblin, Charles H. "A Note on Doubt and Reassurance in Mt 28:16-20." *Catholic Biblical Quarterly*, 37 (1975), pp. 68-75.

Goulder, M. "Characteristics of the Parables in the Several Gospels." *Journal of Theological Studies*, 19 (1968), pp. 51-70.

Grant, F. C. "Gospel of Matthew." *Interpreter's Dictionary of the Bible*, Vol. III. Nashville: Abingdon Press, 1962, pp. 302-313.

Grassi, Joseph A. "The Last Testament-Succession Literary Background of Matthew 9:35 - 11:1 and its Significance." *Biblical Theology Bulletin*, 7 (1977), pp. 172-175.

Green, H. Benedict. *The Gospel According to Matthew.* Oxford: University Press, 1975.

Guelich, Robert A. "The Matthean Beatitudes: 'Entrance Requirements' or Eschatological Blessings." *Journal of Biblical Literature*, 95 (1976), pp. 415-434.

Gundry, Robert H. *The Use of the Old Testament in St. Matthew's Gospel.* Leiden: Brill, 1967.

--- *Matthew: A Commentary on His Literary and Theological Art.* Grand Rapids, Michigan: William B. Eerdmans Publishing Co., 1982.

Hall, T. Hartley. "An Exposition of Matthew 4:21-23." *Interpretation*, 29 (1975), pp. 63-67.

Hamerton-Kelly, R. G. "Gospel of Matthew." *Interpreter's Dictionary of the Bible*, Suppl. Vol. Nashville: Abingdon Press, 1976, pp. 580-583.

Hare, Douglas R. A. *The Theme of Jewish Persecution of Christians in the Gospel According to St. Matthew.* Cambridge: University Press, 1967.

Hare, Douglas R. A. and Daniel J. Harrington. " 'Make Disciples of All the Gentiles' (Matthew 28:19)." *Catholic Biblical Quarterly*, 37 (1975), pp. 359-369.

Harrington, Daniel. "Matthew Studies since Joachim Rhode." *Heythrop Journal*, 16 (1975), pp. 375-388.

Held, Heinz Joachim. "Matthew as Interpreter of the Miracle Stories." *Tradition and Interpretation in Matthew.* Bornkamm, Gunther, Gerhard Barth, Heinz Joachim Held, eds. Philadelphia: The Westminster Press, 1963, pp. 165-299.

Hill, David. *The Gospel of Matthew.* London: Oliphants, 1972.

--- *New Testament Prophecy.* Atlanta: John Knox Press, 1979.

--- "Son and Servant: An Essay on Matthean Christology." *Journal for the Study of the New Testament*, 6 (1980), pp. 2-16.

Hinnebusch, P. *St. Matthew's Earthquake.* Ann Arbor, Michigan: Servant Books, 1980.

Jeremias, Joachim. *The Parables of Jesus.* London: SCM., Press Ltd., 1972.

182

Jones, Alexander. *The Gospel according to St. Matthew.* New York: Sheed and Ward, 1965.

Kealy, Sean P. "The Modern Approach to Matthew." *Biblical Theology Bulletin,* 9 (1979), pp. 165-178.

Kee, Howard Clark. *Understanding the New Testament,* 4th ed. Englewood Cliffs, New Jersey: Prentice-Hall, Inc., 1983.

Keegan, Terence J. "Introductory Formulae for Matthean Discourses." *Catholic Biblical Quarterly,* 44 (1982), pp. 415-430.

Kilgallen, J. J. "To what are the Matthean Exception-Texts (5,32 and 19,9) an Exception?" *Biblica,* 61 (1980), pp. 102-105.

Kilpatrick, G. D. *The Origins of the Gospel According to St. Matthew.* Oxford: The Clarendon Press, 1946.

Kingsbury, Jack Dean. *Matthew Structure, Christology, Kingdom.* Philadelphia: Fortress Press, 1975.

--- *Matthew.* Philadelphia: Fortress Press, 1977.

--- "The Figure of Peter in Matthew's Gospel as a Theological Problem." *Journal of Biblical Literature,* 98 (1979), pp. 67-83.

Kirk, Albert, and Robert E. Obach. *A Commentary on the Gospel of Matthew.* New York: Paulist Press, 1978.

Kodel, Jerome. "The Celibacy Logion in Matthew 19:12." *Biblical Theology Bulletin,* 8 (1978), pp. 19-23.

LaVerdiere, Eugene A. and William G. Thompson. "New Testament Communities in Transition." *Theological Studies,* 37 (1976), pp. 567-597.

Loader, W. R. G. "Son of David, Blindness, Possession, and Duality in Matthew." *Catholic Biblical Quarterly,* 44 (1982), pp. 570-585.

Lohr, Charles H. "Oral Techniques in the Gospel of Matthew." *Catholic Biblical Quarterly,* 23 (1961), pp. 403-435.

Martin, James P. "The Church in Matthew." *Interpretation,* 29 (1975), pp. 41-50.

McEleney, Neil J. "The Beatitudes of the Sermon on the Mount/Plain." *Catholic Biblical Quarterly,* 43 (1981), pp. 1-13.

McKenzie, John L. "The Gospel According to Matthew." *The Jerome Biblical Commentary.* London: Geoffrey Chapman, 1970, pp. 62-114.

Meier, John P. "Salvation History in Matthew: In Search of a Starting Point." *Catholic Biblical Quarterly,* 37 (1975), pp. 203-215.

--- "Nations or Gentiles in Matthew 28:19?" *Catholic Biblical Quarterly,* 39 (1977), pp. 94-102.

--- *The Vision of Matthew. Christ, Church, and Morality in the First Gospel.* New York: Paulist Press, 1979.

--- *Matthew*. Wilmington, Delaware: Michael Glazier, Inc., 1980.

Metzger, Bruce M. *The New Testament: Its background, growth, and content*. Nashville: Abingdon Press, 1965.

Milavec, Aaron. "Matthew's Integration of Sexual and Divine Begetting." *Biblical Theology Bulletin*, 8 (1978), pp. 108-116.

Milton, Helen. "The Structure of the Prologue to St. Matthew's Gospel." *Journal of Biblical Literature*, 81 (1962), pp. 175-181.

Montague, George T. "The Discreet Pneumatology of Matthew." *The Holy Spirit*. New York: Paulist Press, 1976, pp. 302-310.

Moule, C. F. D. *The Birth of the New Testament*. 2nd ed. 1962; rpt. London: Adam and Charles Black, 1973.

--- "St. Matthew; some neglected features." *Essays in New Testament Interpretation*. New York: Cambridge University Press, 1982, pp. 67-74.

Murphy-O'Connor, Jerome. "The Structure of Matthew XIV-XVII." *Revue Biblique*, 82 (1975), pp. 360-384.

Orchard, Bernard. *Matthew, Luke and Mark*. 2nd ed. Manchester, England: Koinonia Press, 1977.

Pamment Margaret. "The Kingdom of Heaven According to the First Gospel." *New Testament Studies*, 27 (1980-81), pp.211-232.

Perrin, Norman and Dennis C. Duling. *The New Testament: An Introduction*. 2nd ed. New York: Harcourt Brace Jovanovich Inc., 1982.

Perumalil, The Rev. A. C. "Are not Papias and Irenaeus competent to report on the gospels"? *Expository Times*, 91 (1979-80), pp. 332-337.

Petrie, Rev. C. Stewart. "The Authorship of 'The Gospel According to Matthew'; a Reconsideration of the External Evidence." *New Testament Studies*, 14 (1967-68), pp. 15-32.

Piper, Otto A. "The Virgin Birth: The Meaning of the Gospel Accounts." *Interpretation*, 18 (1964), pp. 131-148.

Quesnell, Quentin. " 'Made Themselves Eunuchs for the Kingdom of Heaven' (Mt 19,12)." *Catholic Biblical Quarterly*, 30 (1968), pp. 335-358.

Reese, James M. "How Matthew Portrays the Communication of Christ's Authority." *Biblical Theology Bulletin*, 7 (1977), pp. 139-144.

Rigaux, Beda. *The Testimony of St. Matthew*. Chicago: Franciscan Herald Press, 1968.

Robinson, John A. T. *Redating the New Testament*. Philadelphia: The Westminster Press, 1976.

Rolland, Philippe. "From the Genesis to the End of the World: the Plan of Matthew's Gospel." *Biblical Theology Bulletin*, 2 (1972), pp. 155-176.

Sanders, Dr. E. P. "The Argument from Order and the Relationship between Matthew and Luke." *New Testament Studies*, 15 (1968-69), pp. 249-261.

Schweizer, Eduard. *The Good News according to Matthew*. Atlanta: John Knox Press, 1975.

Senior, Donald. "The Ministry of Continuity (Matthew's Gospel and the Interpretation of History)." *Bible Today*, 14 (1976), pp. 670-676.

Sheridan, Mark. "Disciples and Discipleship in Matthew and Luke." *Biblical Theology Bulletin*, 3 (1973), pp. 235-255.

Simpson, Rev. R. T. "The Major Agreements of Matthew and Luke against Mark." *New Testament Studies*, 12 (1965-66), pp. 273-284.

Shuler, Philip L. *A Genre for the Gospels: The Biographical Character of Matthew*. Philadelphia: Fortress Press, 1982.

Stanton, G. N. "Salvation Proclaimed: X. Matthew 11:28-30: Comfortable Words?" *Expository Times*, 94 (1982), pp. 3-9.

Stendal, K. *The School of St. Matthew*. 2nd ed. Philadelphia: Fortress Press, 1968.

Suggs, M. Jack. *Wisdom, Christology, and the Law in Matthew's Gospel*. Cambridge, Mass.: Harvard University Press, 1970.

Tagawa, Kenzo. "People and Community in the Gospel of Matthew." *New Testament Studies*, 16 (1969-70), pp. 149-162.

Thompson William G. *Matthew's Advice to a Divided Community* Rome: Biblical Institute Press, 1970.

Tostato, A. "Joseph, Being a Just Man (Matt 1:19)." *Catholic Biblical Quarterly*, 41 (1979), pp. 547-551.

Viviano, B. T. "Where Was the Gospel According to St. Matthew Written?" *Catholic Biblical Quarterly*, 41 (1979), pp. 533-546.

Waetjen, Herman C. "The Genealogy as the Key to the Gospel according to Matthew." *Journal of Biblical Literature*, 95 (1976), pp. 205-230.

Wallace-Hadrill, D. S. *Christian Antioch*. New York: Cambridge University Press, 1982.

Wilson, G. Todd. "Conditions for Entering the Kingdom According to St. Matthew." *Perspectives in Religious Studies*, 5 (1978), pp. 42-53.

Index of Subjects

This index should be used in conjunction with the detailed table of contents at the beginning.

Index of Authors

Index of Scriptural References

Matthew *(continued)*

Matthew *(continued)*

Matthew *(continued)*

Matthew *(continued)*

198

Matthew *(continued)*

Scripture	*page*	*Scripture*	*page*
25:37	106, 107	26:69-75	117, 124
25:37-40	62	26:75	117
25:40	144	27:1	82
25:41	79	27:4	86
25:44	94	27:9-10	54
25:44-46	94	27:11-14	43
25:45-46	63, 106	27:19	86
25:46	79, 106, 107	27:20-23	43
26:1	18, 57, 85, 122	27:24	86
26:2	80, 86	27:25	26, 44, 45, 62, 86
26:6-13	136	27:27-31	86, 92
26:6-16	86	27:37	92
26:8	124	27:40	86, 93
26:10	144	27:41	102
26:10-13	86	27:42	92, 105
26:18	86	27:43	86, 93
26:14-16	43	27:46	143
26:21	86	27:51	39
26:22	91	27:51-53	86
26:23-24	62	27:51 - 28:3	53
26:25	86, 91	27:52	6, 29
26:26-28	55	27:52-53	87
26:28	86, 89, 90	27:54	29, 62, 86, 88, 93, 151
26:29	78, 86	27:57	47, 122
26:31	91	27:62-66	87
26:31-35	133	28:2	6, 29
26:32	87	28:4-8	87
26:33-35	115, 116, 117	28:7	29
26:37	115	28:11-15	87
26:39	78, 136, 143	28:16-20	38, 53, 55, 61, 74, 87, 102, 103
26:41	9	28:17	62, 87, 124, 133
26:42	78, 86, 136, 143	28:18	54, 91, 113
26:49	91	28:18-20	18, 41, 45, 62, 88, 107, 111, 113, 144
26:52-53	86		
26:53	78		
26:54	86		
26:56	87, 124		
26:57-75	116		
26:63	86, 92		
26:64	94		
26:66	18		
26:69	115		

BOOKS OF RELATED INTEREST
BY BEAR & COMPANY

MARK
Visionary of Early Christianity
by Leonard Doohan

LUKE
The Perennial Spirituality
by Leonard Doohan

JOHN
Gospel for a New Age
by Leonard Doohan

FIREBALL AND THE LOTUS
Emerging Spirituality from Ancient Roots
edited by Ron Miller & Jim Kenney

HILDEGARD OF BINGEN'S
BOOK OF DIVINE WORKS
with Letters and Songs
edited by Matthew Fox

ORIGINAL BLESSING
A Primer in Creation Spirituality
by Matthew Fox

WESTERN SPIRITUALITY
Historical Roots, Ecumenical Routes
edited by Matthew Fox

Contact your local bookseller or write:
Bear & Company
P.O. Drawer 2860
Santa Fe, NM 87504